More Advance Praise for *Nature Matrix*

"Robert Michael Pyle's essays pace the fraught ground between our need for the wild and our growing neglect of it. Filled with his signature mix of insight, wit, and immersive description, this career-spanning collection is a master class in nature writing from one of its finest practitioners. Highly recommended."

—THOR HANSON, author of *Buzz, Feathers,*
and *The Triumph of Seeds*

"Robert Michael Pyle's *Nature Matrix: New and Selected Essays* adds to his long list of books that take the reader on a literary journey of observation and discovery, or even rediscovery, as the case may be. Pyle's detail and specificity with language detail both the mundane and the mythic in the nonhuman world as a way to shake readers out of their too-familiar ways of engaging. *Nature Matrix*, like others of Pyle's works, leads me from the page to place so that I want to immerse myself in nature with something of his keen eye and passion." —DR. DAVID TAYLOR,
author of *An Island in the Stream:*
Ecocritical and Literary Responses to Cuban Environmental Culture

"Written across a span of many years, these essays by Robert Michael Pyle, one of America's great literary naturalists, make for engaging reading throughout—peppered with wit and humor, threaded through with genuine insight."

—THOMAS LOWE FLEISCHNER,
executive director of the Natural History Institute
and editor of *Nature, Love, Medicine:*
Essays on Wildness and Wellness

"Robert Michael Pyle's *Nature Matrix: New and Selected Essays* is a fascinating weave of ecology, history, and ethics. Decades of close observation of life's community yield gripping narratives, each one sparkling with insight." —DAVID GEORGE HASKELL, author of John Burroughs Medal winner *The Songs of Trees* and Pulitzer Prize finalist *The Forest Unseen*

"There is a particular ridgeline that the naturalist-writer walks above two watersheds—that of science and that of what C. P. Snow called the realm of 'the literary intellectual.' Robert Michael Pyle has been hiking that ridge for decades now, and maybe he charts that territory better than any. I go to him often for knowledge of the natural world and for beauty—of language, of voice, of quest, of clear mission. It is so good to have such a range of his essays collected in one place." —JOHN LANE, author of *Coyote Settles the South*

"This collection tracks the career of a fine naturalist who is a celebrant of overlooked and damaged places—irrigation ditches, vacant lots, urban campuses, and 'the suburban jungle'—as sites for natural history observation. Pyle lends his attentive eye to finding wonders in unlikely places and cultivating an ethos of care for the creaturely world wherever he takes his readers." —ALISON HAWTHORNE DEMING, author of *Zoologies: On Animals and the Human Spirit*

" 'Many are given to write; few, to really Write.' In so declaring, Robert Michael Pyle presages his own craft, 'really' writing to beautiful effect in *Nature Matrix*. As he weaves through groves of prose and near verse to scale grand mountains, then rounds the next bend and descends to revel in small beauties—bird, blossom, and butterfly—Pyle opines eloquently to awaken us to wildness and the necessity of its care. Rich stories are loosely stitched together with a life lived in quest. As drops of memoir seep in to nurture wonder, strong opinions make clear this writer's favor of a more feral path. Savor the slow read, as *Nature Matrix* is a master noticer's lifework. Robert Michael Pyle's work merits the sauntering wander."

—J. DREW LANHAM,
author of *The Home Place:*
Memoirs of a Colored Man's Love Affair with Nature

"A remarkably observant, perceptive, and provocative writer, Robert Michael Pyle is among our most eloquent literary interpreters of nature. In prose at once grounded in science and luminous as poetry, Pyle reminds us that a complex and beautiful web of relations is not only where we find ourselves but also who we are. *Nature Matrix* is a brilliant book that inspires a necessary rethinking of our deeply nourishing but increasingly strained relationship with the more-than-human world."   —MICHAEL P. BRANCH,
author of *Rants from the Hill*

"No living American so creatively and competently combines fine literary writing with equally fine contributions to the natural sciences in service to conservation as does Robert Michael Pyle. In *Nature Matrix*, it is abundantly clear that art and science are crafted with equal talent and a glorious sense of inquisitiveness about the other-than-world."   —GARY PAUL NABHAN,
Ecumenical Franciscan Brother, conservation biologist,
and author of *Mesquite: An Arboreal Love Affair*

NATURE MATRIX

New and Selected Essays

ROBERT MICHAEL PYLE

COUNTERPOINT

Berkeley, California

Nature Matrix

Permission is gratefully acknowledged from Oregon State University Press,
Columbia River Reader Press, Beacon Press, and Counterpoint Press for
excerpts on pages 82, 157–158, 175–178, and 241–243, for all of which the
author holds or shares copyright.

Library of Congress Cataloging-in-Publication Data
Names: Pyle, Robert Michael, author.
Title: Nature matrix : new and selected essays / Robert Michael Pyle.
Description: First paperback edition. | Berkeley, California : Counterpoint,
     2020.
Identifiers: LCCN 2019017872 | ISBN 9781640092761
Subjects: LCSH: Pyle, Robert Michael,—Prose. | Natural history.
Classification: LCC QH45.2 .P95 2020 | DDC 508—dc23
LC record available at https://lccn.loc.gov/2019017872

Cover design by Sarah Brody
Book design by Jordan Koluch

COUNTERPOINT
2560 Ninth Street, Suite 318
Berkeley, CA 94710
www.counterpointpress.com

Printed in the United States of America

10 9 8 7 6 5 4 3 2 1

For my grandchildren, and for theirs

Nothing prevents us from exercising our powers of autonomy and rationality in bringing the world as it is gradually closer to the world as it ought to be.

—PAUL W. TAYLOR, *Respect for Nature:
A Theory of Environmental Ethics*

CONTENTS

INTRO

Pyrex, Postcards, and Panzers—
the Birth of Nature Matrix

One of the ways that universities try to make postgraduate students feel special and at home while accruing vast debts for their advanced degrees is to give them an office, or lab, or both. Depending on the size of the department, its budget, and the professor's grant, this may vary from a coat closet to a cranny to a cubicle to quite capacious quarters. The office serves the practical purpose of office hours for teaching assistants, and as a quiet place of study or work on the thesis project.

My first office as a grad student was in a good room facing an inner plaza in the fine old college-gothic forestry school, Anderson Hall, at the University of Washington. My desk faced that of my officemate and lifetime friend, Neil Johannsen. We TA'd for Professor Grant Sharpe, the guru of the time for the field of Nature Interpretation. When Neil left (later to become director of Alaska State Parks), I moved offices across the forestry quad to Bloedel Hall, a striking new facility, all laminated cedar and glass. Not so lucky with an officemate this time, I drew a right-winger of an eastern Washington kid who liked to hunt bobcats, the very negative of my enviro-hippie-commie style. Forestry was polarized in those days between the pulp-and-paper types and the wildlife/wilderness devotees—or Pinchot vs. Muir, as we saw the split. I didn't really enjoy the bobcat-and-clearcut debates, which were unavoidable. But my officemate had the desirable trait of seldom being in residence, especially at night when I mostly worked.

Nor was the setting as amenable as Anderson Hall. The innards of Bloedel were as functional as the outer surface was esthetic. My study space, in the basement, was about as sterile and antiseptic as a room might be. No stone walls or old wooden desks, as are found in graduate student crannies elsewhere: only plastic and cinderblocks. No mullioned windows, either, through which to spy on squirrels and siskins. My desk faced a cinderblock wall. In fact, the only thing in that room with any character or animation at all was a transparent Pyrex water pipe, running ceiling to floor, hard beside my desk. The water flow was intermittent, like flushing; so at first I watched reluctantly, earnestly hoping I wouldn't see something brown coming down that was definitely not an otter.

In time, of course, I began adding some sparing furnishings just to keep me sane while cooped in this cinderblock cell: a poster of a tern in flight, for uplifting inspiration; a woodcut of a forest clearcut, to keep me from slipping into an unconcerned idyll; a color picture of aspen-clad mountains in Colorado, for occasional dreams; and another of a butterfly on a thistle, to bring me back to the reality of my thesis-*cum*-butterfly book. Just for comfort, I added an FM radio for soothing baroque, and a few crispy sycamore leaves on the floor for counterpoint crunching. My officemate did not approve, and stayed away more.

One particular evening, my intention was to concentrate solely on my thesis. I soon knew, though, that I was going to be subverted. I should have stopped with the Colorado aspens. But, feeling a need to cover a part of the big, plastic surface of my desk with something palatable, I had smuggled four postcards into my mental monastery. Three I could glance at, enjoy, and then subordinate to my work: the Haida thunderbird panel, the Glen Canyon moss spring, and the Samuel Palmer sepia. But the fourth one, and I knew it should have stayed home in my playroom, haunted me. It pictured the Lüneburger Heide of northern Germany. It conjured soft smells of heather, the evening sounds—and a throbbing, hurtful memory of an abominable act.

The Lüneburger Heide, a nature reserve south of Hamburg, is much of what remains of the vast heaths that once carpeted large parts of north-central Europe. My wife JoAnne and I had gone there by accident that June, then returned most purposefully in August when the heather bloomed. We had known heather only as sparse plantings around our Seattle campus and neighborhood and were entranced by it even then. You can imagine our joy at finding ourselves in the midst of thousands of acres of solid purple heath.

There was more to the *Heide* than the heather, however. Turning off the autobahn, we rolled on gentle roads through forestland crisscrossed by miles of pleasant trails. In June we had walked these trails for idyllic hours. Returning late in the season, we bypassed them and went directly to the tiny villages of the heathland proper. These villages consisted almost entirely of farms, because some limited farming was allowed in the park (to help maintain habitat for the wild boars), and of gasthauses or *Fremdenzimmer*—places where one could lodge and dine. And such places! Classic half-timbered German farmsteads they were, many with thatched roofs and pigs in the yard. Comfortable, warm, genuinely endemic, and cheap in 1968: maybe three dollars for a warm bed and sumptuous breakfast before the hike.

The hike, of course, being the chief pleasure thereabouts. Oh, not everyone hikes who comes to the *Heide*. Some Hamburgers simply sit around the gasthaus under the rows of mounted deer antlers and capercaillies (*Auerhuhn*), the big, black forest grouse that were more often shot in the past than even seen today. Others drive the few roads in their automobiles, stopping where they can find beer and company, or to shop for the shaggy sheepskins displayed at the junctions. Still other formal visitors from the North Sea cities penetrate the auto-free parts of the park by means of horse-drawn, rubber-tired carriages. But Germans are walkers, and the trails are seldom solitary when the heather blooms and the vacationing families arrive for their *Spaziergänge*. We walked the paths with the natives for the afternoon, surprised at their funny reactions to our American high-top hiking boots.

We paused at the micro-village of Wilsede in the middle of a broad heath. Here was the tiny Magdalena Church, a *Teestube* for sustenance, and a resident artist's gallery, where I obtained the postcard that stimulated these thoughts. By waiting until the first of dusk, we found we were able to have the heath to ourselves. My postcard shows the *Heide* just as I remember it that evening. A lowering sky falls upon a lowering land. Clouds of vapor meet clouds of heather, their textures nearly the same. The white sand path, trampled by the ages yet firm, stretches off into the purpled plain. It is lined, off and on, by unpretentious birches, whose leaves are gold-washed since the heather blooms late in the season. Everything else is horizontal, except for the erect and olivaceous forms of sparse junipers. Beyond all, the black spruce forest swells.

Dark was only threatening, not yet arrived. The hikers had

retired; but the *Heide* creatures were about. One vale held a jumpy family of brown rabbits, browsing their protective cover. Nearby, a courtship transpired: a pair of lapwings, exotically crested plovers of temperate uplands, were conducting the dance prescribed by eons of adaptation to stimulate the mating frame of mind. Did they suppose there was still time for one more brood? The last direct light caught a maroon flash from a lapwing's flank.

We mounted a hillock to watch the tangerine sunset. As we did so, a red fox darted from heather to spruce. The spruces on one eastern ridge emulated castle turrets against the pale sky. Thus the *Heide* experience. Until the morning, when it was shattered.

We happened to drive out of the federal nature-protection area (*Naturschutzgebiet*) toward the southeast, the way we had entered in June. This took us past the trailheads we had discovered then. Incredulous, we saw our vernal footpaths now as great, gouged thoroughfares! Every route that intersected the small highway had been similarly disemboweled.

"What the hell . . . ?" I began, but I knew what. Each trail, previously horse-sized at biggest, had been overlaid by fifteen-foot swaths; and at the sides, engraved in the crushed leaves and violated soil, were tracks—the hateful, hellish tread-tracks of tanks!

After just a few hundred yards there lay a scene of greater plunder yet. The forest will rejuvenate, the trails can be restored. But here stretched a whole heath, or a once-heath, ripped and raped over all of its many fragile acres. Like the arctic mosses, heather is a delicate tissue; and the heath, so like the tundra, is a perishable organism. No life remained on this plundered plain. Only a ring of trees in the center that sheltered a historic, but now anomalous, old *Heidehaus*. Ancient, peaked and thatched, the scenic relic now languished solitary and bleak among the ruins of the land that had nurtured it for centuries.

On still a little farther, the villains were revealed: in an expansive mudflat, a camp of British armored troops. George Laycock's term for harmful invasive species, "diligent destroyers," could be used to no greater advantage than for these professionals. The tank soldiers lounged on their metal monsters, which hulked in a foot of tortured mud. A few, not yet satiated, spun and grinded and clawed, as though some further pain could still be wrenched from the earth, like the murderer who sinks his blade in far more times than necessary for simple dispatch.

We did not speak with them. Soviet tanks had rolled in Prague that spring when the Warsaw Pact countries invaded Czechoslovakia. We surmised that those events, and the many protests around Europe that summer of '68, were the pretense for these maneuvers. Defense, if you will. We had seen the shattered cathedrals at Lübeck and we asked ourselves: "Weren't you satisfied with Germany's culture? Do you have to crush her heather, too?" Naively, we had thought all that was over before we were born. And though we were acutely aware of the horrors of American defoliation in Vietnam, we had hardly expected to find similar biocide in modern Europe.

How can any country establish a land ethic, we wondered, when its very "protectors" sabotage the land itself? The very land that had spawned Gifford Pinchot's vision of forestry. We did not bother to learn where the *Naturschutzgebiet* boundary lay in relation to the depredation. It was all the same, just as redwoods are redwoods, federal or private. The surviving heath was tiny enough that any loss is tragic, inside or outside of formal reserves.

Besides, we doubted whether the British tankmen could not have had the entire park for their lethal games, had they wanted it. The conquering soldier's disregard for the sacred is universal.

But it was driven home with bitter irony that day on the Lüneburger Heide by the signs that marked each tank-gored trail:

NO MOTORED VEHICLES PERMITTED.

* * *

And now, all these years forward, I wonder whether this book
would be here, absent that postcard, that Pyrex pipe. Mostly, in
that office, I worked on drafts and data for my master's thesis,
an interpretive study of Washington State's butterflies. Eventually
this became my first book, *Watching Washington Butterflies*. It was
not without its lyrical notes. But I was, in addition to a forestry
graduate student, a young writer. I had published by that time
a number of essays, most locally, a few nationally. I was eager to
extend my reach as a nature and conservation writer, to make a
name, and maybe a career.

I had read a book that much affected me by Daniel P. Man-
nix, *The Fox and the Hound*, and I'd noticed that it received the
Dutton Animal Book Award in 1967. Looking it up, I found that
this prize was about to morph into the Dutton Environmental
Book of the Year Award. It was to include a generous advance
against royalties and publication by Dutton. This was during
the heady days of major environmental legislation (Wilderness,
Clean Air, Clean Water, Endangered Species, and National Environmental Policy acts), when everything was eco-this and eco-
that. My own first publication between book covers had recently
appeared in the Sierra Club/Ballantine book *Ecotactics*. The
deadline for the 1970 Dutton book was coming up. I thought, I
could do that! It seemed plausible that I could sling together my
published essays, write a few new ones, and have a manuscript.

In fairness to self, it wasn't just the book or the award: I was utterly devoted to conservation, myopically if you will. I already had a taste for the difficulty of making change through other channels, and thought books might be the better way, at least for one of little political patience such as myself. But it was that postcard of the Lüneburger Heide, and the memory of the British Panzers' tread on the tender heath, that pushed me over. I wanted to write that, and I wanted it in a book that people might read.

And so, in secret, certainly from my professor and even from my young wife at first, I began descending into my subterranean study to work on not only what I was supposed to be doing, but also on this putative book. A name occurred to me: *Nature Matrix*, later to be one of the essays. And it came along. My friends were getting stoned, and I was tap-tapping away in my cave beside Otter Slide Falls. Though I could type pretty well (I considered high school typing to be one of the most useful classes I ever took, tied with Local Flora in college), I saved enough from my meager TA's stipend to hire a typist to make a fair copy for the contest.

I asked Victor B. Scheffer, a great wildlife biologist and writer, recent winner of the John Burroughs Medal for distinguished nature writing for *The Year of the Whale*, and a mentor to the young conservation activists around Seattle, if he would write a foreword for the book. Wisely, he declined to do it on spec. He replied that if I actually got a contract, he would consider it. But he did encourage me in the enterprise. So I forged on, finished, and sent it in!

At first, it did pretty well. The editors told me they liked it, and in fact it ended up the final entry in contention. But in the end they felt it didn't really hold together enough to command an adequate audience. Good call!—for a twenty-two-year-old's callow, hurried slumgullion; not without merit, but certainly not ready for publication. In the end they declined to give the award that year, and then they never did. The Animal Book Award was given once more in 1975, and that was that. Well, not quite: the editors and I went on to discuss several additional book ideas, all of which have since been written and published, but with different houses. So the exercise was not the bust it might have seemed at the time. I was disappointed then. But many times since I have been grateful that *NM* wasn't published before time—it was unready, unripe, and lacking a central idea. I put it away, later pulling out some of the essays to publish here and there, and forgot about it.

Until, many years later, I was asked to write a piece for the centennial edition of *Oryx*, the international journal of conservation published in the U.K. by Fauna & Flora International. I had been thinking of updating and expanding upon the title essay from the original *Nature Matrix*, and this seemed a chance to do that. The piece was wrought and published in 2003, and it attracted a measure of international attention (in those pre–social media days) in the old-fashioned form of reprint requests.

Since then, other essays riffing and refracting on related but different ideas and experiences accumulated, some of them collected in *Through a Green Lens: Fifty Years of Writing for Nature*, but others not. I felt that this gathering body, and a few more in progress, clustered well beneath the *Nature Matrix* umbrella. So when Jack Shoemaker, publisher of Counterpoint Press, asked whether I might have a "new and selected essays" up my sleeve, I replied, "Jack, do I have the book for you!" And the title, too.

The present volume contains only two pieces from the original Dutton entrant version: the hitherto unpublished "Mineral King Esthetic," and the above remembrance of the violation of the Lüneburger Heide, which sparked the whole thing. The other selections have either been published elsewhere, and I have felt them worthy of a longer life together in collected form, or they have been newly written on topics that have long concerned me. The older pieces have all been edited to a greater or lesser extent, but are based closely on the originals, with much of the prose intact. Naturally, you will hear echoes of some of my dominant themes over the years, but not, I trust, to the point of outright repetition of theme. Anyway, a few of these things cannot be said too often. My criteria for inclusion were these: substance, depth, freshness, wit, and relevance to the deep appreciation and survival of our complicated green world.

As for Vic Scheffer? It's too late to include a foreword from him, now that I finally have a contract for *Nature Matrix*, nearly fifty years after that first attempt. He died in 2011 at the age of 104—he'd waited long enough for me to get it together. But he had granted a lovely blurb to my book *Wintergreen*, not so many years after my initial pretentious request. And I like to think that if he were still with us, he might accede. I wonder what he would have said.

Nature Matrix

Secrets of the Talking Leaf

The befuddlement of native peoples upon encountering European adventurers stemmed from many unfamiliarities. There were the carved and shiny sticks that thundered and brought blood. There were bright beads and blankets of unknown materials. There were metals that would easily rend flesh or wood. And perhaps as perplexing as anything, there were the clusters of white leaves with marks upon them that seemed to speak. At least, when the interlopers looked at the leaves, they spoke in words that seemed to arise from the clusters. Messages, dictates, deeds, and treaties ripe for breaking all were carried on single large leaves that could be rolled or folded. Whole philosophies were borne in bunches of leaves called books. Talking leaves appeared to carry great power, for they might signify concord or war, beneficence or confiscation, salvation, deportation, or death, depending upon the marks; and sometimes, they moved men to raise their arms aloft and tell of gods.

Sequoyah, a young man of the Tennessee Cherokee, was not the only Indian to wonder over the power of the leaves that talked. But he was the only one to do something about it.

In 1969, I worked as a ranger-naturalist in Sequoia National Park in California's Sierra Nevada. Sequoia, the second-oldest national park in the United States, protects the most massive trees in the world—the giant sequoias. Their relatives, the coast redwoods, are the tallest trees in the world, and many of the ones that remain reside in Redwood National Park in the coastal lowlands of California. When I went to lead nature walks and give campfire programs among the Big Trees, I had no idea where the name Sequoia came from. I assumed it was Indian, of Californian origin. Looking back, it seems surprising that none of the evening programs, guided walks, or interpretive exhibits told the story of Sequoyah in depth. But then, perhaps not so surprising: his was a radical, even deeply revolutionary act; and 1969 was the summer when a hundred mounted rangers with truncheons raided Yosemite Meadows, cracking hippie heads in a display of fervor that mimicked that of Chicago police at the Democratic National Convention a year earlier.

Sequoyah was born in Tennessee two hundred years before, and later transported to Arkansas on the Trail of Tears. He noticed the capacities given whites by their peculiar talking leaves. His tribesmen were divided in their theories: some thought books were conferred on the Europeans by a god who denied them, like so many other things, to their people, thus proving the depressing rightness of European supremacy. Others believed that writing had nothing to do with gods, but was the invaders' own invention. Sequoyah was one of these. Convinced that this tool was within his own reach, he pondered the question and, eventually, worked it out. Using a direct syllabic notation of his own invention, he brought literacy to his people in a remarkably short time and changed their lives.

The wonderfully evocative term "talking leaves" gave the title for Craig Lesley's fine anthology of Native American short stories (Dell, 1991). Reading this stunning collection, we see that the secret exposed by Sequoyah has become abundantly owned by the First People at last. The technical knowledge of a written language, of course, is only the first step in allowing the leaves to truly speak. If all it took to make literature was the ability to write in any given tongue, we would not distinguish between the literary arts and the telephone book. In fact, this is a curious distinction between writing and the other arts: most of the members of many cultures possess the raw materials, since basic literacy is taken for granted as an everyday survival skill like simple math, giving directions, or telling the time. This means that just about anyone is capable of writing up a storm. Yet in art, prolific expression means little if it lacks the personal element that we variously call heart, soul, talent, spirit. Many are given to write; few, to really Write.

To allow the leaves to speak: that is the task. I often tell students that we should aspire to be amanuenses to the land: to let the land speak (in all its voices, human and otherwise), then take dictation, and try to get some of the words right. "How do you know when you get the words right?" they ask.

"You know," I reply. When we do, the leaves not only speak; they positively sing.

But your right words will not be mine. Words are all names for something, and names are as relative as the rain: one minute a downpour, the next mere virga evaporating before it hits the ground; the rain shifts substance and meaning before our eyes. Names, and all words (mere symbols after all), do the same. Listen to the names given the great trees of the Sierra Nevada, for instance. We call them giant sequoias, naming them for their massiveness and their genus, which in turn was named to celebrate a man who performed a giant task. But the botanists have since changed the genus, separating the redwoods into three genera: *Sequoia* now belongs to species *sempervirens* alone, the coast redwood. *Metasequoia* refers to the sole species *glyptostroboides*, the dawn redwood, known only as an extinct fossil species until discovered in living verdure in a Chinese monastery during World War II. As for the giant redwoods, they have been consigned to the new genus *Sequoiadendron*, meaning sequoia tree. Fair enough: *Sequoiadendron gigantea*, known to all as the Big Trees of California. But what were the native names for the largest trees in the world? We can be sure they did not call the biggest one the General Sherman Tree, as we do.

And how are these monoliths known elsewhere, in the arboreta of invading nations, where they might be grown alongside botanical booty such as *Douglasia, Lewisia, Clarkia, Franklinia, Fremontia*, and other living souvenirs of Manifest Destiny? When I lived in England, I often saw the crowns of giant sequoias in their first hundred years, poking through the morning mists, mimicking the village spires. "What are those trees?" I once asked a passing vicar.

"Why," he responded, as if to a simpleton, "they are Wellingtonias, of course! Everyone knows that."

Sequoyah taught a people to master the exclusive tool of their oppressors. The Duke of Wellington defeated Napoleon at Waterloo. Both were honored for their Herculean feats by having their handles tacked onto the biggest trees in the world. (Sequoyah also got the national park, and Wellington, a type of rubber boot.) So it happened that the names of a Native American lexicographer and a British warrior both came to convey a tree that has nothing to do with either one of them.

As naturalists know, it has been anything but uncommon for the so-called discoverers of new species of plants and animals—or anyone they wished to patronize, acclaim, commemorate, honor, or flatter—to carry the names of those organisms into scientific perpetuity. Interestingly, the taxonomist who gives an animal or plant its scientific name is known as its "author," as if the act of bestowing the Linnaean binomial appellation of genus and species were tantamount to breathing life itself into the organism. Not to put too fine a point on this, however, since systematists are rarely Frankensteinian in their presumption. Among the gentlest of people, they are truly enamored of the creatures they attend to, as befits the practitioners of Adam's task.

Even so, the classifiers are possessed of all the venality, envy, whimsy, and ego that beset the rest of us, and the names they give often show it. Butterflies, a group I know fairly well, betray in their names every imaginable motive. Because early lepidopterists frequently boasted classical educations, they felt compelled to use them. So it is that the names of many swallowtails commemorate heroes of the Trojan Wars, while arctic fritillaries bear the names of Norse goddesses and their more southerly cousins embody mythic figures such as Cybele, Aphrodite, Astarte, and Hippolyta. From the number of fauns, satyrs, nymphs, and other Greek and Roman rustic deities found among butterfly checklists, you could be forgiven for thinking that these insects live a constant bacchanal of drinking and mating—though that is, in fact, the case. Yet the observant authors of our butterflies did not always draw their monikers from the European cultural canon. The names of American skippers, for example, include many Native American designations: Hobomok, Pocahontas, Sachem, Ottoe,

Pawnee, Dakota, Pahaska, Poweshiek, Delaware, Assiniboine—
often inhabiting the same grasslands and woodlands where their
namesakes once roamed.

Nineteenth-century explorer-naturalists, in need of financial
backing for their collecting expeditions, named finds for sponsors
or patrons, such as the genus of giant moths called *Rothschildia*
after the financier-naturalist. Lord Rothschild bestowed as well
as received patronyms, naming the largest butterfly in the world
Queen Alexandra's birdwing. The New Guinea giant spreads a
foot in wingspan, and the first female was collected with a shot-
gun. Alexandra, the much-beloved queen consort of Edward VII,
had received an earlier dash of immortality when the influential
Pennsylvania lepidopterist W. H. Edwards named Queen Alexandra's sulphur for her in 1863, upon her marriage to the Prince
of Wales. Edwards named another brilliant western sulphur after
Theodore Mead. An enterprising youth who hoped for Edwards's
daughter Edith's hand, Mead went forth by stagecoach and rail
to bring back butterfly booty for her father. One of these was a
bright copper butterfly, prettier than any bauble, that has ever
since worn Edith's name. She, in turn, became Edith Mead. Apparently, Mead got the words right.

Two books I am working on have brought me nose to nose
with striking examples of viewpoint in choosing the words, again
the names of butterflies. For a Colorado novel with a Magdale-
nian subtext, I looked into the derivation of the name of a completely black mountain species known as the Magdalena alpine.
Was this a devotional gesture by a devout Roman Catholic butterfly hunter? I asked F. Martin Brown, the late historian of Western
butterfly study. "Absolutely not!" Brownie's postcard replied. It
seems that Herman Strecker, the insect's author, was irreligious,
and missed no opportunity to embarrass his best friend, a parson.

So he named the most undistinguished and obscure moth he could find, *jehovah*; and the sooty-winged *Erebia magdalena* was no doubt named, said Brown, to rub his friend's nose in the saint's supposedly besmirched reputation.

The other example also has religious overtones. A colleague in New York performed a revision of a group of small Western forest butterflies called cedar hairstreaks. At the time he was a follower of the Reverend Sun Myung Moon, and he named several new species after prominent Moonies—this to the chagrin of local lepidopterists, since we will be stuck with this inapt nomenclature ever after. But more recently, the same lepidopterist has assisted me in compiling a collection of the late novelist Vladimir Nabokov's butterfly writings for a Beacon Press edition. Many know of Nabokov's interest in butterflies, but few realize the depth of his passion for them or that he was a notable lepidopterist in his own right. My New York friend has lately been completing some of the taxonomic tasks that Nabokov began, by naming many new species of the small butterflies known as blues that Nabokov had studied and loved. But now, having renounced the Moonies, my friend is mining the master's oeuvre for truly Nabokovian labels for the hitherto nameless butterflies. These lovely Latin American blues will bear such delightful and suitable names as *Nabokovia ada*, *Itylos pnin*, and *Madeleinea lolita*.

What have the names of butterflies to do with the craft of fine writing? No more or less than the words we use for worms, or rather the worms we use for words. Consider, for a moment, the way worms worm their way through our lexicon. We say (in an inaccuracy that Nabokov the scientist-wordsman would never have countenanced) that butterflies come from worms, and butterflies are commonly employed (to the point of cliché, as Nabokov pointed out) as a symbol for resurrection. Thus, with only one degree of separation, we link worms with immortality. Yet worms are the very agent of decay in every lore (though we really mean maggots): "The worms crawl in, the worms crawl out . . ." With one word, however twisted from its actual meaning, we manage to convey the entire range of existence from birth to rot to re-birth. And the only thing that makes our meaning clear is con-text: "worm" on its own conveys nothing.

Rather, nothing that we can agree upon. Three examples of worm usage make the point that each of us brings his or her own baggage or bias to the lesson of any given talking leaf, at least until we listen enough to put it in context. First, consider Charles Darwin. This graceful writer's last and, according to Ste-phen Jay Gould, loveliest book is entitled *The Formation of Vegeta-ble Mould Through the Action of Worms* (1881). It describes the very evolution of the landscape in terms of lowly wormworks. Darwin watched worms all his life and admired their industry, behavior, and adaptability immensely. When he heard the term "worm," he thought good things. Second, think of a right-wing Uncle Sam billboard along Interstate 5, between Seattle and Portland, guar-anteed to be more reactionary than thou on any issue. During the first Iraqi invasion, the board's owner asked whether we would be bombing Baghdad if there were spotted owls there, and com-pared Saddam Hussein to a "human worm." That was the worst thing he could think to say about Hussein. Of these two authors, the first, a British naturalist, revered the word *worm* and all it im-plied to him. The other, a Washington turkey farmer, reviled it. You could easily find similarly diametric views over the words bat, moth, cricket, or football.

Now consider a third specific use of the same word, this time in context. When Wallace Stegner lectured in Seattle several years ago, he summed the writer's task by challenging us to "leave the worms of wonder working in the mind of the reader." Was this a positive or a negative reading of the name? The idea of "worms working in the mind" clearly evokes the vicarious discomfort of imagined decay, inspiring a squeamish tickle. Yet by coupling "worm" with "wonder," Stegner deftly twists the sensation toward the positive, even the rapturous. After all, what feels better (to a reader) than wonderment—even riding on worms—twisting its way through the dumbed-down convolutions of our day-numbed brains?

Now we come to the hard, clear relationship between the secret of the leaves that talk and the irresistible human penchant to give names. A name—a word—sitting on its own can convey anything to anyone, depending on personal history, bias, phobia, obsession, experience, association, or whim. Yet surrounded by others, words take root in the soil of context: not fixed, nor bereft of shifting nuance, translucent layer, or alternative meanings (just read Nabokov!), but freed from the footlooseness of the uprooted rune. Like an animal in a zoo cage or a plant in a pot with no hint of habitat, a word on its own can convey nothing beyond its own hide. But as soon as you stick things together—the way you found them in the wild or in some new combo—you get an ecology. Interactions become inevitable. Togetherness of words forces not only context, but also cadence, collaboration, and color, assonance and dissonance, aim, attitude, and altitude. Sentences are family groups, and paragraphs are the neighborhoods they dwell within. A text is indeed a community of words, and the author—not unlike the authors of the names of butterflies or the architects of towns—is responsible for the organization of the living things within the habitat of the page.

Ultimately, then, getting the words right becomes a matter of responsibility. The botanist is responsible for the data that,

properly transcribed, speak truly for the mute leaf pasted to the
talking leaf of an herbarium sheet. So it is with us: as writers, we
speak for that which cannot. Derelict in our duty, we run the risk
of getting the data wrong. When that happens, the leaves lie . . .
and the reader will always know. The secret of the talking leaves
lies not with Gutenberg, nor with Sequoyah; no mere marks on
a page can make what we call language. They give us the means
alone, and from there, we're on our own.

To help define where we are to go, I would like to take two
quotations from Oregonian writer-friends and see how they co-
operate. In the introduction to his sublime book *Having Everything Right*, Kim Stafford compares descriptive Kwakiutl names
for places (such as the bay called "Insufficient Canoe," or the
term for parts of an island separated by an isthmus at low tide:
"Two Round Things Meeting Now and Then") with bland Anglo
names such as "courthouse" or "Vancouver." He invokes the term
hē'ladē, meaning "having everything right," and says it could be "a
portable name . . . It could be what we call Earth. But it will not,
unless we sift from our habits the nourishing ways: listening, re-
membering, telling, weaving a rooted companionship with home
ground." In the other phrase, writer Barry Lopez, addressing the
Pacific Northwest Booksellers Association, enunciated a phrase
that has haunted me ever since: he called us "the community of
writers in service to readers."

Now, it seems to me that if writers were rigorously to seek a
rooted companionship with home ground, so that their words and
names carried the specificity and feeling of the Kwakiutl and the
wit and humanity of a Stafford; and if readers were to recognize
the service rendered by writers such as Lopez and reciprocate
abundantly with their attentions, then we might at last have everything right: at least, much of what is important to writers—that

is, notating the world exactly, and having someone appreciate it when we do.

Yet there are countervailing tendencies that detract from the prospects of our ever realizing *hē'ladē*. Let's take these in the reverse order from Lopez's and Stafford's quotes, first looking at writers and readers, then coming back to the rooted companionship. In doing so, we might be able to chisel our understanding of why we insist on defacing good clean leaves with our marks, and come to a clearer view of how at least we might do it better.

By some obvious measures, writers' service to readers does not seem to be a two-way thing. A tendency toward the devaluation of reading and the displacement of the book as a major cultural form have literary people worried. The field marks can be easily listed: (a) takeovers of independent publishers by multinational corporations and a narrowed focus on the bottom line as a result; (b) the inventory tax, an amazing American manifestation of philistinism, one of the most punitive anti-intellectual devices anywhere, leading to a restructuring of the publishing industry with small printings, early remainderings, and a big fat out-of-print sign as its hallmarks; (c) the rise of ignoble bookbarns, where books are units and writing is product and the resemblance to a real bookstore with informed staff and concern with authors is largely and insidiously ersatz; (d) a declining readership for serious fiction, poetry, and belles lettres; (e) a growing readership for instant oatmeal such as *Bridges of Madison County* and the strident belchings of Rush Limbaugh and glitzy city fables and violent scary thrillers and international plot-plots and angel-fakery and sub-pop psychobabble and cartoons and manuals for successful self-preening, self-aggrandizement, self-abasement, self-absorption, and self-promotion; (f) the much-heralded onslaught of digital text with its interactive alternative to mere talking leaves, the much-ballyhooed information interstate with its invisible substitutes for print, and their supposed outcome, the much-exaggerated rumors of the demise of the book.

Why, you might well ask, should anyone persist in writing for traditional publication in the face of all this? Are we not merely indulging a romantic form of onanism, stubbornly sticking by a dying idyll? Are we to be thought of as bull-headed Luddites for maintaining our loving involvement with paper, print, and all things bookish? Do we poetize in vain, draw characters for oblivion, essay our way into anonymity? So it might seem, as the community of writers scribbles pointlessly away into the autumn of the talking leaf.

And yet, we write on: because, remunerative or not, a book to us is something that we love and aspire to woo, like Theodore Mead and his Edith. To make the leaves speak sweetly—that is the siren. This is not to say that the pleasures and satisfactions of the scrivener cannot be had from disk to screen, skipping committal to the printed page. But to know and love the book is a devotion that will never (in the hearts and minds of many) be replaced by any image romanced from an optical screen by bits, bytes, bleeps, and pixels. Just as it has often been observed that curling up with a terminal will never take the place of a cat, a cup of cocoa, and a book, so will the "publication" of work by electronic means—a marvelous thing in itself—never satisfy the same part of the soul that thrills to share itself in the same medium known by Chaucer and Shakespeare, Colette and Saki, Margaret Wise Brown and Toni Morrison.

When Robert Frost traveled, he took with him the entirety of Bennett Cerf's Modern Library, in great wooden cases that he had delivered to his rooms so that he could select whichever volume he wished to take to bed. He could have had the same thing today from a single digital disk, and had pictures and voices and music to boot. Why do I imagine that he would not have been amused to open his crate and find an e-reader lurking in place of his books?

Books will change, of that there is no doubt. Electronic publishing was the hottest topic at the recent American Booksellers Association meeting, and the rights surrounding it are blowing a maelstrom among publishers and the Authors Guild. There will be fewer paper books published, they say. Yet is that all bad for book lovers? Who would not agree that there is too much published today? The birchwoods of the northern taiga are being raided not only for the tar sands, but also for pulp to fill our mailboxes with tripe, our newspapers with advertisers, and our bookshelves with dross. If much of this can go on instantly erasable screens, how much better for trees, for mail carriers, and for real books, which might again emerge from the crowd.

After all, when big business swallows honored but weak old publishing houses, small new vibrant ones have a way of arising. Fine printing and bookmaking are alive and well, and may come into their own again as mass-produced books diminish. Literary publishing is like a balloon: push it or squeeze it in one place, and it pops up in another. There is a resiliency to Gutenberg's trade. And if the info-boosters were to be proven right and new books did drop out of the picture, perhaps it would be a favor in disguise. We bibliophiles could retreat to the secondhand stores and the ruins of the libraries, and maybe we could actually achieve that elusive and gossamer goal of all readers: to catch up.

In the end, the reasons that books as we know them and writers as we know ourselves will persist are at least two: first, because (in whatever diluted numbers) there will continue to be curious, educated people who love to read, and for whom reading means a book. Second, because a book, though removed from the author by editor, printer, the page and its glyphs, is still—held in the hands and perused and put down and picked up and referred to and lent and retrieved and dog-eared and smelling and dog-chewed and flapping on the porch in a breeze like unruly leaves on a bush—something *real*, a physical object in a way that evanescent images on a screen can never be. An experience with a book is a direct experience. Many people obviously find experiences with computer screens to be real, intense, and satisfying. But it is a different kind of experience: it may be interactive, but it is not interactive with the world. For writers, most of whom spend way too much time in the company of computers as it is, fondling a physical book is like taking a walk: it is a sensory oasis.

When I am asked how I can live without television or a smart phone, I say, "Easy. Why in the world would I want to live even more of my life in front of a screen than I already do? And what sort of input do I really need that I can't find in a good library, a good bookstore, occasional clandestine dalliance with a search engine, and out-of-doors in a perfectly good world?"

"But the information you lose," they go on. To which I reply that in my view, writers are inundated with information. The very last thing in the world that I want, next to hantavirus, is more incoming. Why did writers' retreats evolve, anyway?

And it is this question that brings us back to our second quotation. When Kim Stafford speaks of weaving "a rooted companionship with home ground," he is enjoining us to find time and attention and care for direct experience of the world around us. If there is a shallowness and vapidity to a lot of what passes for writing, it may be because TV, the internet, social media, and all the other amusements and blandishments of our time have seduced us away from a one-on-one with the dirt and the air and our nonhuman neighbors. We have forgotten how to perceive them, let alone interact with them and report on them honestly and vividly. Nor do we have a clue what we ourselves are (hence the success of all the self-self books) in relation to the world around us. That makes it impossible to write personally and honestly. And writing that is not personal and honest is copy fit for telephone books.

I cannot refer to telephone books without mentioning my friend and neighbor Carlton Appelo, who is also president of the Western Wahkiakum Telephone Company. A fine writer and local historian, Carlton employs the annual telephone directories as repositories for his moving accounts of our local pioneers and their vanished communities. Owner of a captive audience, Carlton Appelo is the only writer I know who makes the telephone book work as a medium of literature. Most of us lack such an outlet and must make do with the traditional homes for personal print. Even so, as terminal writers who wish not to be extensions of our terminals, we can resist a world that seems bent on becoming less literary and more removed from the personal, direct response to individual experience. We don't have to have our own telephone books; which is good, since soon there will be no more telephone books.

Some of the ways are simple to voice if not always to perform. Live directly. Allow your knowledge, sensation, response, and experience to draw acutely from the physical surfaces of things, and then dive deeper. Take at least some of your satisfaction from outside of your brain and its attendant machines, every day. Every day, come to your senses—use every one of them at every opportunity. In seeking to serve readers, be one yourself: read widely, abundantly, diversely, demandingly, critically, light-heartedly, generously, without excuse, and more than you ever thought possible. And when it comes time to make your own leaves speak, do so from your own carefully observed, individually encountered experience, in as much particularity of detail as you can possibly recount.

Spend gladly as much time as it takes to get the words right. As *New Yorker* editor William Shawn once told John McPhee, who wondered how Mr. Shawn could take so much time with his copy: "It takes as long as it takes." Read it to someone, to yourself, to your cat, then do it all over again. All this is proof against a world where literary expression threatens to vanish into nothing more than the speed of light.

As John McPhee told me, he answers all of his correspondence, by hand. He asks how could he do otherwise, when the letters he receives are the one actual sign of a bond between the writer and his readers? To live as writers, we must revise our expectations of reward. Few will make their livelihood exclusively or even substantially through their writing, and to expect to do so is probably asking for disappointment and disillusionment. But to pay the occasional light bill or car payment with a writing check is not unreasonable, and viewed in that light, every tangible reward brings jubilation. Royalties are rare; I think of them as funny-money, worth more than other dollars, to be spent for pleasure if possible. Nor should we live or die based on reviews or acclaim. As writer Susan Lardner wrote in the *New Yorker*, "A good writer has no reason to be surprised when the world offers him less in the way of fame and riches than he deserves." Expect calumny and neglect: then if praise comes, it too will be a delight and a surprise.

Sometimes, just rewards jump up and surprise you. When I last taught here at Centrum, many of us laughed along with Robert Olen Butler's remarkable fiction, and wrung our hands and towels with him when none of his five acclaimed novels were in print to be sold or signed alongside other faculty members' books. Some months later, I attended Bob's reading for his new book, *A Good Scent from a Strange Mountain*, at the Elliott Bay Book Company in Seattle, along with five other souls. At dinner afterward, Bob told me that he didn't really mind, because the six had been attentive and enthusiastic, but that it would be nice if this book were to bring more attention to the others, perhaps giving them a paperback future. A few months later, he won the Pulitzer Prize for Fiction. He may never have had such an intimate evening in a bookstore since.

This could happen to you; but it probably won't. It is enough to have those among us who flag the fact that literature lives, and is loved. That means a lot, and it lets us get on with our honorable task of scratching the letters on the leaves. And what, then, is the reward? If great remuneration is unlikely, if critical attention is sparse and praise even thinner on the ground, and if the publishing world we've read about and hoped or expected to join all our lives is changing under our feet like an ice-cream sidewalk in the sun, why bother?

Because of the possibility of achieving *hē'ladē*; or, if not having everything right, then getting enough of the words right that you know you've made something that looks good, reads well, and will stand. As the Blackfeet singer-songwriter Jack Gladstone wrote in his song "The Builder," "You know, building is a risky thing to do / When the work you perform outlasts you." Jack also wrote, in a splendid song entitled "Dyin' for a Metaphor," "That's why we're designed to weave our way / Through the forest of word-lore / Dyin' for a metaphor." These things are true of us, the writers, who are builders. And when we find our way through the forest of word-lore with just the right metaphor, and know that we have built something that will outlast us, we take great joy in it.

And for the same reason that John McPhee answers all his mail. Malcolm Cowley said, "A writer is someone with readers." When you know that you have a reader, one who took time to read your stuff from among all the stuff that's out there, one who chose you over the screen and other cheap thrills, and one who has gone to the trouble of expressing love for your work in a letter, it is worth more than any review or royalty check. At least, it is worth a great deal.

The *New Yorker* recently profiled James Wilcox, a novelist with five well-reviewed books to his name who is nonetheless living in near penury. James B. Stewart's article closed with a letter Wilcox received from one devoted reader, a pregnant woman whose father had just suffered a heart attack and who couldn't sleep in the heat. In part, she wrote: "I'm clutching to the things that I love. And I love your books ... Please write another novel fast because I can't sleep ... Is that a lot to ask? I'd do the same for you."

Such are the real rewards. If not a letter from someone sleeplessly awaiting your words, it might be a comment from a workmate, unsolicited praise from a partner, or a kind word from someone who accidentally picked up your story, thinking it was a recipe. Even an unkind word. Anything to prove that you have broken through the incandescent screen to connect with another human, that you got enough of the words right to make the talking leaves shimmer and rustle in the breeze. When that faint whisper shouts above the cacophony of the information gridlock, not only for yourself but for someone else, then you know why you write, and you know that writing (and all it means) will never die as long as literate creatures litter the landscape, committing senseless and random acts of reading.

I am currently completing a long project inspired by the rich and many Bigfoot traditions. One of the schisms I have found among the true believers is that between those who would kill a Sasquatch to prove its existence and those who don't think it's worth skirting the moral brink to do so. When I recently interviewed Dr. Grover Krantz on this point, the Washington State University anthropologist and Bigfoot seeker said that if he had a chance to pull the trigger it would be the hardest decision of his life, and he would regret either outcome as long as he lived. But he believes that the discovery and subsequent protection would warrant the life taken. When I asked him about the morality of killing a possible hominid, he said that the animal's apparent lack of tools renders it not human, from an anthropological viewpoint. Many other serious searchers agree with that opinion. Language, of course, is considered more advanced than tool use, and many Northwest Indian traditions speak of Bigfoot as having language. Whether the animal exists corporeally or metaphorically, it is a powerful presence. Yet its seeming lack of tools, fire, and talk makes it liable to be shot to prove its existence.

Perhaps this would indeed lead to ultimate protection, and one hesitates in any case to make comparisons between human ethics and the metaphysics of monsters. After all, if Grendel walked today, he would not exactly be embraced by the ACLU, munching the heads of Thanes being a capital crime. Yet it is instructive to remember that many episodes of imperial genocide were justified on the basis that the victims were savages who did not even possess language. Of course they all did—often languages whose subtlety and range of expression surpassed that of their conquerors. Yet, lacking a written language, they were dismissed as sub-intelligent. And because they had not mastered the secrets of the talking leaf, they were powerless to combat violent change through the power of the pen. Not that it would have been enough: Edward Bulwer-Lytton's quotation, after all, reads in full: *"Beneath the rule of men entirely great*, the pen is mightier than the sword." That's a big if. Even so, Sequoyah recognized that power—the advantage given the whites by written documents—and he believed that it was obtainable.

In search of the pen's power, he went into the woods deliberately and pondered the problem. Twelve years later, he emerged not with a *Walden*, but with the means to make one: the only syllabic alphabet ever perfected in its entirety by an individual. The literacy he was able rapidly to bestow upon his people led to the eventual confederation of the Cherokee Nation after removal to Oklahoma. When Sequoyah joined treaty talks in Washington, D.C., he was asked why he had made his written language. Jeremiah Evarts wrote this contemporary account of his reply:

> He had observed that many things were found out by men, and known in the world, but that this knowledge escaped and was lost, for want of some way to preserve it. He had also observed white people write things on paper, and he had seen books; and he knew that what was written down remained and was not forgotten. He had attempted, therefore, to fix certain marks for sounds, and thought that if he could make certain things fast on paper, it would be like catching a wild animal and taming it.

Sequoyah was right. What is written down is not forgotten. It is powerful, and it can change everything. It is also all we have.

Note: I wrote this essay as a craft lecture for the Port Townsend Writers Conference at Centrum, Port Townsend, Washington, delivered in the summer of 1994. As I gave it on my birthday, poets Marvin Bell and Garrett Hongo did their best to disrupt it. When I got to the part about worms, Garrett stood up in the rear and shouted, "You're not going to tell us about *worms*, are you?" Then Marvin stood and played a fanfare on a plastic toy trumpet, and Garrett went on, "At least not until we sing 'Happy Birthday' for you, you're not!" Everyone sang it, and that pretty well did it for my presentation.

A Mineral King Esthetic

The black-and-white bullets shot past, faster than birds are supposed to fly. Snatching the scrap of cellophane I released onto the breeze, one of the long-winged darts took it aloft perhaps a thousand feet, then dropped the shiny trophy. It shimmered as it drifted through the blue Sierra sky. Before being lost in the sugar pine tops, the cellophane filled the bill of another pied sailor that once more launched skyward with the toy. All the while, half a dozen non-players exploded through our vision, clicking and flip-flopping like mad, exultant racers. These bicolored speed freaks were white-throated swifts, and their watchers were a group of visitors to the top of Moro Rock, a granite dome in Sequoia National Park. As a ranger-naturalist for the National Park Service, I recruited the artful swifts as thrilling interpreters of the Sierran scene. The tourists and I shared pleasure over the playful performance between stone and sky.

Each time I climbed Moro Rock to show off its swifts and

its views, I found myself distracted. All perspectives beckoned, from the high summits of the Great Western Divide on the east to the wilderness redwood forests vaguely visible on the south. But in the southwest there lay special intrigue, inviting my imagination again and again. For there, twenty miles away through the resin mist, lay Mineral King. I could just make out its mountain rooftops.

The ranger-naturalist's daily work consists of the stuff from which great vacations are made. Nature walks took me deep into Big Tree groves, across the lush meadows called "gems of the Sierra" by John Muir, down into marble caves of wonder and up to high-country lookouts such as Moro Rock. But I longed to see corners and stretches unpeopled. So on days off, I backpacked into remote sections of the granite parkland. Through my work and my leisure, I experienced many of the intriguing features of Sequoia and Kings Canyon national parks. I was trying (vainly, of course) to embrace the entire Sequoia experience in a single summer. All along, I wanted most especially to visit Mineral King, whose mystique sailed up the rivers on the wings of a swift.

Mineral King. In 1969, the name recalled a dozen recent articles, scores of fiery altercations, and the introduction of a classic environmental law case pitting a planned superresort against wilderness. All implications of a powerful land-use battle, each saturated with iron economics and acid emotion so contradictory that those to judge must be bewildered. No further summaries are needed of the political and legal aspects of the fray, no further catalogs of the ecological travesty purportedly in store, no more bared ledgers in prediction of recreational treasure to be lost or gained. The Sierra Club and Walt Disney Enterprises, the residents of the valley and the café operators in Three Rivers, the backpackers and the skiers, all had been represented and pleaded for repeatedly in widespread print. As a college activist, I was no stranger to this battle, and many others. But I was also seeking to educate myself as a naturalist, and that's how I wanted to encounter the place. I wanted to experience, take in, and form for myself what I called a Mineral King Esthetic.

From Giant Forest, where my wife JoAnne and I lived in a small Park Service tent house, Mineral King was within relatively ready access. The distance is forty-five miles on rather unusual "highways," however, and JoAnne had only one day off a week from her job selling curios for Fred Harvey, the park concessionaire. We had, therefore, some trepidation about undertaking a one-day visit, including getting-there time, knowing that the King required much more, even for a cursory look around. On a Thursday in late July, I spent my first of two days off exploring a few of the many miles of trail in the glorious Big Tree groves of the Giant Forest Plateau. When I came home, I found our car packed with hiking and camping gear, and JoAnne, home from work, sitting on the porch with an excited "Let's go!" look on her face.

This was a good idea. There was still an hour of light remaining and we hoped, by scurrying down the steep and curvy Ash Mountain road into the valley below, to be able to travel at least some of the still trickier Mineral King road while vision held. Petrified eastern tourists in front maintained a conservative speed for us. We were delayed further by a special meeting that occurred just past Amphitheater Point, where one passes out of forest and into the oak-and-yucca chaparral. It was our first tarantula, gingerly plodding across the warm asphalt. We stopped, leaped out, and set the furry creature into the shrubbery by the road. Then I invited it onto my boot, where the great chestnut spider was photographed. Its spinnerets brandished on an uplifted abdomen, the tarantula was obviously upset. So we left, thinking it a wonderfully exciting rendezvous. As we drove down the mountain we were followed by the lengthening shadow of Moro Rock, Sequoia's monumental, silvery exfoliation dome of granite, jutting out of Giant Forest.

At Three Rivers, the voluminous Kaweah River's three forks coalesce, and the Mineral King Road leaves the state highway. It was dark by the time we regained mountain altitude and the oaks changed back into giant sequoias and white firs. The road's primitive, serpentine nature revealed itself in the headlights and the shocks. The express superhighway proposed through here was madness, I could see already. Not only would sequoias fall to the bulldozers, but also thin and bony soils would rebel—as would the citizens, when their tax backs broke under the state subsidy for such a folly. We rolled past Atwell Mill and Silver City, specters of a former kind of time. We made a simple camp at Cold Springs Forest Service campground, at the foot of Mineral King Valley.

Morning sun shone through a roof of fir and pine and into a bower of red currant and leopard lily. Cold Kaweah water on our faces made the morning clearer in our eyes. Looking up from the stream, I was surprised to see a forest of aspens lying snapped in flattened, frustrated palisades. Quaking aspens have evolved very limber trunks and can weather a snowy niche hostile to other trees. Their defeat here told dramatically of the extremely rigorous winters served up yearly in snowballed Mineral King. Consecutive avalanches challenge any winter resident; recently one of the Disney surveyors had been killed here by an avalanche. This hardly portended anything good for the proposed massive ski facility. Yet the plan called for five to ten thousand visitors daily to be concentrated in this wild, fickle ice-crusher.

Where Monarch Creek merges with the East Fork of the Kaweah on the valley floor, the Mineral King spectacle came out in full: massive, implacable peaks on three sides; a narrow green valley running up toward a graceful gap on the south, slit all along by wild canyons, and life zones mingling in floral richness. Rustic cabins, unfinished or faded red, told of earlier arrivers to live with the King. What the settlers took was little, and they left behind nothing more but a scattering of pretty cabins that might as well have grown from the red soil itself. I tried not to think of the plastic, aluminum, and shoddy veneers that would replace those weathered boards if Disney came in. In fact, I tried not to think about Disney at all for the next few hours.

Faced as we were by numerous glorious possibilities, we elected to start right there. So at eight, we left the cabin cluster and headed up an easterly slope of sagebrush and lupine. In early exultation JoAnne sped upward. I wanted to dawdle, to "ramble" as the British say, so I could see and hear the place, smell it and taste its summer ripeness; so I could feel the way it still was. An olive-sided flycatcher buzzed "Pick THREE beers" from a hidden perch. I thought of the swifts and was glad they'd sent us here.

Padding along past rosy pussypaws, I noticed bracken fern among the sagebrush, a strange combo brought about by the meeting of the higher and the lower alpine elements. Soon, however, open space was replaced by thick scrub of manzanita, bearing the "little apples" that give the plant its Spanish name. These fruits, and the protective cover of the brush, attracted rufous-crowned sparrows in numbers, the rich auburn of the manzanita trunks echoed in their caps. Looking back at a parent and immature bird scratching in the trail gravel, I was dismayed to see the veil of smog from the west, which penetrates the vision far into the High Sierra. My eyes shifted back around, and scanning the valley from

this first higher viewpoint, I was reminded sharply of the Grindel-
wald Valley near the base of the Jungfrau in Switzerland—only
without the tourists and their trams.

Flowers decked the trailside. Mariposa lily was easy to pick
out of the confusing brocade, with its triad of heliotrope-on-ivory
petals. Scarlet penstemon launched from a ledge. A trail crew
passed carrying power saws, picks, and spades. Happily for me
they took the Timber Gap trail, while I was continuing on toward
Sawtooth Peak. The efforts of these Forest Service employees are
appreciated, but I didn't need their noise that day over the calls
of ubiquitous robins. Otherwise I was alone on the trail; that is,
except for those who hang their shingles in the valley and tolerate visitors such as myself, such as marmots sunning in a rocky
draw and the flicker laughing from a cherry copse. Twisted, giant Sierra junipers dotted the slopes, their affinity with the giant
sequoias obvious in their russet trunks and bluish, scaly foliage.
Twisted, metamorphic rocks underlay the trail, gneisses, schists,
quartzite, and slate.

This meant that these mountains were not wholly a result
of the recent orogeny that produced the present Sierra Nevada,
but actually were remnants of a much older range. The first Sierra consisted of upthrust ocean sediments, most of which were
stripped away hundreds of millions of years ago. Fragments such
as these rocks in Mineral King, known as roof pendants, were
preserved, and metamorphosed by the heat and pressure of the
rising, molten pluton that would eventually extrude to become
the younger, granitic mountains.

One of my colleagues gave his weekly campfire talks in the
park on this topic. My own fireside talk, on Sierra birdlife, came
to mind when the ruby crown of a Cassin's finch glistened from a
dewy meadow, a Nashville warbler's color bespoke the rising sun,

and a pair of house wrens conversed in a snow-broken juniper, attracting a third who gave a different call and approached as I walked on. Overhead, a green female rufous hummingbird led two rusty males through an aerobatic pursuit. The trail reached the level of a snow bed on the creek and tunneled simultaneously into a snowbrush ceanothus brake. Not far below to the right, in a rocky draw, lay a fat pair of yellow-bellied marmots, doing nothing but delighting me, and that unintentionally.

Trailside vegetation switched to chinquapin, underscored by a yellow morning glory. Chinquapin, known by the golden ventral surfaces of its long, lance-like leaves, was a favorite with the children on my nature walks in the park, and I was glad to see it here. Now soft, green, and unimposing, the prickly fruit hardens into a botanical pincushion more formidable than a chestnut bur. Steller's jays and chickaree squirrels eat this fruit, I am told. The jay should have no problem piercing the spiny hull and extracting the tasty kernel within, but the chickaree's methods elude me if its face remains unpierced. But then, pumas do eat porcupines!

Groundhog Meadow was scored by two rutted trails, one heading south to Crystal Lake, mine proceeding north and east to Monarch Lakes. A sizable snowfield formed an impermanent pergola over the stream. Where the meltwater seeped into boggy soil, lush growth of corn lily burgeoned and blue butterflies harmoniously flew among mountain bluebells. Among the sedges bloomed Sierra star tulips, downy cream and pale lilac, their parts in threes. The trail wrapped around a low cirque and over a scree of sharp cobbles. Even the rockslide was alive, brightened by an alighting western painted lady butterfly, all salmon and black. Looming above were particularly ragged crags; at my feet, lemon wallflowers and a deep purple larkspur, both potential nectar for the rare short-tailed black swallowtails that plied the breeze below me. They crossed a dissected, some say "rotten" snowfield, which I saw was mine to negotiate as well. For me it would be more tenuous. l had to leave the trail to cross it, and soon I arrived at the head of the cirque, where I was greeted by luxuriant blooming heads of blue elderberry and by vermilion patches of paintbrush and red columbine.

The high country was officially introduced by a bird I had sought fruitlessly on many an alpine trek—the gray-crowned rosy finch. I especially like birds, such as these and redpolls, which flash just a hint of bright color from otherwise dun plumages. Somehow in the boreal north and the cool alpine, such packages of muted beauty seem more appropriate than flagrant color spectacles. I had that also, though, in the form of a great magenta clump of mountain pride (Newberry's penstemon). This flower forms a fine brocade along the General's Highway in Sequoia in June, but is later replaced by bright pink mustang clover. Here, the season retarded, the pride had just reached its peak. A clearwing bumblebee sphinx moth raided these colorful pitchers for nectar, its guise likely warding off the birds that prey upon moths but eschew bees. Over patches of yellow stonecrop flitted a pair of green hairstreak butterflies. Most mountain walkers never see these common things, and would be doubtful if told that there were emerald-green butterflies in these north-temperate mountains.

Leaving the trail was a decision of some finality, as I was not to regain it all the way up. I headed east and up into a second cirque bowl, this one pervaded with the scent of marsh willows as the plants became fewer and browner, the crags more jagged. The few remaining trees looked weather-pummeled, their branches trending eastward in response to winter westerlies. Then into a higher, wet, white, green, and pink hollow, and across a blinding snowfield up a steep southeastern gap choked with yellow columbines.

This is the alpine species; it varies from a delicate butter-yellow to a deeper shade infused with pink. A few summers later, in the Rockies, my fellow graduate student Russ Miller would show that these color phases are driven by the dominant pollinators, whether sphinx moth or hummingbird, in a given vicinity. Marmots piped. Yellow-bellied marmots pipe, rather than whistling like the hoaries of the Rockies.

I came into a stony, grassy swale with a few junipers on the south side of the main Monarch drainage. Immediately above me was the transition from juniper to foxtail pine, a five-needle species with red, reptilian bark. By the time I began the ascent of the fifth cirque, I came to the rather obvious realization that these many "cirque bowls" were, in fact, glacial steps—hollows plucked out by a single glacier, not just at its head, but all up and down a steep valley of jointed rock. When I felt there could be no more rises, there always materialized still another step. The sixth was bisected longitudinally by a wide and shallow stream coursing over polished rock directly beneath the prominence of Sawtooth Peak. This topography reminded me of John Muir's *My First Summer in the Sierra* and his first glimmers of alpine glaciology (as opposed to the continental he already knew from Wisconsin) and how it functioned, a study that would occupy much of his life.

Few nature experiences from our travels in Europe of two summers before will I remember as keenly as the Lüneburger Heide, the great heaths of northern Germany. So when I came upon red heather high in the fastness of Mineral King, I knew it already in kind and rejoiced at its purple presence. The flowers were larger and opened more broadly than those of the German prototypes (*Cassiope* vs. *Erica* and *Calluna*), but their bell-shaped corolla and needly, low green foliage showed their kinship to heathers in general. The heather grew abundantly in a high, wide gap to the south, out of which flowed many streams, some broadening into ephemeral pools of unthinkable clarity.

There was another generous snowfield to cross as I skirted this gap, trending east, certain only of the general direction I wanted. The sapphire Sierrasphere had not diminished in hue; it transmitted the summer temperature well, and I was warm. Each expanse of white occasioned several stops to rest my eyes and scoop a handful of grainy snow, called firn, with which to slake my thirst and ice my forehead. I had to be careful in this: the weird rufous patches of algae known as red snow were all about. It makes a striking sight where their masses have migrated to the surface of the snow, as they do in the day. The dusty snow only benefits from the addition of these rose highlights. But the red snow algae are supposed to be bad to eat, causing vile effects upon the stomach. Once, as I knelt to examine an especially scarlet patch of algae, I found a track. Then several, pacing toward a willowy slope. They were not very distinct, just clear enough to show that their maker was a bobcat. I was excited by the nearness of such a magnificent beast. Then I thought ruefully how ludicrous it was that the animal would be totally protected just a mile away over the crest of Sawtooth Pass in Sequoia National Park, while here on Forest Service land it could be killed at any time, in any way. How many times must that cat, with a home range of many square miles, have crossed that invisible line, oblivious to its significance?

The last couple of hundred feet of the 3,500 feet I was to ascend that day came as a scramble to a high, foxtail-piney rise capped with heather, a violet penstemon, and a chipping Oregon junco. The promontory itself was granite; this meant I had crossed a geologic contact somewhere and was now standing on 150-million-year-young Sierra rock #2. The nature of my substrate was not as important, though, as the fact that it was there at all, supporting me on high.

Dominating the south was Mineral Peak itself. Just as impressive, though radically different in countenance, is Sawtooth. How many Sawtooth Peaks might there be in the world, I wonder. As many as there are Deer Creeks, or Hidden Valleys perhaps? Surely none, however, that more deserve the hackneyed name than this. The day being limited, I topped out on a sharp shoulder summit between Sawtooth and Mineral peaks. Mineral is a horn carved from iron-tinted veneers of stone stacked very high. Sawtooth, like nearby Mount Whitney, has the skin of a quarry pile—small, bare boulders rolled into a warty, slaggy hide. It's the sort of place one expects to see bighorns, not butterflies. Yet gray-brown arctics, just a little darker than the wind, live hardy lives against the uninviting backdrop of the granite matrix. I watched one battle the currents along with tiny, dusky Shasta blues, almost impossible to distinguish from the speckled rock once they alighted.

Now, for the first time since she had bounded past me down in the sage, I saw JoAnne—tiny against the bony, snowy, upper flanks of Sawtooth. Obviously she, like me, was on no kind of a trail. I worried a little for JoAnne, but just a little. I knew her savvy for the highlands was great and that she was a better hiker than I. I watched her progress. When she was within signaling range, we somehow communicated our mutual desire to meet at the west end of Upper Monarch Lake.

Had I remained on the trail back at the first snowfield I encountered, it would have brought me to the foot of Lower Monarch. In my solo pathfinding I had passed instead behind a long ridge that hid the usual route from my view. When finally I came out onto this rocky peaklet, I found myself several hundred feet above and south of Upper Monarch, on the shoulder of Mineral Peak. Singing from a stunted pine-top, an eloquent white-crowned sparrow enhanced the clarity of the air. I leaned against a thick, slanted pine and allowed the breeze to cool my overheated body, as it blew the columbines and heather, the mountains and the water, and my mind. JoAnne and I met, after our respective scrambles downward, at the foot of Upper Monarch Lake. Dry sandwiches vanished with quantities of very cold water drawn straight from snowmelt. "Refresh" is a strange word to use in the wilderness, for one is always fresh there. Maybe replenish, or refuel. Anyway, while doing it, we were stunningly occupied by piercing patterns of ice melt. Indigo potholes and palest blue pools punctuated the quasi-polar expanse. It was hard to leave the ice. Cross-country took us down snowfields and rockslides.

We regained the trail somewhere near the point of earlier loss. Once taken, the path was a visual, if not pedal, delight. The warm day had brought many-gallon rivulets down every available drainage, the trail serving well to water huge flower gardens that no one tended. Our feet ignored the sharp-rock trail; our minds bathed in columbines, larkspurs, and corn lilies. This was balm for the weary. Thoreau spoke of wild pleasures as "barks and tonics," and so they are. One such for us was an aggregation of blue butterflies, involving several scores of winged jewels of four different species. Male butterflies often gather at muddy or wet sandy spots to extract salts through their soda-straw "tongues." Disturbing them in passing, we became immersed in a veritable blue haze, reminiscent of a similar swarm we encountered several years before in western Colorado, involving tens of thousands of participants.

As the last of the blues were left behind, we met a young couple, Jim and Barbara Muff, whom we had seen fishing at the lakes.

They were the only other people we encountered on this, one of the notorious "hiked to death" Sierra trails. We walked down together and, near the bottom, we paused to contemplate the valley's future. Jim, who hiked here often and knew the Disney plans explicitly, outlined several phases of the intended development for us. We had just been through an unfaked, unstaged true-life adventure. Thoroughly steeped in the day's sensations, along with the King's more brash and muted beauties, these Disneyfied details seemed not only horrific but utterly out of proportion with the resources available.

"Do you see the point where Monarch Creek runs into the Kaweah River?" Jim asked. The juncture was sharply inscribed in silver against a background of arboreal jade: a point of such simple glory that even the tiny dirt road and the few campsites looked anomalous. "That spot," he continued, "will be the hub of the entire thirty-five-million-dollar complex." Jim tried to speak with the leaping enthusiasm of the developer and entrepreneur. "The lodge will actually span both creeks"—his words becoming rueful—"which will be lined with concrete and stones for five hundred feet in each direction, to make a natural-looking setting here in the wilderness."

Driving home that afternoon through hot chaparral, the air gold-infused by the setting sun over the San Joaquin, we did not know whether we would return to Mineral King that summer; or ever again, if the worst came to pass.

As it turned out, there would be two more visits before we headed back north at summer's end. Sometime earlier, during a day spent on tour duty at Sequoia's beautiful Crystal Cave, supervisory park naturalist Jack Hickey had asked me if I might be interested in flying over the park. The Park Service leased a light plane and a pilot for purposes of aerial fire patrol, and it was aloft

daily throughout the fire season. Rangers were permitted to go
along if there was room available. I responded enthusiastically,
and a date was duly reserved.

So on Friday, August 15, JoAnne and I drove to Three Rivers early. We were to meet the pilot at the teensy Three Rivers
airport at 9:30. By 10:00, we were getting worried that he might
have forgotten to stop for us. It was always over 100 degrees in
the valley and foothills deeper into the day, but this morning was
still comfortable. Acorn woodpeckers glided between field-dotting
oaks. As the day grew warmer, people came to splash and plunge
in a deep pool on the lazy, California sycamore–lined North Fork
of the Kaweah River. But our anticipation was sky-high and we
were beginning to despair. Abruptly, a small green plane landed
from the north.

From it emerged Jim Josephson, who was to be our pilot for
the next three incomparable hours. We fueled and took off into
the now hot, lazy morning. The first few minutes aloft were spent
circling the oak-and-orchard lowlands, gaining altitude. As we
turned east, we passed over Kaweah Lake. It glittered, but showed
muddy drawdown hems as well. Striking southeast, we traversed a
great expanse of blue and California black and live oaks, trending
higher into Jeffrey pine and white fir. It seemed a very short time
until we were in Mineral King country, which we easily picked
out from the surrounding peak land by Sawtooth's stony scimitar
and blunter, blacker Mineral Peak close by. For our benefit, Jim
circled close around the two mountains. From above, our entire
route of the previous trip was visible. He executed a low swoop
the length of Mineral King Valley's green crease. Quickly we
skimmed pristine White Chief, then rose to cross alpine Farewell
Gap. Immense slopes of red talus, soft patches of tundra, and serpentine lakelets made the passage one of the most transfixing of a

flight that was later to include close-ups of the Great Western Divide, the classic glacial Big Arroyo and Kern Canyon, Whitney's crest itself, and the whole of the wild Kings Canyon wilderness. It was a heartrending passage, for unlike those places, Farewell Gap and its snowy, vaulting cataracts were not sacrosanct. The Disney plan called for great armies of steel towers to scale twenty-seven heights from valley to summit. It seemed a travesty at the time, though we too were violating White Chief's wilderness in a metal contrivance. I almost felt an impersonal satisfaction when later, while passing very close to Mount Whitney's eastern face, we saw the wreckage of a plane that had been denied its impetuous penetration of the wild mountains. But one was enough.

The summer waned. In Giant Forest, the meadows that John Muir had so loved metamorphosed from low spring carpets of pink shooting stars to tall, waving fields of carrot-like Queen Anne's lace. The several families of white-headed woodpeckers that had lived in our tent house dooryard had brought up their broods and vanished. When weekends grew few, I knew we should get back to Mineral King. The time we chose was toward the end of August. One night before we were to leave, JoAnne didn't feel well and decided to spend her day off resting. Nevertheless, I had a delightful companion: Dr. Gertrude Tank of Corvallis, Oregon.

A retired professor of dentistry, the seventy-seven-year-old Frau Doktor Tank still spent each summer hiking as she has done her whole life in Europe and America. I invited her to finish her month-long stay in Sequoia by hiking with me at the King. With Betty Etson, a manager for the Fred Harvey store, we drove down the mountain through blue elderberry, buckeye, and redbud. While the berry was still in bloom, the latter two trees were already coppery and crisply autumnal, telling of the advancing season in the lowlands. At 10:30 we arrived in the valley and camped in the heart of it.

Next morning, we might have driven a mile farther, but chose to walk when walk we could. It was better that way. We could catch the balsam air wafting from black cottonwoods along the wayside. We could both covet and have the treasure trove of gold in the valley bottom: goldenrod, groundsel, sneezeweed, and a buckwheat. Red and purple rimmed the roadside in the person of paintbrush and asters. As the trail began, I noticed a gathering of cheery white-crowned sparrows in among thickets of prickly gooseberries. The white heads of the composite pearly everlasting and the umbel Queen Anne's lace can look similar from a little distance, but here they grew side by side, giving close comparison. A little farther along there dripped and bubbled a tiny stream-garden of bracken and small willows, fabricating the lushest of greens, even so late.

Gertrude and Betty left me far behind, as had JoAnne before. But in their rapidity they couldn't have missed the spectacle I saw next. From the rocky soil of the trail-cut sprang a glorious cluster of lemony blossoms, looking like some strange, out-of-place exotic from a florist's hothouse. The Sierra blazing star astonishes the wilderness traveler with its exquisite form and brilliant hue. A broad flower with knife-like petals radiating outward from a center spray of dozens of waxy stamens, it is well named. Several clumps adorned the trail for a few tens of feet; they were the only ones I encountered all summer, and the first of my life. We didn't have *that* in Botany 113!

The unobscured sun was as intense as the blazing stars that day, so I enjoyed a water-pause at spectacular Franklin Creek Falls. This was one of a score or more falls lacing the day's walk— all quenching, in those pre-giardia days. Hereafter moisture was abundant in seeps and freshets, each fostering a lush garden. A cool breeze carried me into a meadow of mint framed by blues and purples of larkspurs, lupine, and another first for me—gentians. Of a species called explorer's, they were the same chalky blue as the lycaenid butterflies flitting over trailside seeps.

The valley narrowed. Its bottom was snow-filled and deep, the sides supporting gnarled junipers outlined against the white V below. The upper slopes opposite were Tyrolean in aspect, yet ungrazed. The trail crossed a scree of shining slate, which clinked under my worn boots. Between clinks I heard the grouped, sweet whistles of the yellow-barred, streaked finches called pine siskins. These were hosted by a very little pine that had found a tenuous foothold upslope.

I caught up with Gertrude and Betty as they ate their late lunch. We paused to rest and absorb the *Heidi*-esque scene. Here the carpet was woven scarlet with columbine and paintbrush, there yellow with coneflower and daisy; under all, a verdant fabric of sedges and grasses, becoming autumn straw in the upper ends of sunny vales. We were a mile still beneath the pass that had been our original destination, but we decided to descend because of time. That we did, after gazing long at Vandever Mountain on the west, Florence Peak on the east, and the great green crotch that is Farewell Gap in the middle.

Each thing that bid us stop earlier deserved a return visit going down. We marveled anew at the blazing stars, just closing for the evening. Nearby, on a bank that held a festival of flowers, Gertrude pointed out more gentians, of which I couldn't get enough. Along with the blue explorer's she discovered the Sierra gentian as well. This species is tinted deepest purple, my favorite color. Once more pausing at Franklin Creek, I dipped graham crackers in the alpine ice water. Creek dogwood quivered mildly in the waterfall's breeze beside me. Brown towhees skittered into the manzanita and out again and a dust devil swirled as we reached the car.

Rolling back into Sequoia's forests we talked a little, thought a lot. My mind followed paths of history. The old-time characterizers, in the days of Albert Bierstadt and George Perkins Marsh, spoke of the American wilderness in terms of sublimity. Such descriptions have passed out of common usage in the utilitarian literature of preservation ecology. Yet the experience I had undergone may certainly be called sublime, esthetically and ecologically. Surely Mineral King will change in some ways, some year, no matter how the current development controversy would be resolved.

For even if a montane Disneyland were defeated, the valley camping facilities would need to be expanded. Although Mr. Disney, some say, would never have let it happen, the Disney Corporation hopes to introduce five to ten thousand people per day into Mineral King. Such numbers would require a truly park-wrecking road. But even if Disney's proposed superhighway were denied, the visitors will likely multiply. For the battle is serving to popularize Mineral King, if nothing else.

So we were fortunate to have seen Mineral King exactly as it was, that summer of 1969; it will never be quite the same again. But if Congress reads the issue as I and many others do, at least there will still be a Mineral King—instead of the alpine Anaheim envisioned by poor Walt's avaricious outfit.

Note: In the late 1960s, I was attempting to fashion a made-up general studies degree in natural history and conservation at the University of Washington. Finally finding a sympathetic dean, I saw it all come together in a BA called "Nature Perception and

Protection." This essay, or a longer version of it, served as my senior thesis for the College of Arts and Sciences. This is its first publication. As for the place itself, Congress did the right thing, and Mineral King was annexed to Sequoia National Park. I hear that it has changed little. I have not been back in the fifty years since.

A Different Day
on Beetle Rock

The great, underappreciated natural history writer Sally Carrighar wrote beautiful and sensitive books in which she described some of her most beloved places and their denizens. *One Day on Beetle Rock* (1944) was later adapted to film by Walt Disney, attempting to show with photography what Carrighar had done with words. Both movie and book, through very different means, illustrated the lives and doings of the creatures of a wild park place—Beetle Rock, in Giant Forest, Sequoia National Park, California.

I was a ranger-naturalist in Sequoia during the summer of 1969. My lodging, with my wife JoAnne, was about half a mile through the Big Trees from Beetle Rock. Drawn by glorious Sierra sunsets and the prospect of tranquil evening walks, I visited Beetle often. I found it very different from what the book and the movie had prepared me to expect. Though it may sadden Sally Carrighar, I would like to describe Beetle Rock today—and to say why I think it has changed and what it implies about the health of the National Park system.

Visitors to Sequoia traverse the General's Highway. This winding way enters the chaparral of oak and yucca near Fresno on the north and Visalia on the south. From these points, the road snakes up gradually into forests of giant sequoia and white fir, past the General Grant Tree in Kings Canyon and the General Sherman in Sequoia, finally meeting itself in the middle. The highway never penetrates the upper mountains that make up most of Sequoia and Kings Canyon national parks, so auto traffic is concentrated in the forests when it grows hot in the valley below. Sequoia's hub is Giant Forest, a village located near all the major attractions for drive-through tourists: General Sherman (the world's largest tree), Crescent Meadow (John Muir's "Gem of the Sierra"), Lodgepole Visitor Center, the viewpoint on Moro Rock, and a literal drive-through sequoia.

Giant Forest is a great plateau of granite. In some places, the sugary white stone juts out in typical Sierran exfoliation domes. While none is as large or as well known as Yosemite's Half Dome, still Moro Rock is a very imposing landform. Several lesser monoliths stud the other edges of Giant Forest Plateau. One of these is Beetle Rock.

Beetle Rock protrudes little and is actually rather shield-shaped, like a beetle's carapace. Hence its name. It enjoys a perch on the very western border of Giant Forest, poised thousands of feet above the San Joaquin Valley, free enough from the forest to possess a truly panoramic view. Standing on its sandy surface, I tried to re-create in my mind the wild conditions that surely did exist there at an earlier time. But as I said, I found it different. What follows is an account of one of my visits. I'm afraid it was typical.

I had just finished guiding an afternoon nature walk on the popular Congress Trail of the Big Trees. Arriving home at our small but sufficient tent house on a hill near Giant Forest Village, I remembered that JoAnne was working late at the concession store where she was employed. Since I had no evening program to give that night, I decided to doff my uniform for comfortable Levi's and walk through the woods to Beetle Rock to photograph Steller's jays and the sunset. To get there, I had to cross a wide, deep ravine. Once up on the other side, I watched the pristinity of the scene fade as I entered rows of tight concession cabins. The way led through a great cluster of rustic cottages, past the lodge amphitheater, and finally to the Beetle Rock Recreation Hall. This large pine dance hall, game room, and theater, built for the concessionaire's employees and guests, sat right next to Beetle Rock itself.

Emanating from the dance hall came classical "sunset music," provided by the concessionaire for the enjoyment of guests on the rock. I settled onto a flat stone to enjoy the western sky, just beginning to blaze. Placidity was short lived. I was the first person on the rock, but was soon joined by dozens of visitors. Many sat quietly in anticipation of the impending glory, intensified by the light brown haze over the valley. But many did not. First, I was unnerved by a childish yelping. One game of tag evolved into whole clumps of loud and rowdy people, parents and children alike, raising their voices in a manner ill befitting the contemplative scene. This persisted until dark. One large family ignored the sky scene entirely, while consuming a large quantity of Polaroid film on shots of one another engaging in raucous antics. The film backing was discarded, although the salts it bears are both attractive and toxic to deer, which frequent the area at night.

On my right, a boy threw a cola can down the slope of the

rock. Following the clanging, shining object with my eyes, I was amazed to see a thick stratum of glass, paper, and metal refuse on nearly every ledge and recess of the rock! I reprimanded the child for his careless action while his father looked on blankly, later denying any obligation to retrieve the can.

I tried to escape the clamor of the callous crowd by immersing myself among jays on a manzanita-covered ledge a bit to the north. Admiring the azure birds, I uncased my camera and lens. My topic for evening amphitheater programs was "Birds of the Sierra," so I was always trying to boost my store of good bird slides. But even the bold jays fled, retreating to high and distant Jeffrey pines, when unleashed dogs came bounding menacingly across the granite. Once again, an admonition to the sheepish owners. Then, just as I decided my off-duty ministrations were over, and I would be able to enjoy the sunset, another father and son scaled the gentle face from below and arrived in front of me. In their hands were large bunches of wildflowers (which scarcely grow on Beetle at all). I gave them the same explanation of protected natural objects that I dispensed every day all summer to those carrying armloads of vanishing sugar pine cones.

"Whaddya mean I can't pick flowers?" asked the man. "What's a national forest for, anyway?" Amid the drone of human voices far too loud, the reflections of broken pop-bottle glass and flip-top tabs shining brighter than the crystals of quartz in Beetle's matrix, I watched the crimson, smoke-stained sun melt into a tangerine sky. As the others departed and it finally became quiet, I considered remaining to watch for the appearance of the stars—surely that would be the same as always. Then, from the dance hall just behind me, there rose the piercing wail of a rock band . . .

What has happened to change Beetle Rock from how it was

in Carrighar's day? I maintain that the decline of Beetle Rock experience and the assault on its ecology are not by any means entirely the fault of the National Park Service. Uniformed rangers are dispersed through the park as far as the budget allows. Even so, it is simply not possible to have a ranger present every time an infraction is about to occur. Such things have been going on ever since people came to the parks, as evidenced by several of Sequoia's once-rich marble caves that were destroyed by visitors in the last century. Such violations of nature have always been a part of the makeup of one large segment of park visitors. Today, increased visitorship concentrates such instincts, so they are felt the more. But the problem cannot be attributed to greater crowds alone. My experience leads me to believe that illegal actions by tourists are seldom intended as such. *Almost always, offenders plead ignorance of the very regulations they are breaking, or of the purpose for which they were established.*

Typical remarks I have received are these: From a family prevented from removing whole armloads of giant sugar pine cones, "You mean we can't take these home to New Jersey? I thought they'd make great souvenirs since we can't get 'em back there." From two grown children brandishing knives while climbing a sequoia root-swell, when asked if they were cutting their initials in the bark, "No, but we're going to. Dad said it would be fun." And from a woman picking a large bracken fern unabashedly while four rangers looked on and listened in amazement, "I'm just getting a *few*. That's okay, isn't it?"

I contend that the national parks are in serious jeopardy from vandalism, removal of natural objects, the feeding, killing, and harassment of wildlife, and a multitude of other illegal actions, and that the cause (or at least, excuse) for this behavior is mainly ignorance. If this is true, then it seems to me that radical innovations are imperative to acquaint park visitors with park purposes and policies. We must cure ignorance.

There are a number of simple things we can do immediately to relieve the situation. First, all things contradictory to serious park protection must be removed. Already-initialed trees and rocks should be restored, for example, to reduce invitation to further vandalism. The actions of park and concession employees, not always exemplary, must be regulated for the same reason; no concession operations should be allowed to deface park property, for this makes a mockery of rules. And obvious hypocrisy in "educational" materials must be perceived and removed. For example, in Sequoia, as in most parks, campfire programs are provided each night both by the park ranger-naturalists and by concession personnel for lodge and cabin guests. A film shown frequently in Sequoia, being so obviously appropriate, is Disney's adaptation of *Beetle Rock*. On the whole this is another "delightful," though stereotyped, animal adventure. However, in one scene there occur no fewer than five blatant violations of park regulations. While encountering various denizens of Beetle Rock during a picnic, a family is shown feeding and handling a fawn, tearing foliage from shrubbery, throwing objects at a bird, and littering: all clear violations of regulations. At no time are the characters upbraided for their actions in any way. How, I would ask, can park officials expect visitors to obey little-publicized rules when even dear old super-conservationist Walt pays them no heed?

The lack of proper publicity is another matter to be remedied. The Park Service has too long demonstrated its reticence to "overburden" the visitor with regulatory instructions. I can cite these specifics: Each car entering a park is given a pamphlet that contains, very briefly, park purposes and rules, but no effort is made to assure that each visitor actually reads the contents of the pamphlet. Inside the park itself, rules are seldom displayed. In Sequoia, for example, occasional DO NOT ENTER signs on barriers and DO NOT FEED THE WILDLIFE signs along the highways and in the meadows are about the extent of the posting. I have been highly impressed by the large, attractive signs that I have observed at many stopping places in the Swiss and Italian national parks, illustrating in several languages and in tongue-spanning pictures exactly the sorts of behavior expected and prohibited. Why cannot these be provided in American parks?

A third area of deficiency is found in the enforcement of regulations; I seldom witnessed the levying of a sufficient fine or even a serious reprimand. Usually, after being cited by a ranger who was concerned by an infraction and happened to witness it, the guilty parties merely made a perfunctory visit to the office of the chief enforcement ranger—after which they were often released without a fine. If regulations are to have any meaning at all, they must be enforced regularly, consistently, and more earnestly.

Useful as these suggestions might be, they are nevertheless prescriptions for treating the symptoms of visitor abuse—not its cause, which is ignorance. In the courts, ignorance of the law does not hold up as a valid alibi; yet in the national parks it often works. Therefore it seems that the best means of protecting our parks from—and for—people lies in the elimination of their essential ignorance. I propose that no citizen of literate age or condition be admitted to a National Park Service–administered area without possession of a certificate of knowledge concerning basic park purposes and regulations.

If this sounds at first like a radical abridgement of the rights of the American citizen, consider the following analogy: our highways are publicly owned and are administered by various public agencies and levels of government. Everyone has access to them.

Yet no one may legally operate a motor vehicle upon the highways without first having proven his or her ability to do so without jeopardizing others. No one argues seriously that this procedure limits his or her constitutional rights. Driving restrictions do restrict, but driving is considered by the public and by the courts to be a privilege, rather than a right. The basis for this idea is the mass good in balance with the convenience of the individual. Think what the roads would be like if highway regulations were treated as cavalierly as those for the parks.

Conceptually, the use of national parks is also a privilege, not a right. In some democracies (including this one), access to certain ecological preserves within national parks is denied to everyone but essential scientists and managers, and legally and rightfully so. Sections of our own military reserves, which are public land, are likewise totally unavailable for public entry, for different reasons. Once again, the underlying principle supposedly served by this limitation on personal freedom is the good of the whole—an object of democracy. In this context, licensing of park visitors ceases to appear as a fascist imposition and becomes a democratic imperative.

To elaborate on the idea, no one old enough or able to take the test would be permitted entry to a park without such a license—which might be called the "park-pass." Once issued, this park-pass would indicate to all that the bearer had demonstrated knowledge of the manner in which he or she is expected to behave in a national park, national monument, national recreation area, national historic site, or other National Park Service (NPS) area, just as a driver's license assures one's fellow drivers of proven competence and safety on the roadway. I can foresee two great benefits that would accrue directly from the adoption of such a system.

First, virtually all park visitors would have had mandatory exposure to the particulars of park regulations and appropriate comportment. This would surely result in large-scale reduction of the number of infractions, from the very day the system was activated, simply because people would not have to guess how to behave in a given circumstance. Second, license-holders could no longer plead ignorance of regulations that they had violated. Thus, once apprehended, they could be punished as if it mattered—which it does.

Naturally, the mechanics involved in executing this plan would be complex. But they are not insurmountable, and I believe the benefits would far outweigh the effort and expense entailed. Such a scheme as this might work to envision and undertake the park-pass plan:

1. The park-pass would be issued upon successful completion of a simple examination.
2. The examination would be administered at a variety of public offices designated by the regional directors of the NPS, including Park Service and other Department of Interior offices and centers. Examination forms could be distributed at post offices, as are Civil Service and Internal Revenue standard forms. Take-home tests need not be ruled out, for if the examinee were to certify by a signature that the answers were his or her own, then he or she could be held legally responsible for their content. If administered on this level, costs could be low. [This was written before the internet arose. These days, it might chiefly be done online.]
3. Once bestowed, the park-pass need be renewed only at very infrequent intervals. Like road safety habits, the park

ethics involved should, once they are put into practice,
lodge firmly in the visitor's mind.

4. A fee may or may not be levied for issuance of the park-pass;
    with a small fee, the program should be self-supporting.

5. Depending on future decisions regarding fees for general
    park use, a special rate for seniors, renewable annually or
    for life, could be incorporated into the park-pass.

6. As far as the economics of the plan are concerned, no mat-
    ter what the cost of its adoption, it could not possibly exceed
    the current cost, in dollars and grief, to both rangers and
    visitors.

7. Now I would like to propose a potential park-pass exam-
    ination. I have chosen objective testing means and feel this
    to be inevitable for practical processing purposes, as well as
    to prevent discrimination against those with limited facility
    with the language. The parenthetical Xs refer to correct
    answers in this multiple-choice example.

Park-Pass Examination

This park-pass test is being given to help you learn the purposes
and regulations of our national parks and the reasons behind
them. For each question, please check the letter of the answer you
feel is right (just one for each).

1. National parks and monuments are:
    a. The same as national forests.
    b. Administered for multiple use, including logging, min-
        ing, and grazing.
    c. Places where nature is as fully protected as possible,

with compatible recreation encouraged but other uses prohibited. (X)

d. Basically for recreation, where people may do as they please to enjoy themselves in the outdoors with little restriction.

e. Especially for scientific purposes, where all recreation is discouraged.

2. In a national park or monument, visitors may:

a. Take *no* natural objects whatsoever for souvenirs or other purposes without a permit. (X)

b. Take tree cones and rocks, but not flowers, berries, or mushrooms.

c. Take anything for hobby or souvenir purposes—minerals, butterflies, flowers, etc.

d. Take what they need, but not more.

e. Take things for scientific purposes, without a permit.

3. Animals in NPS areas:

a. May be fed if one is careful.

b. May be handled if one is gentle, but may not be fed.

c. May be killed if not desirable, such as snakes, spiders, and slugs.

d. Are entirely protected, except fish where fishing is allowed, biting insects, and dangerous species that are actually attacking. (X)

e. Are there for the public's use as regulated by the state wildlife department.

4. Trailbikes, motorcycles, jeeps, ATVs, and mountain bikes:

a. May be used wherever practical without getting stuck.

b. May be used only on roads and trails, to prevent erosion.

    c. May be used only on *designated* roads and trails, never in sensitive habitats. (X)

    d. May be equipped and ridden as the owner desires for maximum enjoyment.

    e. May be used in "waste areas" anytime: dunes, beaches, marshes, etc.

5. Trash, garbage, and refuse:

    a. Should be buried, especially in the backcountry.

    b. Should be discarded where it is not likely to be seen.

    c. May be dumped anywhere; the rangers are paid to collect it for your convenience.

    d. Should be saved until a proper trash or recycling container is found for it, or taken home. (X)

    e. Must always be taken home with you.

6. Visitor conduct in NPS areas:

    a. Is entirely up to the visitor.

    b. Should never be overly noisy or rowdy, in or out of camp. (X)

    c. Can be city-like and undisciplined in camp and at places where many people gather, but not on trails in wilderness.

    d. Should be as in any park or playground—uninhibited.

    e. May certainly be loud and boisterous, in keeping with the recreational theme, as long as no one complains to the ranger.

7. Carving or painting of initials or slogans on natural objects and buildings, cutting trees and shrubs, and use of guns in parks and monuments:

    a. Are all perfectly acceptable—a park is a place to let go.

    b. Are different kinds of things—the first two are okay, but not the last, for safety's sake.

    c. Are frowned upon, but are not punishable offenses.

    d. Are all basic American citizens' rights, which may not be restricted.

    e. Are all forms of vandalism, for which one can be strictly punished under federal law. (X)

8. Campfires in NPS areas:

    a. Are a tradition and are encouraged anywhere, anytime, with any wood that can be found.

    b. Are potentially dangerous; may be built only in designated places and must be carefully extinguished. (X)

    c. Are safe these days; forest fires are no longer a danger thanks to Smokey's campaign.

    d. May never be built, under any circumstances, due to fire danger and wood shortage.

9. Camping in national parks and monuments:

    a. Is the real reason for the parks—anyone is encouraged to camp wherever there is space.

    b. The above is true only when designated campsites are full.

    c. May be done in trailers and campers on any pullout or back road, since not enough campgrounds have been built.

    d. Is restricted to tents, and lean-tos made of brush and boughs.

    e. Is restricted to designated campsites and back country zones; no trench-digging or bough-cutting allowed. (X)

10. Pets and small children:

    a. Must be restrained—pets always on leash, children under control of a parent; pets prohibited on most trails. (X)

    b. Are not allowed in national parks and monuments.

    c.   May run freely—they need the exercise and fun.

    d.   Are not restricted as long as they don't hurt the wild animals.

    e.   May be loose in campground, but not elsewhere.

Other questions of better construction might well supplant mine. But the ten examples given here make a good base, in that they embrace much of the material we need to communicate. And there are certainly other forms an examination might take. Programmed instruction, a powerful and promising new educational tool, might be employed here with great success. It presents the material, tests the learner, and corrects the answers simultaneously, allowing for an eventual 100 percent score for all, at their own speed. It could well do the job better than a plain test, though it would require sophisticated testing expertise to construct.

Since the illiterate, young children, and many non-English or ESL speakers clearly could not understand the suggested exam, it would be proper (and feasible) to construct alternative tests in different languages and on several levels of comprehension, age, and ability. These should vary to meet differing experience quotients as well, such as rural versus urban. This is a vital consideration in the context of NPS goals to attract a more diverse visitorship.

Modern testing and measurement research should be incorporated first to establish the test's goals and objectives, then the test itself built to satisfy those goals. Of course, a booklet of preparatory information should be available for study, as with driver's license testing. If, as would surely occur, certain individuals could not handle any of the test options, there could be temporary park permits issued so that they could visit the parks in the company of one who holds a park-pass. This would provide for short-term foreign visitors, the illiterate, the developmentally disabled, and young children.

It is only a matter of personal conjecture at this point as to whether or not a park-pass plan as I have presented it would work. I think a powerful assumption can be made that it could, and I deeply hope that it will have the chance. I'd like to think that if Sally Carrighar could come back in some more enlightened future, she might recognize Beetle Rock and smile.

––––––––––––––––––

Note: I wrote this piece for *American West* magazine in reaction to my shock, as a young ranger-naturalist, at just how much depreciative behavior by visitors I experienced, and how wanton it was. Some might think *reactionary* is just the word for this piece, and that my formula is merely authoritarian. All these years later, people problems in the parks are both better and worse. Even more people come, but innovations such as shuttle buses and digital devices have diminished some impacts. On the other hand, Trump's extended government shutdown demonstrated just how close to the surface truly appalling park behavior lurks, when supervision is suspended. So while aspects of my plan may be naive (perhaps acceptably so; I was twenty-three when I wrote it), I continue to think something like this may be both necessary and helpful.

When I returned to Sequoia a few years ago for a ranger reunion, I was able to see how very different the human footprint has become in Giant Forest Village. Almost all the housing has been removed, both for rangers and the many cabins for visitors, along with the dance hall, parking lots, and much else; and trails have been redesigned. The result is far less intrusive, as well as less democratic, as the only lodging options are distant and much more expensive. But I suspect Sally Carrighar might actually find Beetle Rock closer now to what she remembered in 1944 than it was in 1969.

Joys of the Suburban Jungle

Thanksgiving, 1966. Midnight on Mercer Island. We lay on a fragrant mat of big heart-shaped leaves, yellow and brown, in a grove of black cottonwoods, attempting to nap. My newly wedded wife JoAnne and I had decided to hike back and forth across Lake Washington in order to walk off our massive meal. We had a hell of a long way to go and we were already tired.

Then it began to rain. We got up stiffly and walked on. By daybreak we were back in our University District apartment, having hitchhiked the last bit across the Evergreen Point Bridge in a drizzly dawn. As I dived into the Murphy bed, I had time for two thoughts before oblivion. First, that my after-dinner whim had been a dumb one. Second, that there was an awful lot of open territory over there across Lake Washington.

JoAnne and I were sophomores at the University of Washington in Seattle. We had it in mind to study natural history, as much as our advisers would allow, and we reveled in the novel flora and fauna of this new green land. But, as in Colorado, whence we'd come, we'd lived in town, far from the seductive hills, too poor to reach the wilderness often. The cottonwood leaves we knew then were chiefly in Friday-night parking places in leftover groves between tracts.

Now, farther west, we hitched a lift to the Cascades or Olympics whenever we could. In between, we took our nature where we could find it, among the scraps of land close to home. The Arboretum (the "Arb"), the Montlake Fill, Green Lake—these made the city tolerable. But when we finally equipped ourselves at the first REI store, and were eager to try out our gear, we had to go a little farther afield—camping in the Arb was frowned upon. So we caught a bus to Bellevue, to explore some of the de facto wildland we'd seen looming on that long night's trek. Bridle Trails State Park turned out to be as good a place as anywhere to get lost, get soaked, and decide we still needed a good tent.

And on JoAnne's birthday in August, unable to get away to Mount Rainier as planned, we followed a tip from Janice Krenmayr and hiked in Redmond instead. Her *Footloose Around Puget Sound* told of an old redbrick roadway through a perfect rural valley. It made a memorable day, replete with red-tailed hawks and longhorn Highland cows.

We were not the only ones to seek nature near the city. Some of our professors did the same. On a fine day, Dan Stuntz would pack up his fungi class and take us 'shrooming in Denny Park on Lake Washington and in Juanita, where chanterelles abounded in the deepwood about a seminary. Or Frank Richardson would lead his mammalogy class on vole-trapping expeditions in Cherry Valley near Duvall, yellow warblers and sunshine illuminating the Oz-like morning. Somehow it all seemed invulnerable, back then.

When we left Seattle, JoAnne for Alaska, me for England, we went with a sense of nature abounding near our adopted city, and a plan to return. She discovered real wilderness in Alaska and remained. And I, seeing in England how well people and the countryside can coexist, was shocked when I came back years later to find the Puget Sound sprawl as bad as any I had left behind in Denver. I fled to Portland, then the deep country, and seldom looked back.

A couple of years ago I went to Redmond to try to see a vermilion flycatcher, the first ever recorded in the region. The fiery red mite made quite an impression in the snowy January landscape of the Eastside of Lake Washington, and hundreds of birders came to spot it. I never did (though I later saw many others, in their proper habitat, in warm Mexico). But I did get my first good look at the Eastside in years. The bird had sensibly selected a bit of set-aside open space along Bear Creek for its bivouac. But all around, forever it seemed, the countryside had traded places with condominiums and automobiles and the further modifications that they and their inhabitants require. Where had that Thanksgiving countryside of yore gone?

I grew up in Hoffman Heights, a postwar subdivision on Denver's hem. Sam Hoffman built his big new towns on the farmed-out edges of several Midwest cities, shrewdly greeting the hordes of returning vets with sound but modest new homes big enough for their quickly expanding families. Hoffman's premise was this: the cities are done, and the country is inconvenient. I'll give you the best of both in that grand new creation, the suburb. A lot of people bought the idea, and his houses sold fast. Hoffman's idea was not new, of course. As early as 1885, Baron Walter von Richthofen, an uncle of the Red Baron of World War I, had announced plans for Montclair, "a beautiful suburban town." In his prospectus,

Richthofen attempted to lure investors to his prairie plats with the following come-on, remarkably true to today: "Denver has now become so large and closely built a city that it seems impossible, within its boundaries, to fully enjoy the pure air and delightful climate." He went on, stating the suburban theory perfectly: "A great want has been a pleasant suburban town combining the advantages of country and city, where both health seekers and pleasure lovers might at leisure enjoy surroundings at once tasteful and convenient to Denver."

My grandmother Grace Miller ended up near Montclair around 1925, lured by that logic. But before that she bought her first house on Naomi Place next to Ravenna Park in Seattle, with the same idea: to situate oneself away from the smokes of town, yet within easy streetcar reach of the center (as Ravenna then was).

The ideal was fairly easily reached when the suburbs were small and truly on the edge of civilization. Montclair abutted the Great Plains, as Hoffman Heights had in its time; Ravenna backed onto an ocean of old growth. Where the plan begins to break down is when growth reaches the point that either the suburb becomes the city (as both Montclair and Hoffman Heights have done—both are now historic districts) or the countryside itself retreats, sealed off from suburbanites by miles and miles of themselves.

In reality, the majority of Americans have grown distant from nature. Most of us have a greater or lesser need to rub up against nature and open countryside, especially those whose minds and spirits have been abraded by the rough edges of modern urban life. As Valerie Martin suggests in her short story "The Consolation of Nature," in the end, only nature herself can restore a sense of safety. Biologist E. O. Wilson terms this innate desire to connect with other forms of life our "biophilia." In short, nature is therapeutic.

Second, when we completely preempt wild habitats, even common species of plants and animals drop out. As we fail to have daily contact with the elements of natural diversity, we cease to care about it. This becomes cyclical, extending the wave of extinction before the engine of our own alienation until we exist divorced from our coinhabitants of the earth. I call this the Extinction of Experience: the less we see of nature about us, the less we concern ourselves with keeping it. And as we all should know by now, we cannot long survive apart from the rest of nature.

Happily, some have always recognized this. From the historical park plans of the Olmsteds to the greenways movement of today, visionaries have long sought to bring nature to town. Mike Houck, urban naturalist for the Audubon Society of Portland, has become a guru in this field. His annual Country in the City conferences have attracted planners and open-space advocates from all over the world, and have become expositions of enlightened development. Portland, with its five-thousand-acre Forest Park, makes an appropriate setting. Both economists and naturalists have come to agree that concentrating people within largely natural areas makes sense. The alternative means spreading people so thin and far as to create a no-man's-land that is neither urban nor really rural. Townscapes with nature intact also take visitor pressure off first-line nature reserves, national parks, and wilderness.

The success of maintaining habitats for humans and other species together depends largely on our ability to develop a love of damaged lands. Opportunities for setting aside virgin places near population centers have mostly vanished. But the chance to renovate secondhand landscapes as open space and habitat is one that could be taken much more often. That Ravenna, Schmitz, and Carkeek parks were saved for Seattle in their forested glory is a credit forever to farsighted people. That the Montlake Fill, Magnuson and Burbank parks, and St. Edward's Seminary are now fine urban wildlife centers on Lake Washington could scarcely have been foreseen based on their former uses. As a boy of the suburbs thrashing in Denver's wake, I survived on hand-me-down habitats, mainly an old ditch snaking through beat-up former farmland. Now, a resident of the ravaged landscape of logged-off Willapa, I still seek nature's gentle stimuli in a landscape hard done by. What I have found is that wilderness is essential, but that in its absence, the secondhand lands will do for the time being.

Richard Mabey, the British naturalist, describes such places as "unofficial countryside." They are the wastelands, the abandoned flats in the post-industrial landscape, the vacant lots. Perhaps especially the vacant lots. I suspect that far more people have gotten in touch with their own biophilia on vacant lots or along an old ditch than in all the formal nature reserves.

So that which survives in our midst will be a sum product of all three: the old parks and greenways; the latter-day nature reserves, wetlands, and open spaces; and the random patches that happen to remain undeveloped. From that quick vermilion flycatcher trip and freeway glimpses of nearby Factoria, I was not sanguine about finding much in the way of such leftover life on the Eastside.

But I went to do just that—to investigate whether much of nature survived in the Northwest's newest conurbation. I left I-405 in midtown Bellevue and headed east. I had decided to ignore the guidebooks, the park maps, and other direct clues, and to follow my nose. And I began, not surprisingly, in a vacant lot.

Traffic was heavy on NE Eighth Street, the day wet and

blustery. Trying to decide which way to go at 124th, I saw yellow globs through my window. It had to be pussy willows. I pulled over, got out, and found a vacant lot on the southeast corner worth having a look. Cottonwoods and Douglas-firs formed a canopy over the patch of rough grass, Scotch broom, Styrofoam, and bramble. One side was fenced. Over the wire hung the saffron stems of rain-slick madrona and the shiny leaves of its bushy relative, salal. And there were the pussy willows—soggy catkins, smeared with yellow pollen, looking like bumblebees caught out in the rain. Next to them, the other early flower of the Washington spring, Indian plum. Its unfurled leaves, the freshest green imaginable, stood up to the rain; its white flowers hung in odoriferous chains. Merely a vacant lot. I could have spent the day there. How many more were there like it in Bellevue?

I struck deeper into the suburb. Before long I crossed a creek labeled with a fish sign. Circling blocks, I found this Kelsey Creek at various points in its muddy plunge toward the lake. The rains had brought it to freshet, so that it throttled the bankside grasses and sloshed the rip-rap in the creekside backyards. From one crossing I could see an old barn and a wet white horse moldering by a wood in a little pocket of ruralia. Farther on, a western tributary encircled the backs of apartments on Eighth. An exercise trail ran along the edge of set-aside wetlands. The waterway, in anxious spate, emerged from a swamp and a wood, where the path led. Pine siskins and black-capped chickadees worked the new alder catkins for insects. Algae painted the fir trunks chartreuse. Houses leered through the screen of branches, but the creek and its riparian sanctuary were holding their own. As I drove out of the lot, Garfields and Bart Simpsons vied for attention from apartment windows. Living where they do, these people would be better off spending their pennies on a Roger

Tory Peterson field guide, but I wondered how many ever take a look out back.

The infilling along Bel-Red Road was phenomenal to me. Dover Station. Country Creek. Ridgemont. One house, a 1950s outpost with auto bodies, uncut brush, and dangling hazel catkins, held out as if a reproach to the new town opposite, topped with fresh cedar shakes and driveways full of shiny toys.

The Lake Sammamish Parkway couldn't see the lake. Villa Marion. Chandler Reach. Sammamish Landing. Then the fancy heathers and cypresses ran out into brambles and broom, alders and willow, and I found myself alongside Marymoor Park. This substantial slice of Official Countryside grew out of Willowmoor Farm, and a goodly chunk of it is still willow moor. Much of the rest is now developed for recreation; but, as with most parks, adaptable wildlife will use it nonetheless, and the best times to visit are those when everyone else stays home. So there were no whizzing bicycles at the velodrome, but masses of mew gulls glided overhead like the cottonwood fluff that was months away. Crows, starlings, robins, and mallards inhabited the soccer fields, ducks the flooded parts. Ornithology in the suburbs is often a matter of paying homage to elegant opportunists, especially in the rain.

The Marymoor Windmill stood battened against that rain above the Sammamish River. Before the lakes were lowered when the ship canal between Puget Sound and Lake Washington was dug (1911–1934), the windmill stood at water level. Chiefly decorative, it never ground grain or pumped water. Now it is newly decorated. The northernmost of its eight sides is richly clad in bright lichens.

In the brown water, a crisp black-and-white common goldeneye steamed past a covey of coots. I could have followed it downstream ten miles, all the way to Bothell Landing, along the

green Sammamish River Trail. Never mind that the more suitable name we knew in the 1960s, Sammamish Slough, has since
been yupped up to River—it is still one of the great lowland walk-
ways in the region. Thanks to floodplain and farmland preservation legislation, much of its way winds through undeveloped
pastures, woods, marshes. And if I had a week, I could hook into
the Burke-Gilman Trail for passage around Lake Washington
into the city, or take the Tolt Pipeline Trail for a long easterly shot
(through rapidly developing woods) all the way to the Snoqualmie
River and the foothills of the Cascades. It seemed there was something left after all.

As I rambled the hinterlands of Greater Redmond, I felt al-
ternately depressed by the rate of our species' proliferation, and
heartened by signs of care on behalf of others. Summerwood.
Morning Meadows. English Hill. The names of subdivisions
always seem to co-opt the essence of that which they erase, or
else try to sound English, borrowing on that country's partially
earned reputation for a sympathetic countryside of charm. As the
"several new Redmonds" that the crusty conservationist Harvey
Manning predicts eat away at the moraines, plateaus, and ravines,
the landscape that results is anything but English. Only restraint
and maturity can bring that. The one seems in short supply, and
the other takes time.

At least there seems to be a thought spared for the fish. Trib-
utaries of Bear Creek were signed as "excellent salmon streams,"
and announced as being in *our* care. This is good. But I kept
thinking that if we are to care for the salmon, I wish we had more
say about what goes on upstream. Time will tell. If the tribes of
salmon and settlers can survive together, perhaps names such as
"Country Creek" and "Summerwood" will be earned.

As the day waned, I wished that I could visit the old redbrick road again, to see how its valley had fared. I had little hope of finding it after all these years, having long ago lost my *Footloose*. But as I came out of the Old Fall City Road—flooded fields, tufted with orchard grass and hardhack, backed by old-growth cedar stumps with springboard slots and springing hemlocks—and headed up 196th, there it was. I parked and walked the maroon stripe of the old brick roadway.

Big houses claimed portions of the south end, but there was still a vine-hung farmhouse and barn with an orchard, crowded with mauve crocuses and shielded by a cedar hedge. Across the way, a modern squireage stood for sale. Its two tall maples hosted a cacophonous mass of starlings and crows, almost drowning out the traffic's thunder from nearby thoroughfares.

The brick road led, straight but for one jog, for one-and-a-quarter miles. Pastures and wooded hills looked unbroken on the east, though ranks of condos marched across the western horizon. The Highland cows were gone, but the red-tails still plied the air. And little Evans Creek still flowed through a valley largely made of small farms and wetlands red with osier dogwoods the color of the road. Frogs cluttered, towhees said "*screee!*," and marsh wrens buzzed on the marsh. A cattery was loose among the streamside scrub: pussy willows by the bushel. Relics of possums past joined the moss and mortar in holding together the cracked and rutted bricks of the old roadbed. Yes, it was still rural. Nice little houses at the north end, up on the western moraine, had been condemned by the massive gravel workings over the hill, where bulldozers whistled with irritating regularity: a NIMBY that didn't work. But the valley was somehow intact. And at the end, a handsome blue enamel sign with King County's crown informed me that the road was built in 1913 as part of the transcontinental Yellowstone Trail connecting Boston and Seattle. As the longest remaining brick highway in the county, it was designated a King County landmark in 1983. Since then it has been shored up. I could only hope that its landscape would fare as well for another twenty years or more.

The Yellowstone Trail ends at Arthur G. Johnson Park, open space acquired through a combination of a 1967 bond issue and a donation. Park development funds, happily, have not been forthcoming, so one can walk an old field thatched with buttercups and plantain, into a wood scented with sweet fir-terps and the cat-pee perfume of Indian plum. Sword ferns reached up to mingle with licorice ferns on a moss-clad maple, where a winter wren loosed its amazing polysyllabic song. The floor was laced with lady ferns and fuzzy leaves of saxifrage, purpled by the recent freeze. Three green cascara leaves hung like a limp sail among a mat of dewberry vine. Low sun emerged to light up a circlet of four firs and two cedars: standing in the middle of them, I felt myself in a powerful place left over from nature's retreat.

As the day closed down, I happened upon the old Juanita Bay Road, where Ninety-Eighth has been routed inland above the shoreline. The previous route, now a wooden walkway, carries one right over the marshy shore. Here, at dusk, a Virginia rail coughed from cattails where redwings plinked, unwilling to give up the day. Using the last light, a big feeding flock of bushtits and chickadees mined the pink buds and catkins, the old brown cones of alders. Seattle skulked off to the west, as cormorants clung to rotting pilings like so many skinny vicars. Clean mallards, and mallard-oids in all their bastard motley, hoped for handouts at the Jack in the Box that stands at the northern end of the walk. I returned along the slippery wooden sidewalk, sniffing the good methane stinks of the swamp, and called it a day as a light rain resumed.

The morning came bright and windy. I broke down and

consulted my Harvey Manning. He steered me to Lake Hills Greenbelt Park, a long, sprawling open space between Larsen Lake and Phantom Lake. The broad gravel trail leads through the red haze of working blueberry farms, the bushes as old as I am. In summer its edges go pink with cosmos planted for goldfinches. Minute green buds lined the cinnamon sticks of Douglas spiraea, their brown heads promising the sweet pink puffs to come. From a footbridge I watched Kelsey Creek being born and a pair of hooded mergansers ruddering offshore in the stiff breeze. Slaty coots, nipping off fresh grass shoots, gave me the red eye. Coyote scat in the path was gray with vole fur, would be blue with berries in late summer; it seemed to bear no relation to a nearby load of unfurry dog shit. This, I thought, is what we have accomplished in a million years: to turn wild dog sign, odorless and interesting, into something disgusting. When I got to the trailhead, I found cardboard pooper-scoopers available for walkers. This was definitely Official Countryside.

At the ranger station, I overlooked community pea patches from a patio where special gardens for butterflies and hummingbirds awaited the summertime. Judging from the plants, this should be a fine place to spot anise swallowtails, red admirals, and many other bright wind-sailors. I was going to have to revise my opinion of available nature in the Eastside suburbs.

But Harvey had mentioned old growth right there in Bellevue. Right where his *Footsore 1* told me to look, I found Phantom Creek debouching from its artificial course into the wilds of cornily named Weowna Beach Park. I followed it down toward Lake Sammamish. Rounding a massive rootwad from a downed Douglas-fir, I came to a moss-upholstered maple with golden-crowned kinglets tinkling in its boughs. A hollowed totem of a cedar stood beside a fir fully fifteen feet around. "Old growth" may be a stretch, except in relative terms, but there are some big trees and, if not the full diversity of an ancient forest, at least some of their associates. All of a sudden I found myself in a semblance of big bush that could have been a slice out of the Olympics foothills—just four miles from Bellevue Square.

Hanging over the gorge from a madrona handhold, at last I could hear no traffic—until a seaplane roared off the lake. An early midge hatch glimmered against fire-blackened boles. A round, brown polypore fungus on a broken hemlock resembled a perfectly toasted marshmallow; old ones on the ground were flat and black like overcooked shiitake. A moss suitably called *Hylocomium splendens* made a downed log into a forest ridge; lichens the color of Key lime pie daubed a stump that was a Gotham of life. Here was a "vacant lot" that could serve as a primer on the old-growth issue. It wasn't wilderness but it was wild.

If Weowna was the antithesis of the sterile suburb, how about the heart of the place? I knew I could visit Kelsey Creek Park with its white barns, or Bellevue Nature Park on Mercer Slough (not yet River), and find more in the way of nature. According to Harvey, the several parks departments had done a fine job. But I was curious about the city center—for a prisoner of Bellevue Square and its environs, would there be anything to see?

So I concluded my expedition at Downtown Park. The Lake Hills Connector took me there across acres of wild wetlands. Then, at the freeway, one enters the unremitting *urbs*. Downtown Park borders Bellevue Square on the south. A broad lawn stippled with crows and vetch earns the green patch on the map. But the primary attraction is the pink gravel path rounding pink concrete waterways and waterfalls on several levels, the whole punctuated by cadres of pink obelisks—lamp standards—alternating with plane trees. The effect is very formal. Did it have anything to do with nature? I was unsure at first.

As I watched the pleasing flow of water over the pink rim of the fall, I remembered that water falls much the same everywhere and that this was no more artificial than the "old growth" outflow from Phantom Lake, which had been rerouted for convenience. There was no doubt that the curves and ripples and soft plop of droplets moderated the starkness of the mall and high-rise scene beyond. And this is true of fountains everywhere: water is the principal palliative we have.

Then I remembered something else. It was in a concrete pool such as this, the Drumheller Fountain on the University of Washington campus to be precise, where one day in February of 1966 I encountered my first bufflehead duck. That warm ball of floating fluff, plumed in crispest black and white, seized my imagination. It was just what a nature-loving urban exile, deep into his first Seattle winter, months from the nearest butterfly, needed. And it began a love affair with birds that has now run a quarter of a century.

There was no bufflehead on the pond at Downtown Park just then. But there could be any day. There were gulls, and the nutmeg hanging seed balls of sycamores. And as I left, I noticed a tiny, brambled vacant lot hunkering against one corner of the park. Perhaps the last one in downtown.

To live in the suburbs is to know change. As in my home district of Willapa, where it doesn't pay to become too attached to any one tree, your landmarks and hangouts are here today, gone tomorrow. Flying squirrels leave, tough gray squirrels come in. We settle for something less than what there was. The suburbs are not, after all, the countryside. But with planning, care, and willingness to spend good money and land on nature, something worthwhile can survive.

If you will seek out these special places that a friend of mine calls the "cracks in the grid"—official and otherwise—you need not be cut off from nature because you, and a great many others, live here. The suburban ideal, at least in this sense, can work—to the extent that the human metastasis can be contained and kept from wiping out all that we wish to keep. An old saying of my grandfather's about Sunday dinner applies nicely here. "That was mighty fine, what there was of it," he would say, "and there was plenty of it, such as it was."

Note: This essay was, like any portrait of place, a picture in time. My friend Kelly Fine, who lives in Bellevue, has brought me up to date on these places. Post-Microsoft and all the rest, many of the "random patches" have been lost or soon will be. But the parks remain, even if some of them are being eaten alive by English ivy. As for Weowna Park, Kelly says she positively relies on it. "These woods are a narrow island in the suburbs," she says. "A narrow island where noisy eagles nest!" Long may those narrow islands last, in suburbs everywhere; and long may walkers stride the red-brick mile of the Yellowstone Road.

Eden in a Vacant Lot

SPECIAL PLACES, SPECIES, AND KIDS IN THE NEIGHBORHOOD OF LIFE

And *freedom* is this September field
Covered this far by tree shadows
Through which this child chooses to run
Until he chooses to stop . . .
—PATTIANN ROGERS, "Concepts and
Their Bodies (The Boy in the Field Alone)"

In a culture where growth and the advancement of "civilizing" forces against the frontier have always ruled, empty ground has represented little but an opportunity for more growth. The precarious condition of undeveloped land in modern cityscapes threatens the basic tie between humans and the rest of nature, as expressed and achieved by children in their preferred haunts. As the vacant lots go, so goes a source of intimacy and education that contemporary culture can scarcely afford to lose.

From the observed fact that a city abhors a vacuum, a peculiarly American vocabulary has arisen: *raw land* is a real estate term connoting acreage that is ripe and ready for conversion from a natural or undeveloped state to an "improved" condition; *waste ground* is acreage that may have had a productive use in the past but is now unused and therefore "wasted"; and perhaps the oldest and most widespread such term, *vacant lot*, is a tract, often platted or lying within a matrix of developed property, that remains ungraced by human structures and is therefore "vacant."

Unlike all these terms, which usually carry negative or at least unappreciative implications except in a speculative or opportunistic context, the phrase *open space* is generally applied positively, suggesting that the land in question has value for the very reason it is open. Yet open space may apply to the very same plots as raw land, waste ground, and vacant lots. Recently I heard a hybrid moniker—*open ground*, which conveys all the ambivalence we as a colonizing culture have felt about such places.

Alone among these labels, *vacant lot* elicits widely affectionate following among one special group of users—children who have vacant lots in their lives. It is my premise here that nothing is less empty to a curious, exploring child than a vacant lot, nothing less wasted than waste ground, nothing more richly simmered in promise than raw land. Yet too many adults seem to have forgotten the vacant lots of their growing-up years. In a word, the young and the grown often have different values about open ground.

In my classes and lectures, I make a point of asking the audience members or students whether they can remember a particular place where they made early contact with the land as boys and girls; a place they went repeatedly to play, explore, sulk, or think; a small, particular corner of the landscape where they went to make forts, catch creatures, and mess about with water and plants.

In most groups, most hands go up. I then ask them to picture the place and to tell me something about it. Commonly, the special spots are watercourses, such as creeks, canals, ravines, and ponds; a big tree, clump; brush, bosky dell, or hollow; parks, especially undeveloped ones; and old fields, pastures, and meadows. Very often, the term *vacant lot* is employed to define the place in question. In fact, insofar as most of my listeners have urban or suburban backgrounds, most of these sites of initiation are vacant lots of some sort. They share the qualities of nearness, wildness, secretiveness, and possibility. Most people can relate the details of the spot and tell stories from their places that surprise even themselves with their remarkable clarity and nuance, and the deep affection aroused.

Next I ask a question whose answers tend to arouse feelings of both sadness and solidarity: How many can return to their special places and find them substantially intact? A recent example brought a typical outcome. In October 1999, I addressed a group of managers, scientists, rangers, engineers, teachers, activists, and others involved in the future of the Cherry Creek Watershed in Colorado—the same watershed in which I grew up. When I asked the first question, almost every hand flew up. The participants' faces showed pleasure, excitement, and even reverie to be invited back into their childhood haunts—the very places that had lured them into their current professions and involvement with watersheds. But when I asked the second question, fewer than ten hands went up in the audience of three or four hundred. Almost everyone's special place had been spoiled or greatly changed, and all those fallen faces told the story. As the following discussion showed, they took some comfort in the fact that others shared their concern and distress over lost landscapes, and everyone emerged from the exercise bolstered in the common belief that such places must be saved wherever possible.

My own convictions along these lines came from a modest place indeed, an artificial watercourse that transects Cherry Creek on its run from the mountains to the plains. The High Line Canal emerges from the Platte Canyon in the Colorado Front Range and flows some seventy-five miles to its terminus in a small Platte tributary. A historic irrigation ditch that once was Denver's major water diversion, the canal now flows intermittently and peters out near Denver International Airport. In an era of "epic liberties taken with water," as Marc Reisner put it in *Cadillac Desert*, his epic history of western water, when sixteen major tunnels carry western slope water to the Front Range cities, the significance of the High Line has shifted from water transport to recreation. But in the 1950s and '60s, "the ditch" played a massive role in my growing up.

As denizens of the easternmost postwar subdivision on Denver's hems—an expansion of the small town of Aurora—we dwelt within a rigid grid of new streets laid down on farmed-out prairie. The Rockies attracted me mightily, but I lived on the Great Plains side of the city. From the day my older brother Tom came home and announced the discovery of a neat ditch full of intriguing wetness and greenery, the High Line Canal became my constant haunt, friend, and focus. Its tangled growth and sinuous path made the perfect getaway from the raw young suburb. Free to roam after school and in summer, I fled the town for the ditch every chance I got.

In the summer of 1954, Tom and I found ourselves caught out in a devastating hailstorm that broke the backs of cattle in the field next to us with hail the size of softballs. Small boys with no protection, we were literally in mortal danger. Tom swept me into a massive hollow cottonwood tree, and it saved our lives. Even so we were badly bruised, and he was concussed. Ever after, the hollow tree situated the center of our universe, and the canal took on even greater power.

When I left our ordered block and crossed an embryonic park, a set of tracks, U.S. 6, and a farmer's field or two to reach the canal, what I found was an unordered world of brown and green mystery. Long, broad-bladed grass hung over the banks and waved in the current. Chocolate wood nymphs flip-flopped among those grasses, big black-and-white admirals glided through the willows above, and still higher, their visual echo on the wing, the voluble, iridescent magpies. Orioles, flickers, kestrels, and kingbirds kept us constant company if we kept our slingshots holstered. I envied the few farm kids who actually lived along the canal, and did my best to live what I imagined was their lives, while watching out for rough big boys and the ever-threatening farmers and ditch riders.

Over the coming years, I sought out the winding, cottonwood-shaded watercourse for purposes of exploration and play, alone and with friends; discovery of crawdads, birds, and butterflies; sulking and kicking the dust through a troubled home life; hiding, camping, fort-building, stealing corn, cooking out, and pretending every kind of life in the out-of-doors; and ultimately, walking and parking and petting with girlfriends. But even in high school and later, when the chief social attractions lay in the town, I took myself to the fields and banks that had brought me up as a naturalist. I thought I was the only one, but I was wrong. Of my few peers who later became involved in life sciences—a vet, a zookeeper, a federal wildlife agent—all attributed their interest at least in part to the High Line Canal. And so I believe it goes, for such places everywhere.

I have told the story of the High Line Canal and its impact on myself and others in *The Thunder Tree: Lessons from an Urban Wildland*. Attempting to capture the canal's overall import, I wrote: "Had it not been for the High Line Canal, the vacant lots I knew, the scruffy park, I'm not at all certain I would have become a biologist . . . The total immersion in nature that I found in my special spots baptized me in a faith that never wavered, but it was a matter of happenstance, too. It was the place that made me."

What is most germane here is the way in which the canal changed as Aurora, Colorado, grew from 40,000 to some 400,000 people. Fields, marshes, farmyards, and woodsy gulches all went the way of the D-9 Caterpillar blade. It is true that these rampant losses first inspired me toward conservation activism; it is also true that the efforts of many who loved the canal and what it represented brought about eventual protection for a few sites and consecration of the ditch riders' road as a part of the National Trail System. But much of the charm and fundamental fascination of the place were lost, and as they went, the canal's ability to influence the lives of children diminished. If such changes matter at the High Line Canal in Colorado, then the cumulative effect of millions of special places lost all across the continent must be vast.

The intense connection that children form with particular places is no secret. Peter H. Kahn Jr. investigated the origins of children's connections to the natural world through analysis of both physical and social sciences, concluding that these bonds are fragile and subject to stresses peculiar to contemporary culture. Gary Paul Nabhan and Stephen Trimble, David Sobel, and Kim Stafford have all explored "the geography of childhood" (Nabhan and Trimble's title), including detailed descriptions of their own places of fort-making, escape, and discovery. Sobel's "labyrinthine passages in the rhododendrons" and Stafford's "path threading through nettle and alder" show how these writers owe their naturalist lifeways to their hearts' own places.

The recognition of the importance of outdoor experiences for the young greatly predates these contemporary thinkers, however. From the late nineteenth century to the mid-twentieth century, nature study, as a formal element of school curricula, overlaid this bush savvy with actual pedagogy for many American children. The quality and depth of such instruction varied widely, of course. But most American schools employed Anna Botsford Comstock's *Handbook of Nature Study* (1911), and I have collected dozens of less ambitious but similar texts from the same era. While the nature study movement certainly did not produce a nation of sophisticated naturalists, it did ensure that most students received at least a framework of tutelage on which to hang their own outdoor discoveries. Flora and Fauna went right along with the Three R's.

The goal of accelerated mathematics and science instruction for all students both before and after World War II, peaking during the Cold War, all but extinguished natural history as a standard curriculum unit. Hard, numerical sciences took its place, and the observational approach fell into disrepute. Even the term "naturalist," revered in John Burroughs's day, became something of a derogation, implying a soft, nonscientific, and even sentimental approach toward an abstract nature. Never mind that descriptive natural history and systematics could be conducted with as much rigor as outright experimentation; they quickly became passé and lost support in the schools.

My own intense interest in natural history was certainly not accommodated at school, except by a few exceptional teacher-birders who offered a lifesaving afterschool ecology club. I was obliged to make do with books (including those dusty old nature study texts, which I began collecting in junior high school),

National Audubon Society pamphlets, and truly self-guided
walks. Nowadays, children may have formal environmental education to augment the classroom. Sophisticated in some respects,
employing water-quality tests and other modern techniques with
which Anna Botsford Comstock was not familiar, environmental
education nonetheless fails to replace the forsaken nature study
of earlier times. True, some innovative teachers employ map-
making, tracking, and other field-based exercises. But outdoor
education's common emphasis on games, teamwork, and motion
militates against deliberate and ruminative natural history. Kids
get lessons on ecological relationships, without much basic knowledge of the related organisms and their life ways—not even, or
especially not, their names.

Few students (or teachers) have even the most basic acquaintance with their local fauna and flora when they graduate. As
David W. Orr put it in *Earth in Mind*, "Even in this time of ecological concern, high schools, colleges, and universities continue
to turn out a large percentage of graduates who have no clue how
their personal prospects are intertwined with the vital signs of the
earth." Nor is ecological illiteracy limited to the cities. A friend of
mine from a rural logging and farming family recently told me, "I
cannot believe the people who have lived in this area all their lives
long who do not know a salamander from a salmonberry." If this
is true in the country, how much more critical must our ignorance
be in the cities? This is not an academic question, as the population concentrates more and more away from the countryside.

In modern times, the special places sought out by the young
have furnished an alternative education parallel to the classroom.
All children are autodidacts, their subjects depending on the
available curricula: if it is the streets, they will become streetwise;
if it's computers, they'll be screen wizards. But if what is at hand is

a scrap of the wild, at least some children will become naturalists before ever receiving instruction. Though this natural tradition is intuitive and associative rather than rote, and employs self-generated vernacular nomenclature (where I live, water striders are "skippers," and cinnabar moth larvae are "tansy tigers"), it triggers not only knowledge but also intimacy with nature among the young.

As cities began to grow in earnest, the demise of traditional field studies placed an increased burden on open spaces: if kids were going to become acquainted with nature, it would have to take place mostly out-of-doors, on their own time. Yet even as nature study faded, eclipsed in the shadow of Sputnik, the postwar housing spurt claimed woods and fields at a rate never before seen. And even as increasing numbers of families left the farmlands for the cities, the cities grew out to subsume their farmland edges. And as special places retreated before the growth of the suburbs and the towns moved to or became the cities, many children were left in little physical contact with the world outside their homes, schools, and shopping malls.

To begin to imagine the consequences of the destruction of urban open ground frequented by children, we must first consider the actual services such landscapes provide. The first that comes to mind is play. For much of our history, when children have been left to their own devices, their first choice has often been to flee to the nearest wild place—whether a big tree or brushy corner in the yard, or a watercourse or woodland farther away. This is where they can imagine and enact adventure, construct forts and intrigues, and hunt crawdads and bugs. In aboriginal societies this kind of play was essential for forming basic survival skills: today's crayfish and minnows are tomorrow's game and pot-fish. As the needs for bush skills evaporated, the atavistic pleasure in such play did not, and it continues to connect us to our hunting and gathering past, to our evolutionary legacy.

Second, I think of nature literacy. In tribal times, a close knowledge of other species was essential to survival. Most people grew up knowing many of their nonhuman neighbors, or if they didn't, they were in serious trouble. The argument can be made that because survival is no longer dependent on the individual's sophistication in the ways of the wild, we need not bother to foster it. My response would be that collective ignorance leads inexorably to collective indifference; and from there, it is not many more steps to ecological depreciation and collapse. In *Walking the High Ridge,* I argued that "Maybe excepting only human population and acute chemical pollution, the greatest threat to a sensible environmental future is nature illiteracy."

The third and perhaps most important service rendered by the vacant lots, creeks, and back forties is literacy's partner, intimacy. Widespread public intimacy with the natural elements of our surrounds gives us an opportunity to avoid the Extinction of Experience. The extinction of experience postulates that daily contact with a diversity of experiences—botanical, zoological, cultural, architectural, social—leads to an appreciation for the elements of a rich setting, if only implicit; to concern over threat to those elements; and ultimately, to the desire to conserve. But when common species disappear, they might as well (in one sense) be wholly extinct for those with a narrow radius of reach. Further, when variety thus drops out of the local scene and a sameness sets in, the sequelae may include widespread ignorance of the world's diversity, followed by disaffection, alienation, and apathy. These are not the states of mind that inspire conservation activism. So local extinctions continue, leading to still flatter and more depauperate environments and still deeper isolation from richness. The extinction of experience is thus a cycle whereby impoverishment begets greater impoverishment.

The ultimate result of the extinction of experience might resemble a super-urban condition described by Ashley Montagu and Samuel S. Snyder in *Man and the Computer*: "The city has become a wilderness in which human beings lose their humanity because inhumanity has become the way of life of the city—indifference, disengagement, and isolation." It is just this state of disengagement that makes the extinction of experience such a threat today.

A broad social construct like the extinction of experience is difficult to test analytically, consensus on its reality lending itself more, perhaps, to a common recognition of shared experience than to controlled experimentation. However, a strongly suggestive indication of the degree of natural change (which I call ΔN) can be apprehended by examining the response of the butterfly fauna to change in a given locality. Butterflies, because they are often ecologically specific, conspicuous, popular, and well known, have been used increasingly as effective indicators of ecological and biogeographical richness, uniqueness, and health. As habitats are developed, homogenized, and fragmented, numbers of individuals and of species decline. Furthermore, ΔN derived from local butterfly extinctions can be read as a measure of the suitability of habitat to influence the young, as it is often the insects, and in particular the butterflies, that arouse the curiosity of children, as expressed in the making of collections and observations, as E. O. Wilson has written.

I have studied the butterfly fauna along the High Line Canal in Aurora, Colorado, intermittently, from 1959 to the present. Over forty years I have observed and documented changes— some additive, most subtractive. Annual butterfly counts for the past twenty-five years have added to this database. By 1970, I had

recorded one-tenth of the North American butterfly fauna along
the High Line Canal. In subsequent years, when I accounted for
apparent and imminent local extinctions in my study area, I found
that the Auroran extinction rate (40 percent) was higher than that
calculated for Staten Island (23.6 percent), Orange County, California (21.25 percent), or San Francisco (7.6 percent), as I deter-
mined in a paper on urban insect extinctions. Since then, a few
of the species have reappeared, others have dropped out, while
new species have been recorded. But chiefly, the additions consist of erratic, adventitious irruptives and immigrant species and
generalists, unreliable from year to year, while colonial habitat
specialists have dropped out. For example, the High Line Canal
Fourth of July butterfly count has recorded the national high for
the introduced European cabbage white (*Pieris rapae*), a great gen-
eralist, for several of the twenty-five count years; whereas a colony of the related, specialized Olympia marble (*Euchloe olympia*),
formerly abundant in certain places, has vanished.

     If we further characterize ΔN by considering the area in hect-
ares (A) and the time (T) over which the extinctions (E) were in-
curred, such that $\Delta N = \%E/A/T \times 1,000$, then a measure of the
intensity of loss can be gained. By this formula, a nature reserve of
1,000 hectares that loses one species out of a fauna of 100 through
stochastic processes over 100 years would have a ΔN value of 0.01.
The four urban areas considered above would have ΔN values of
roughly 0.11 for Staten Island, 0.14 for Orange County, .80 for
San Francisco, and 143.0 for the High Line Canal in Aurora.

     Since the area (A) may relate more to biological consequences
(e.g., island extinction theory) than cultural, it could be excluded
from the equation. Doing so flattens the numbers somewhat. Calculating and including the radius of reach for particular human
populations, or selecting equal-sized sections of land to compare,

would also change the final numbers. However, the relative order remains the same. And even allowing for a large margin of error, these figures suggest that *the opportunity for experiencing nature in the cities studied has diminished measurably, most of all in the most rapidly suburbanizing of them.*

Furthermore, the homogenization of urban faunas and floras proceeds largely through the loss of small, marginal remnants of formerly widespread habitats. Insects are able to persist under these conditions longer than megafauna: the last habitats for both the Olympia marble and the bronze copper (*Lycaena thoe*) in Aurora were, respectively, an old field and a marsh fragment in a vacant lot. And since urban children obtain most of their natural contact in exactly these kinds of places, we may conclude that their opportunities for natural discovery decline in proportion to urban butterfly extinctions.

Finally, factoring in the high proportion of biologists, conservationists, and other resource professionals who gained their initial inspiration through contact with insects, ΔN as indicated by urban butterfly extinction may be considered a reliable index of the extinction of experience in action and a predictor of its effects. While it is not possible to demonstrate that environmental leaders will no longer arise from the streets of contemporary Aurora, it seems reasonable to conclude that the likelihood that young Aurorans will become avid naturalists and conservation voters has been reduced in parallel with the town's butterflies and the diversity they represent.

An important corollary of the extinction of experience holds that its effects operate especially strongly on those whose radius of reach is small—people who cannot easily reach beyond their neighborhoods for stimulation. This means, among others, the poor, the disabled, the very old, and the young. Future environmental activists emerging from the burbs are likely to be those children whose families can afford to send them away to camp or to take frequent sallies to the countryside, or those with a special place within walking or biking distance from home. When what you see on your block is all you get, the extinction of experience can have especially baleful consequences.

These consequences go beyond the initial cycle of the extinction of experience. When experiential contact with nature, in the broadest sense, is diminished, negative impacts spread out to every cultural level. Physically, youngsters suffer from the absence of exercise in fresh air that outdoor scrounging traditionally provides. The current epidemic of early onset obesity owes much to sedentary, often electronic, substitutes for outdoor play. This too creates a feedback loop, for the more slothful a child grows, the less likely he or she will be to seek physical play beyond the television or computer room, and the more likely he or she will habituate to recreational, even compulsive, eating.

We can further infer that nature-deprived children suffer intellectually, at least on some levels. Clearly, mental development does not wholly depend on abundant contact with plants, animals, soils, and rocks. Many people achieve keen intellectual powers in largely indoor settings. However, I would argue that breadth of awareness, facility of reasoning, acuity of observation, and the kinds of associative skills that enhance cerebration may all sharpen as a direct result of biological and geological exposure. Support for this and similar conclusions appears throughout the growing literature on biophilia, from E. O. Wilson's original expression of the hypothesis in 1986 to a gathering of essays on the subject edited by Kellert and Wilson in 1993. In a recent statement on the cultural effect of biophilia, Steve Kellert maintained that human powers of creativity and imagination, as well as our emotional well-being, owe much to the non-manufactured world. [Note in 2020: And see all the work since by Richard Louv, especially *Last Child in the Woods: Saving Our Children from Nature-Deficit Disorder.*]

If Kellert, Wilson, and others are right, then the places that arouse biophilia must affect us *emotionally* as well. The young people I know whose lives are rich in natural experience seem to be on firmer, better-balanced footing—and to be happier—than those whose universes orbit strictly around people and made things. Besides, as I know from my own experience and an abundance of testimony, the pain of losing one's special place is a deep and abiding betrayal that never fully recedes. It follows that preventing such losses will head off great hurt. In more positive terms, those on intimate terms with wild places find the world emotionally richer.

It is no large stretch, then, to imagine that the loss of contact can be morally depleting. We're not talking about rearing a generation of Saint Francises, and it is true that much outdoor play (especially among boys) involves testing cruelty and destruction. Nor is it the case that naturalists are good and urbanists are bad, ipso facto. But there is arguably a moral and ethical dimension that emanates or prospers in the light of personal immersion in the wholeness of the physical world. After years of study of human attitudes toward other life forms, Kellert concluded that "the more we plumb the depths of nature, the more we encounter its unrivaled capacity to nurture the human body and spirit."

The moral element has also to do with the maturation of ethics to extend beyond the strictly human realm. Cogent propositions of a moral relationship with the natural world may be found in Aldo Leopold's "Land Ethic," William O. Douglas's *Wilderness Bill of Rights*, Roderick Nash's *The Rights of Nature*, and Christopher

Stone's "Should Trees Have Standing?" Each of these thinkers makes a clear case for an advanced moral universe that takes into account the extra-human. Surely such an ethic would be more likely to develop in a nation that preserved its points of free and easy contact with rocks, trees, and wilderness—or in Leopold's inclusive term, the land, in small parcels as well as large.

Depletion of our natural context, both in quantity (or time) and in quality (or depth) of exposure, may interfere with the development of these and other human qualities. As Montagu and Snyder wrote in *Man and the Computer*, "separation from nature leads to a view of it that is wholly disengaged, even alienated, and frequently hostile. This is a pathological state, a morbid dissociation from what should always have remained a vital involvement with nature." Conversely, everything that acts to reconnect human culture with nonhuman nature counteracts the pathology. But in a macabre extension of the theory, the increase of sociopathic behavior actually accelerates the extinction of experience. Sadly, another factor must now be considered when it comes to children and nature—their personal safety.

Cuts, scrapes, and broken bones as unwanted trophies of outdoor adventures have always been with us. But now the panoply of perceived threats has expanded to include abduction and personal harm at the hands of adults. These specters are not new but were so rare in former times as to represent nothing more than a cautionary bogey. With population expansion and crowding, the frequency of assaults—or its perception—has increased to the point that few parents are comfortable allowing their children anything like the outdoor freedom and latitude that my generation took not only for granted but as an essential birthright. Whether or not violent incidents represent a genuine danger or one largely projected through sensational news coverage, parents think that the woods are unsafe. Recently, I met a woman, an academic sensitive to the natural world, who nonetheless would not permit her seven-year-old outside the family's cul-de-sac unaccompanied. This would have been sheer torture to my friends and me. I feel strongly that had I not enjoyed the freedom of the canal, I would not have become who I am. The loss of footlooseness among the young must be counted every bit as much a tragedy and a challenge as the loss of places in which to be footloose.

Now, in addition to the absence of formal nature study, the retreat of diverse habitats from the home ranges of the young, and the shrinkage of those ranges due to security concerns, we are experiencing the rise of the virtual in place of the real. Television has long commanded much of children's discretionary time: *The Mickey Mouse Club* and *Spin and Marty* certainly competed with the backyard for me, more than forty years ago, when only four TV stations were available in Denver. But in the past ten years, computer games, the internet, and other forms of secondhand entertainment have come to occupy an ever more enormous portion of childhood's hours. It is easy to poke fun at the man I saw speaking on his cell phone in a butterfly house in Seattle, ignoring the vast blue morphos shimmering all around his head in favor of his current wireless crisis; after all, electronic narcissism is everywhere on the street corners and freeways. But I was disturbed to see two brothers buried in their Gameboys as our Boeing 777 passed over the sunlit and unobstructed mountains, icefields, and calving glaciers of Greenland and, more so, to have the flight attendant ask us to lower our window shades, the better to see the video screens. [Note in 2020: And now?]

I have also found disquieting a rash of technical papers describing the boundless wonders of "class field trips in cyberspace." One such article contended that "Increasingly, technology is being used by educators to take students on 'virtual' excursions to a variety of fascinating places." I know that some of these electronic field trips furnish elegant and participatory instruction. "Journey North," for example, allows students anywhere to follow the migration of monarch butterflies and birds, as well as flowering rates, throughout North America, as they contribute their own observations. A videodisc is available that takes students "afield" with Lincoln Brower and his helpers studying the field ecology of monarchs. Used together, these could be powerful tools for understanding a subtle and remarkable organism and its world—especially if the kids get outdoors to see actual monarchs in an actual milkweed patch. There is the key: the electronic element should serve as a spur and a link for real-world watching, rather than a substitute. But not all of these media include the field component. At the same convention of science teachers where I was buoyed by an excellent exhibit of a hands-on program called "Kids in Creeks," sponsored by the Bonneville Power Administration, teachers spoke of principals content to let CD-ROMs, HyperCards, and the internet take the place of messy field trips with their insurance and staffing problems.

Of course, electronic mediation pertaining to natural history may effectively convey facts and impressions and generally reinforce interest in animals and geography. But when the world comes edited for maximum impact and bundled into quick bites, it fails to convey the everyday wonder of the much-maligned ordinary. Just as real life does not consist primarily of car chases and exploding buildings, quotidian nature is much more about grasshoppers in the pigweed than it is rhinos mating on a pixelated screen. Even butterfly houses and zoos, though they present a kind of primary experience, bear some culpability here. Displays of extravagant animals behaving dramatically in captivity and on television can spoil the young for the real thing outside their door. Those big, brilliant blue morphos in the tropical house should not erase the fascination of finding equally bright but tiny spring azures among the dogwoods by the ditch.

But what ditch? Ay, there's the rub. For when the ditches and creeks are all sent down the storm drains, concreted, or sprayed, they are lost to the children. Lucky is the child of the city or suburbs who still has a richly inhabited ditch, creek, field, or forest within walking distance of home. Nor, I emphasize, do parks and nature reserves make up for what I call the secondhand lands or hand-me-down habitats, which correspond to what British naturalist Richard Mabey described as "the unofficial countryside" in his book by that name. Parks are normally too manicured and chemically treated to offer much of interest to the adventuring youngster. And as for nature reserves, they might as well be paved over for all they offer in the way of boundless exploration. For special places to work their magic on kids, they need to be able to do some clabber and damage. They need to be free to climb trees, muck about, catch things, and get wet—above all, to leave the trail. Such activities are normally proscribed in reserves and for good reason. I support the strict protection of natural areas wherever possible, for the careful perpetuation and management of scarce elements of diversity. But the unofficial countryside—the domain of unsupervised outdoor play—needs to be recognized and protected among the built landscape, as well as the official preserves. As I put it in *The Thunder Tree*, "We need to recognize the humble places where this alchemy occurs, and treat them as well as we treat our parks and preserves—or better, with less interference."

In making such assertions, I also recognize the assumptions they depend on. One of them is the actual extent of vacant spaces.

It is possible to cruise timber to determine board feet of stump-age but much more difficult to measure the current availability of potentially special spaces for children, or the amount and quality of open land that is necessary to ensure the kind of child-habitat encounters that allow them to develop caring attitudes. Further-more, we do not know with precision the degree to which vicar-ious and virtual experiences with nature may compensate for direct contact or the depth of impact when contact is thwarted. To some extent we are dependent here on our deductive powers and considered speculation operating on anecdotal observation. This is an important caveat when considering my conclusions. But until robust data become available, it seems reasonable to assume that rapidly expanding suburban development and experiential vicariance intensify the extinction of experience cycle.

If this is so, what about practical antidotes and alternatives to the loss of special places? For the children have not so much been cast out of their little Edens than the garden has been pulled out from under them. If we can agree that the prelapsarian state of accessible vacant lots is worth getting back to, then just how do we put them back, and keep the ones that remain?

Maybe the greatest challenge is to identify and protect the special places. Since secrecy is one of their hallmarks, such places are seldom well known by adults. They also tend to be humbler than the places conservationists fight for. But even when the va-cant lots and open ground beloved of children do enter the land-use discourse, they seldom command the power or resources to save them. Typically, the development value of the site is so great as to simply sweep away all other concerns. Rare success stories usually involve major private donors, the presence of endangered species, or some sort of "miracle" of cooperation or progressive planning.

In a little-visited library belonging to an outdoor education center, I found George Selden's enchanting book, *Tucker's Countryside* (1969): a classic allegory of last-minute salvation presented as a children's story. In this modern fable, the children save the meadow from the developer by shaming the chairman of the town council with the "discovery" of the founder's homestead. "A matter of the deepest historical significance," he then blusters, before pronouncing that it will be left as it is, "as a natural shrine in memory of the great pioneer." But the children prevail only with the assistance of the animals, who help them plant bogus evidence leading to the historic designation. In land-use reality, the magic element is generally missing, and the political imperatives are less malleable to the people's will.

Saving special places as individual causes célèbre can sometimes succeed, but it is tedious, expensive, and risky. And even when the children seem to prevail, the ultimate outcome can be undermined by hard realities. Not long ago, Jewell Wetlands, a relictual Valhalla not far south of the High Line Canal in Aurora, Colorado—one of the last undeveloped tracts for miles around— came under threat of development. Many considered its replacement by hundreds of condominiums inevitable. But local parents and others organized, raised the money in partnership with the city, the drainage district, and the state lottery, with assistance from the Trust for Public Land. In a stunning victory, they bought the prairie remnant, cattail marsh, and its willow-and-cottonwood fringe for open space and flood control. The children, whose afterschool and summer habitat it was, celebrated to know that they would continue to explore and play and learn at Jewell. And so they shall. However, the many interests involved, the prior damage from off-road vehicles, vandals, and filling, the unstable gully and other perceived dangers, and the diverse clientele for the new park led to extensive changes. Volunteers by the hundreds helped landscape a handsome and functional place combining some natural grassland and marsh with drainage and park features. The Aurora Jewell Wetlands were heroically saved for the pleasure of the many. But in the process, the wild tangle and its invitation to uncontrolled discovery were largely lost. Now, boardwalks and butterfly gardens replace sweet surprise, the deepest fort nook became an interpretive site, and the creek falls in concrete runnels. When tradeoffs prevail, sacrifice happens.

How much better if planners incorporated unmanicured open spaces in their urban growth master plans. Unfortunately and ironically, exactly the opposite often occurs, for a conservation rationale: to prevent sprawl at the edges of towns, the "New Urbanism" has embraced the concept of infilling with gusto—maximizing the density of development inside of cities instead of allowing it to dribble out the edges as always before. While infilling may help to maintain city limits, it is anathema for the lovers of vacant lots and "waste ground." This conundrum is currently the subject of intense debate in Portland, Oregon, a city that is very green but that also pushes to grow beyond its legislated urban growth boundary. Though it is considered a naughty word in Portland, this conflict is nothing else but an expression of overpopulation: just too many people living in one place to maintain what they all came for.

A partial saving grace in Portland is the vigorous effort by urban conservationists to build on the city's original Olmsted Brothers plan, which included a forty-mile loop of green space. While the loop was never finished and many gaps exist, Portland visionaries led by urban naturalist Mike Houck have expanded it to a 140-mile linked loop of habitat nodes and corridors. If they are successful, they may counteract the negative effects of infilling to a meaningful degree. But corridors by themselves will not save every child's special place. They work only for children who happen to live nearby; for unlike birds, kids need habitat right there, underfoot.

The creation of corridors can be a cost- and ecology-effective technique for maintaining the connection between cities and their natural underpinnings. But they work best for children if they are linked to intersecting, concentric, tangential, or parallel paths and if they are studded with many large and small clots of unimproved habitat. Just as corridors linking archipelagoes of habitat islands support more species than isolated patches can do, they also have the attribute of expanding available urban wildland beyond the actual acreage of the ground involved. This method thus has the added power of extending the radius of reach of children farther and farther as their powers of wandering increase with age. The High Line Canal offered what seemed unlimited scope for exploration to a child of the 1950s, though it was all technically off-limits.

Even as the habitat along it was built up, a public greenway of some sixty miles was developed, eventually connecting with other trail systems, creeks, and gullies crossed by the canal. Thus today the Canal trail offers a greater extent of access for children than we ever had, even if its amplitude for natural discovery has been much reduced. The diversity too could have been maintained if more habitat nodes had been saved. [Note in 2020: Today, the vigorous efforts of the High Line Canal Conservancy are aimed at saving what's still left, and restoring some of what's been lost.]

In the 1970s, I lived in Seattle and became acquainted with green places that my mother had known as genuinely wild many years before. I imagined a twelve-mile "green circle" that would link these through the severed and frayed remnants of another uncompleted Olmsted plan. The "green leaks" grew, however, along with Seattle and the University of Washington. One bright light in this diminishing scene has been a fervent citizen campaign to daylight Ravenna Creek, which runs out of the same Ravenna ravine my mother haunted as a girl and empties into the vestigial marsh at the margin of Union Bay, my naturalist's retreat when I was at the university. An upscale shopping center and a distinct lack of imagination by the owners stymied the original plan for the daylighted stream, but other routes have been plotted, and the momentum gives hope for eventual success. What could mean more for children's experience than bringing back the creeks they once lost?

Nor are vacant lots an irreplaceable resource. In a presentation to the Natural Areas Association meeting in St. Louis in October 2000, Yale forest sociologist William Burch discussed opportunities inherent in urban problems. Thanks to downtown decay, Detroit is presently plagued—or blessed—with some thirty thousand vacant lots. "We're creating a national forest in inner-city Detroit," Burch quipped. This statistic is seen as a large negative by urban advocates, but I too find it exciting: often the first to suffer from the extinction of experience, perhaps the inner city will also be the first to discover the treasure in abandoned land. Never mind that most of the tree stock in these new "forests" is composed of ailanthus, the "Tree That Grows in Brooklyn"; kids on adventure are not hobbled by native species purism.

Since restoration of built and paved habitats is feasible, and since many urban organisms (even semi-specialists) may recolonize restored sites or be reintroduced, extinction of experience need not necessarily be forever. Frayed and severed connections can be rewoven. And we must remember that children themselves are powerfully adaptive organisms: for them a washing machine box can be a cabin, or a thicket can become a jungle. Children are masters at making mountains out of molehills and trackless veldt from a prairie-dog town in a farmed-out field. But they are also connoisseurs of surprise, mystery, and wildness writ small. The planner who attempts to plug in a structured playground or park in place of a scruffy canebrake or a sumac patch with a pond will fail.

Our cities need to maintain the natural habitats of children—undedicated, unmanaged, undeveloped ground where unplanned, unsupervised, and unexpected discovery can take place. Realtors will continue to call it "waste ground." But in my view, nothing is less wasted than ground where the hand of man has held back and the minds of boys and girls can engage with plants and animals and dirt, nothing more sacred than land that is yet raw and ripe with surprise.

Equally, we need to restrain the impulse to "improve" open land into developed parkland. When children go down to the woods and fields, will their experience be signed, led, guided, planned, and programmed? Or will it be a spontaneous exercise of connection between the land, the water, and their own imaginations, with all the chance in the world to simply *be*, with nothing between themselves and epiphany but the length of the day and dinnertime?

It may be that, given the demographics and politics of contemporary America, such expectations are simply unreasonable. After all, the tamed experience of nature (though inferior, in my view) is better than none. Maybe the only way to "save" such land from off-road vehicles, vandals, developers, and other rascals is to tame it. Maybe. But to a curious kid, wildness is not replaceable by artifice, and kids who encounter wildness may become people who care.

Children know what is interesting when they see it. What I fear is that in the absence of intriguing places to prowl and in the presence of a growing peer obsession with gadgets, they will forget to remember what it is.

We who can remember our own creeks and vacant lots should recognize all they represent. In our earnest desire to maintain our own children's Edens, we must remember that children everywhere, not just those of privilege, have such a need. To begin to reverse the loss of special places, we have no choice but to admit the primacy of untended ground in our cultural landscape. And once we accept that, we must take the following direct actions on behalf of the vacant lots and their like:

- Ask our kids to tell us about their special places, maybe even show us.
- Inventory the unofficial countryside within a mile's walk of our homes and in other neighborhoods.
- Seek to influence our planners and decision-makers to take into account the extraordinary occupation rate of vacant lots, the infinite investment value of waste ground.
- Fight doggedly for these places whenever the threat arises, by all available legal means, until developers and commissioners realize that it won't be easy to wreck them.
- Bully parks departments into leaving well enough alone when it comes to wildland "improvements."
- Organize parents and older siblings to be on hand for exploration sessions—not *with* the children, neither leading nor organizing and definitely not supervising, but close enough to satisfy themselves that the kids are safe.
- Limit the amount of time spent indoors in front of the television, the computer, and even books.

- Encourage nature reserves and environmental education programs, but do not allow them to take the place of spontaneous adventuring on rough ground.
- Build constituencies and partnerships among nonprofits and agencies to imagine and assemble kid-habitat corridors and green circles richly studded with habitat nodes and to plug the green leaks as opportunities arise.
- Work with naturalists to characterize the species-rich sectors remaining in our towns and neighborhoods, for these will be the same places where vital experience may still be found.

We must do all this, and above all we must remember Calvin's pronouncement to Hobbes, after the comic-strip lad and his tiger had suffered a particularly trying day: "The world's not such a bad place," says Calvin, "when you can get out *in* it."

Note: The Cherry Creek Watershed Conference I mentioned above, where most of the participants had lost the special places of their youths, took place in 1999. Twenty years later I again addressed that gathering. By now, many of the attendees had changed. Once again I asked the same questions, and the results were surprising. Nearly half of the five hundred people present responded that they *could* go back and find their magical places still intact. I'd like to think that this happy finding suggests that sensitivity and action toward saving childhood's enchanted spots really have increased. For example, the vigorous current efforts of the High Line Canal Conservancy are aimed at saving what's still left of my own youth's Valhalla and restoring some of what's been lost. They are already having good effects.

As for the discussion of local butterfly extinctions as a measure of overall loss, all this will only increase with climate change, agricultural intensification, and neonicotinoid pesticides, as several long-term studies of collapsing butterfly faunas have recently shown.

And of course the disaffection of the young from leafy green reality in favor of electronic surrogates only intensifies each year, with every upgrade. And yet, yesterday I watched two young boys prowling the margins of a rapidly evaporating pond. That impulse remains, and we must count on it.

Nature Matrix

At the outset of the twenty-first century there is no longer any doubt that a strong individual sense of connection to nature and natural processes is utterly essential to the healthy coexistence of humans with their biological neighbors and physical setting. We also understand that just as such a sense has paled, withered, and is finally failing, so is our ecological condition collapsing and our future contracting. As Steven Sanderson of the Wildlife Conservation Society has put it: "Wild nature is in deep distress, and whatever their occasional protestations, the international institutions charged with Earth's care are not managing it with an eye on 'sustainability.'" Sanderson also identifies a condition that I consider to lie at the very foundation of the ecological crisis, alongside overpopulation and economic disparity: "In the foreseeable future, most of the world's population will not know nature in any direct way."

All aboriginal cultures were peopled by excellent naturalists, or else they perished, both as peoples and as individuals. Feudal oppression was made more tolerable by people's knowledge of the countryside and its supportive systems, enabling bare survival under privation. When the majority of the population of most regions was agriculturally based, and settlements largely rural, most people still connected with the physical world on a daily basis. Even deep into the industrial era, the American Nature Study movement, and parallel educational practices in the U.K. and elsewhere, sought to promote essential familiarity of common people with local flora and fauna. But after World War II, flight from the countryside to the city, combined with overpopulation and mercantile expansion, frayed the remaining relationship. Today, as the virtual finds its apotheosis at the expense of the real, the separation has progressed to a point where reattachment may be impossible, and long-term survival of human culture is not at all a foregone conclusion.

The assumption that responsible behavior toward the environment is closely related to people's feelings of personal connection to nature finds support in nearly every conservation history or bio-philosophical treatise from the 1940s to the '90s, from Aldo Leopold and Marston Bates to John Hay and Victor B. Scheffer. It finds its fundament in E. O. Wilson's 1984 biophilia hypothesis, which posits the existence of an innate affection for living things, developed to a greater or lesser extent in all human beings. Biophilia works, according to Wilson, because "to the extent that each person can feel like a naturalist, the old excitement of the untrammeled world will be regained," and because this "formula for re-enchantment" can lead to conscientious behavior. Many related authors (Rachel Carson, R. M. Pyle, David Sobel, Gary Paul Nabhan and Stephen Trimble, David W. Orr, Stephen R. Kellert, Peter H. Kahn Jr., Mitchell Thomashow, and John

Flicker, for example) argue for childhood bonding with natural places and organisms as the essential key to arousing biophilia and concomitant caring behavior. The principle is so well established as to be considered canon in many quarters, although in practice it is increasingly observed mainly in the breach. The idea gained its own name with the 2005 publication of Richard Louv's *Last Child in the Woods: Saving Our Children from Nature-Deficit Disorder.*

To an alien observer, it may seem that humans pay great obeisance to their ties with other species today. After all, the majority of cultures are still dependent upon daily contact with their physical and biological surroundings for their food and shelter. In fact, many of the rural poor in developing countries still rely on a close knowledge of nature. Even Western industrial society attends conspicuously to "nature" in the context of outdoor recreation. Natural history and environmental writing have never seemed healthier in terms of books published and programs in universities and field institutes. Sales of field guides remain robust, and titles proliferate annually. Membership rises in bird, butterfly, and native plant societies at a respectable rate, while birding and butterflying make larger and larger contributions to ecotourism around the world. Vast numbers of people participate in gardening, angling, hunting, and other outdoor pursuits. Nature-oriented television commands respectable market shares, and parks and visitor centers attract hordes of holidaymakers, day-trippers, and schoolchildren in search of fresh air and information as well as recreation. Conservation societies thrive, and the incipient green theology movement brings spiritual concerns and energies to bear upon the more-than-human world of "the Creation." If all this is true, how can the contention be made that people need to reconnect with nature?

For one thing, the above refers chiefly to the temperate,

industrialized world, where leisure activities are supported by disproportionate resource consumption. Arguably the societies most distantly removed from direct daily dependence on lands and waters are also those where conspicuous nature recreation emerges, and where the vast preponderance of world resources are consumed. From North America, and other aspirants toward its standard of living such as Japan, comes most of the relentless pressure on the biosphere for ecological services, biomass consumption, and genetic resources from the wild.

In contrast, a great proportion of humanity occupies less developed countries in the Global South, where poverty often prevails and few can afford to abstract their relationship with nature into avocation or recreation. While some such cultures still live in relatively close concert with their surrounding ecological communities, more and more peoples find their traditional relationships forced into unsustainable patterns through overpopulation, hardship, externally driven resource mining, and financial and agricultural colonialism taking advantage of an imposed cash economy. For example, as a biologist in Papua New Guinea, I observed many examples of the breakdown of traditional patterns of "bush" resource use and husbandry under the malign influence of oil palm plantations, mining, logging, and other introduced forms of cash generation, extraction, and dependence. Social disintegration inexorably follows.

For another thing, I see a discrepancy between apparent connection and real depth of contact. Listing birds and cultivating roses, while benign and admirable activities, do not necessarily equate with profound association. In many parts of the world, notably the most developed, contemporary society lacks a widespread sense of intimacy with the living world. Nature-based recreation commonly results in superficial contact, as demonstrated in the extreme by the competitive sport known in Britain as bird "twitching," whereby the organism itself becomes a mere game-piece for a tally. The landscape parallel presents a family in a motor home ticking off the Grand Canyon before emptying the holding tank and motoring on toward Zion. Many tourists, members of natural history groups, and participants in country-side pursuits merely skim the surface of the landscape, reaping a shallow reward and a weak relationship; there is a continuum, of course, from casual to devoted. Yet the great majority of the people associate with nature even less. At least the skimmers are aware of nature around them. As for the others, whose lives hold little place for nature, how can they even care? People who care may make choices to conserve; but people who don't know, don't even care. What is the extinction of a condor or an albatross to a child who has never known a wren?

Shallow contact with nature leads to shallow solutions for conservation. During a recent hotel stay, I picked up a card on the pillow asking patrons to consider reusing their linens in order to save water and detergent. This is doubtless a positive development in the hotel industry. However, the card was grandiosely titled SAVE MOTHER EARTH! If people feel that they are discharging their responsibility as conservationists by sleeping twice on their sheets in a premium hotel, the overall effect could be counterproductive. Likewise the level of interpretation in most visitor centers, the depth of detail in environmental education, and the penetration of media representations of nature often approach the shallowness achieved by the casual bird-twitcher. This is not always the case, and examples exist of admirable depth achieved in these fields, but those do not reach many people. Not that full immersion guarantees epiphany either: people who spend $8,000 to travel to Antarctica and view emperor penguins up close may forge a deep personal connection thereby, examine their lives, and act accordingly; or they may remain blind to the impacts and implications of their elite choices in the seductive glow of the southern summer. Intimacy with nature is only a starting point.

On the opposite side, obvious examples of our estrangement from nature abound: the mass toleration of expansive, even ubiquitous pesticide usage, including widespread home and neighborhood toxins commonly believed to be far safer than they arguably are; the proliferation of large, heavily fuel-consumptive SUVs, huge personal diesel and gasoline pickups, and four-wheel drive trucks; general acceptance of off-road vehicles, jet skis ("personal water craft"), leaf blowers, and other two-stroke engine devices that severely pollute the air and the soundshed; indifference toward habitat loss in and around human settlements; societal consent for laws governing mining, grazing, forestry, industry, waste disposal, and transportation amounting to license to pollute and destroy; and an overall embrace of affluence, economic growth, consumption, waste, and sheer human expansion to a degree that cannot conceivably be sustainable in any form we would want to live with.

Furthermore, many individuals suffer from a deep-set antagonism toward nature that cannot be helpful to conservation. Of course, our relationship with other species is inevitably double-edged. We sometimes find ourselves in the position of trying to conserve animals in one place that kill or conflict with people elsewhere, or even in the same places, such as elephants or tigers. Many other species, especially certain herbivorous insects and exotic invasive species, are important competitors with humans for food and fiber, and others serve as vectors of disease. Agricultural response may prove necessary, but can cause enormous by-kill of non-target species. Mass spraying may also have toxicological consequences for public health greater than the potential epidemiological danger from the targets, as seems likely to occur with the current West Nile virus scare and the chemical reaction to it. Just as dangerous, our fixation on a relatively small number of pests and enemies leads to a general hatred of insects: clearly a maladaptive attitude in a world where most of life is insect life. Surely, if meaningful connection is to be forged, we should seek to avoid such polar abstractions. Even as we seek ways to protect essential resources from competitors, our schools should inculcate widespread public equanimity toward all nature. This is the only stance that long-range human adaptability will tolerate.

The loss of everyday intimacy and tolerance both stem partly from the rapid decline of children's contact with their special places. Many authors have described how important their wild nooks have been in their growing up and connecting with nature, going back at least to George Eliot. In *Middlemarch* (1871), her characters' way "lay through a pretty bit of midland landscape, almost all meadows and pastures, with hedgerows still allowed to grow in bushy beauty . . . the high bank where the ash-trees grew; the sudden slope of the old marl-pit making a red background for the burdock . . . old, old thatch full of mossy hills and valleys with wondrous modulations of light and shadow . . . These are the things that make the gamut of joy in landscape . . . the things they toddled among." One hundred years later, Richard Mabey coined the term "unofficial countryside" to refer to the postwar secondary habitats, often abandoned industrial sites or marginal urban waste ground, where children can still find "the gamut of joy in the landscape" when officially protected natural areas are not to hand.

In fact, the "official countryside" of parks and reserves often fails to deliver intimate contact to the curious young because of fences, mandatory paths, no-net rules, and other restrictions. Botanic gardens and zoos can play a role in rebuilding the bridges between people and other species, to be sure, as they always have. However, such artificial assemblages of largely exotic species share some of the same liabilities as reserves and protected areas when it comes to romancing intimacy. They are useful for gaining firsthand acquaintance with an array of organisms from various distant habitats. But without the context of the local, they may not mean much more than Disney World. It is the opportunity for the young to explore, dig, prowl, play, catch, and ultimately discover, among local plants and animals, that truly forges connection. In this sense, a vacant lot may be more valuable than a nature reserve or an arboretum.

Such humble, hand-me-down habitats have traditionally played an enormous role in acquainting the young, in particular, with the more-than-human. When urban and suburban infilling and edge sprawl displace the vacant lots and other open ground, children lose the opportunity to make meaningful contact close to home. Such losses conspire with the seductive tug of computer games, the internet, overscheduling, and parents' fear of real or imagined dangers to limit children's free-ranging outdoor time. I fear that all these influences will lead to a generation of youths with no personal bond with a particular place they can call their own, and this in turn will begin to breed a populace that cares less and less about its physical surroundings. I believe that the innate drive toward biophilia is a reality, along with the impulse of the young to reach in that direction. Recently, in a shopping mall, I witnessed a group of boys skipping stones over a pond, just as any bunch of lads in the country may do. Only the "stones" were quarter-dollars, and the "pond" was an artificial, geometric water feature in the mall. The boys told me they had no outdoor place to skip stones, nor any experience at it, yet they had spontaneously recovered the quarters from the fountain, not to keep and spend, but to skip over the water's surface. What might it have meant for these boys if their encounter had also featured frogs, reeds, dragonflies, and the smell of wet mud?

The decline of individual and corporate connection with the world itself leads to a cycle of loss and disaffection that I have called the Extinction of Experience. Essentially, the extinction of experience syndrome works as follows: when common species of plants and animals (as well as cultural, architectural, or any other features of diversity) become extirpated in one's everyday environs—within, that is, one's radius of reach—one grows increasingly inured to their absence. (The radius of reach is smaller for the poor, the very old, the very young, and the disabled.) That is, as the richness of the neighborhood diminishes, the power of that neighborhood to fascinate, arouse, excite, and stimulate also passes into dullness, ennui, and apathy. Those who know and recognize less, care less, and therefore act less, leading to still more losses. The sequelae to extinction and alienation are further loss and greater detachment, round and round. So the extinction of experience precipitates a cycle of disaffection, degradation, and ultimate separation from nature.

It is also important to note that an element of the actual wild is vitally important in heading off the extinction of experience. This follows from E. O. Wilson's observation that "People can grow up with the outward appearance of normality in an environment largely stripped of plants and animals ... Yet something vitally important would be missing, not merely the knowledge and pleasure that can be imagined and might have been, but a wide array of experiences that the human brain is peculiarly equipped to receive ... on Earth, no less than in space, lawn grass, potted plants, caged parakeets, puppies, and rubber snakes are not enough." We must also now add, neither are virtual images. The shimmering pixels on a computer screen can never substitute for the shimmering scales on a butterfly's wing. Direct, personal contact with other living things affects us in vital ways that vicarious experience can never replace.

Particularly because the common modern condition is more biophobic than biophilic—as illustrated by robust sales of household biocides, benighted rural attitudes toward predators, and many other behaviors—the way toward an enlightened state vis-à-vis other species is steeply uphill and crooked. Yet if the mechanisms of the growing disconnection are clear, how may the consequences be demonstrated? Empirically, since one-on-one contact between the human mind and extra-human life is the ticket to awaken biophilia, and assuming Wilson is right that the awareness and refinement of this condition can lead to behavioral modification in favor of conservation, then the larger implications of a depauperate outdoor setting should be clear. Wilson further states that "to explore and affiliate with life is a deep and complicated process in mental development," and that "to an extent still undervalued in philosophy and religion, our existence depends on this propensity, our spirit is woven from it, hope rises on its currents." It follows that hope, spirit, and existence all suffer when the affiliation is forfeit. So another definition of the extinction of experience may be the failure of biophilia. "Is the exploration of the natural world just a pleasant way to pass the golden hours of childhood," asked Rachel Carson in *The Sense of Wonder* (1965), "or is there something deeper?" We can agree that, indeed, there is something deeper. Plumbing its depth is another matter.

I have attempted to quantify the extinction of experience by employing the rates of extinctions of butterflies in four urban areas to represent the degree of natural change, and as an indicator of lost opportunity for contact. The data showed that the opportunity for experiencing nature in these places has diminished measurably, especially in the most rapidly suburbanizing of them. While it is not possible to demonstrate that environmental leaders will no longer arise from the streets of a place with a high factor of loss, it seems reasonable to conclude that the likelihood of youngsters becoming avid naturalists and conservation voters has been reduced in proportion with their hometown's butterflies and the diversity they represent.

Reconnecting with nature is not a matter of reversing the fall, getting back to Eden, or approximating the peaceable kingdom. These states never existed. The fact is that people have always been at odds and in competition with the wild in many ways. But we have also coevolved with every other species with which we have been in longtime contact, and for most of our evolutionary history, the struggle and cooperation commonly involved the death of individuals but no real threat to the species or its supportive matrix. The balance that aboriginal peoples are routinely said to have existed in, vis-à-vis nature, owes largely to a preindustrial state, low population, and relatively low-impact living. The respect toward nature that such cultures are commonly assumed to have exhibited (for example, Native Americans) may be real or romanticized. But when technology advanced, as with Clovis points, so did human impact, perhaps to the extent of Pleistocene overkill of large North American mammals. Nonetheless, Barry Lopez considers the "way of being" of native peoples to be fundamentally different from the way modern naturalists are tied to nature. He believes that ever since Gilbert White, naturalists have been "searching for a way back in to nature," while native peoples "have been at pains not to leave." Whether or not this applies generally in complex indigenous settings, the principle and the metaphor stand: our challenge now is to find that way back in, while reducing the cumulative impacts of the Industrial Revolution and population increase facilitated by industry and agriculture.

Dedicated people have taken up that challenge in unjaded earnest and to good effect. Much of this work falls in the realm of restoration. To take just one example among any number of notable retrofittings of habitat for people and other species, consider the Limberlost. This extensive swampland in northeastern Indiana gained international fame through the enormously popular novels of Gene Stratton-Porter in the early twentieth century, such as *A Girl of the Limberlost* (1909). Yet, by 1916, most of the Limberlost had been drained and converted to arable fields. After the better part of a century of elegiac existence in the novels alone, the Limberlost is now being reassembled, reflooded, and reforested with native species by Limberlost Swamp Remembered, a group begun by one local farmer, Ken Brunswick. Even lost life forms may have a future, such as the spectacular reintroduction of the large blue butterfly (*Maculinea arion*) into England from Sweden, after extinction of the British subspecies and recovery of its habitat through applied ecology spearheaded by ecologist Jeremy Thomas. In an American counterpart, I have suggested the experimental reconstitution of the extinct Xerces blue (*Glaucopsyche xerces*) from the nearest surviving genotypes, now that its last-known habitat in San Francisco's Presidio is being restored.

But such resurrection ecology will never reverse the majority of human-mediated extinctions, nor will community-based restoration efforts reverse disastrous global trends that will ultimately undo all of our best efforts without adequate address. Likewise, no matter how many people take up natural history or outdoor pursuits, nature conservation will not advance without massive collective will for large-scale change. Gardening and birding won't do it, if basic behavior remains the same. When I see butterfly watchers driving gas-guzzlers, I question their fundamental understanding and devotion to the necessary revolution in consumption. Birders who vote for non-conservation candidates do not vote for birds. The current high popularity ratings for George W. Bush among the American public do not square with other polls that show most Americans are deeply concerned about the environment, for he and his cabinet choices constitute the worst conservation administration since Ronald Reagan's.

The plain fact is, in the military/mercantile climate that now prevails, world culture will never become connected to nature in a way that will ensure survival. Exxon Corporation took a typical stance in the aftermath of the *Exxon Valdez* oil spill, whose casualties were sea otters, seabirds, marine life, salmon, and human fishing communities: business first. The November 2002 oil spill off the coast of Spain may have equivalent impacts, and an equivalent attitude may be expected. *The New York Times* reported in 2002 that "the Bush administration has approved construction of a geothermal power plant in the Modoc National Forest, a remote volcanic field near California's border with Oregon that local tribes consider sacred," reversing a Clinton administration decision. A Native American spokesman meeting with the director of the Bureau of Land Management and the chief of the Forest Service reported that they expressed sympathy for the Native Americans' plight. "They said they recognize our culture," said Gene Preston, chairman of the Pit River Tribes, "but also the culture of capitalism." As long as the culture of capitalism trumps the commonweal, natural and cultural diversity will deteriorate. "Humankind" as an entity, let alone the rest of nature, has no legal standing, shareholder votes, or seats on corporate boards. Therefore, the only reconnection that will be truly significant must also be radical.

Every national economy, and the global economy of the North American Free Trade Agreement, the General Agreement on Tariffs and Trade, the World Trade Organization, and the European Economic Community, assumes growth to be the only acceptable state of affairs. But a permanent state of growth means continued carbon release, ozone depletion, human population expansion, aquifer depletion, toxic contamination, resource depletion, species extinction, class partition, warfare, disease, and, ultimately, breakdown. A cliché among business people is "if you're not growing, you're dead." But in ecological, epidemiological, and oncological terms, beyond a certain point, if you're still growing, you're going to be dead. The radical, steady-state precepts of Zero Population Growth, the E. F. Schumacher Society, and other movements that challenge the grow-until-you-bust paradigm are not much in fashion today. One who argues this position, Murray Bookchin, considered in 1989 that our addiction to growth shows that we live in "an inherently anti-ecological society." The mercantile, deeply philistine ethic that drives the global business and political culture cannot help but subordinate the so-called natural world to the immediate commercial opportunities of the one species that insists upon an epistemology that places it in some other world by itself. Because all others aspire to follow where the United States leads, the most frightening prospect for the biosphere is that China, India, and other populous regions may succeed: all those cars, plastics, silicon chips, pesticides, concrete pourings, and high rises, speeding the metastasis along.

So the kind of radicalization I believe is required has two chambers to its heart. First, a new, responsible economy that addresses economic disparity without feeding the drive toward perpetual growth and acquisition. There is no question that the alleviation of poverty must precede, or at least parallel, conservation. But it mustn't be a matter of the have-nots matching the haves, which would simply lead to a quicker collapse. Rather, both must approach a sustainable mean that will be much more than most enjoy now but very much less than some command. As the preeminent Korean poet and social thinker Ko Un said recently, addressing the Association for the Study of Literature and Environment (Japan) in Okinawa, there will be no peace for people or for the rest of nature until "an ethic of minimal ownership" prevails. But the current state, enunciated by poet Gary Snyder at the same conference, is exactly the opposite: "the elevation of greed and gain to an iconic prominence." Not everyone agrees that a viable conservation future is incompatible with corporate capitalism. Steven Sanderson, president of the Wildlife Conservation Society in New York, believes that greater private investment in conservation, codes of conduct to shift "the behavioral canons of economic growth and development," and novel pragmatic alliances between NGOs and the corporate sector may give nature, and us, a chance at a decent future. But this presumes such qualities as a corporate conscience, restraint, and an awareness of limits. While an enlightened "natural capital" approach may work on a modest and local scale, global corporatism shows no signs of possessing or living by such traits.

Second, an all-out campaign is needed to reduce ecological illiteracy, which is epidemic and is another form of debilitating poverty. For the fact is, the majority of people are connected with nature in their lives, whether they know it or not: they necessarily consume that which comes from nature, and their recreation, avocation, or work often binds them closer. But they are also deeply, profoundly ignorant of the working parts of the world around them, and thus prevented from having any sort of close relationship with extra-human nature. Whereas it was once considered a good thing for people to be at least roughly acquainted with their local flora and fauna, this pretense has long since dropped away. The number of people who have even a rudimentary knowledge of their nonhuman neighbors, just their names, let alone their ways of life, is vanishingly small. This is truly the crux of the crisis, as I see it. Because if the people were closely acquainted with the plants and animals they live among and depend upon, the eco-crimes they permit and abet and conduct and sponsor daily would not be so easy to bear, let alone countenance. Conversely, the development of a political and economic system that depends upon infinite growth could only have arisen in a state of grievous loss of common knowledge. That loss was the true Fall.

So how far have we fallen? To be sure, extraordinary changes in conservation ethics have occurred over the last one hundred years. The plumes of wild birds are no longer used in millinery, and more animals are hunted with cameras than high-powered rifles. However, diminishing protection of wetlands and the growing "bushmeat" trade offset such gains. While eloquent voices (such as E. O. Wilson's) have spoken out for the primacy of understanding the dimensions of biological diversity while there is still time, survey and classification efforts have only been weakening, and major regional centers closing down. The closure of the Nebraska State Insect Collection is merely one recent American example, mirrored widely. At a time when the need for knowledge has never been greater, the tools for knowing are withering; and it has become a cliché that many species will become extinct without ever having been described. This, at a time of unmatched affluence in the developed world! But in one sense, this outcome is not surprising. Aldo Leopold in *A Sand County Almanac* (1949) wrote that "land-use ethics are still governed wholly by economic self-interest, just as social ethics were a century ago." Half a century and more forward, that fact has not fundamentally changed. As Barry Lopez enjoined us in 2001, "Recognize that a politics with no biology, or a politics without field biology, or a political platform in which human biological requirements form but one plank, is a vision of the Gates of Hell."

Yet we're still falling, both in the developed and developing worlds. Most demographers predict that the world population of humans will level off at eight to nine billion near the year 2050. Can we wait to establish a new and closer relationship with what's left then? I don't think so, because not much will be left, and societal suppleness will be much reduced in all regimes, should we survive to see such utterly unsustainable numbers.

I am not sanguine that a better path is still possible. If it were, however, it would have to recognize something else enunciated by Leopold: "The 'key-log' which must be moved to release the evolutionary process for an ethic is simply this: quit thinking about decent land-use as solely an economic problem. Examine each question in terms of what is ethically and esthetically right, as well as what is economically expedient." In the end, for any paradigm shift to succeed in time, it must embrace the central tenet of Leopold's Land Ethic: *"A thing is right when it tends to preserve the integrity, stability, and beauty of the biotic community. It is wrong when it tends otherwise."*

This brings us finally to a vision for a new and wholly different ethical regime. I call this dream Nature Matrix, a term that recognizes the only acceptable long-term way for us to view the rest of the natural world: as completely, irreducibly bonded into a functioning body that we cannot escape. I use the term "matrix" in the biological sense, meaning the intercellular substance that binds all the rest, similar to how Wilson employs it when he says that "other organisms . . . are the matrix in which the human mind originated and is permanently rooted."

Nature Matrix has six essential elements:

1. *Land Ethic Basis.* Every decision is subject to the essential test of the Leopoldian doctrine: "A thing is right when it tends to preserve the integrity, stability, and beauty of the biotic community. It is wrong when it tends otherwise." There is, of course, room for interpretation here; but reasonable persons in possession of real knowledge about "the biotic community" (see (2) below) will eventually come to judge most cases alike. Even so, enigmatic instances would arise such as eucalypts in California: harmful invasive exotics overall, but essential for overwintering monarch butterflies that have adapted to their groves in the absence of the original coastal forest structure. Panels of ecologically sophisticated citizens will explore and settle such disputes on a place-by-place basis.

2. *Nature Study.* "Nothing makes sense except in the light of the local floras and faunas," according to E. O. Wilson, and Korean poet Ko Un says, "Nature hates modern education the most." Education will be based on natural history, with all other topics taught in relation to it. Far from the exception it is today, environmental education forms the core of the new pedagogy, both at home and in the schools. Basic educational goals include not only literacy and numeracy, but also essential acquaintance with the ecosystem of home. Children come to know many of their local plants and animals on a first-name basis as a matter of course.

Higher education once again emphasizes and honors the survey and cataloging of natural diversity, as well as the extended study of their lives and interrelationships once they have been classified. Nature Matrix places human culture and history in their relative importance to the larger world. The arts are held in equal regard and are practiced in cooperative synchrony with the sciences.

3. *Local Focus.* As Leopold recognized, the main split in conservation is between local and federal or state control. As a resident of a rural, resource-dependent county, I can affirm this fact today. Country people devoutly believe that local control is the best and only acceptable kind, and that left to their own devices, local folks will do the right thing. In practice, this seldom happens. The urban tail wags the resentful rural dog, with regulations that often don't fit. And if local authorities do try to exercise control, it is often subverted by economic self-interest, myopia, lack of power, and absence of ecological knowledge. Thus governmental regulation has necessarily imposed limitations for the larger good, as in game laws. But such restraints are temporary, due to changes at the responsible agencies and ruling commissions. Lacking place-specific knowledge, regulators are often unequipped to render decisions tailored to local biological or social conditions. In Nature Matrix, the essential units of decision-making are locally informed but centrally monitored according to (1) above.

4. *Consensus Rule.* One reason conditions remained stable in many Papua New Guinean villages far into modern times is that decisions were made by consensus, not by majority rule. It takes forever to reach consensus, so not much damage is done in the meantime. Not until democracy and a

cash economy were imposed in the twentieth century did this pattern erode, a pattern that also tended toward sustainability in a state of high natural diversity. Of course, totalitarian corporatism leads to the same ecological pass. Nature Matrix replaces both capital-controlled democracy and autocracy with a "biocratic" form of rule by mutual consent. Change, progress, and innovation will be slow and highly conservative in a sense almost opposite to its common political connotation today.

5. *Communitarian Justice.* Human rights are understood as underlying Nature Matrix, and extended to the broader community of life. These do not include the right to accumulate wealth and material goods or profits in violation of the Leopoldian doctrine, nor the right to reproduce without limit. Economic development seeks a standard of minimum rather than maximum ownership, and an ideal of *enough*, rather than having it all. Equitable distribution of wealth and population control are achieved through individual responsibility, restraint, and personal empowerment growing out of (2) above, rather than by coercion. Private property rights are subordinated to the good of the whole, and a sense of community well-being is cultivated in place of the familiar drive for individual acquisition. Freedom recognizes and implies responsibility as well as autonomy. Religious choice is free, with spiritual energies encouraged to look to the care of the here and now, rather than solely toward some hypothetical hereafter.

6. *Ecological Restoration.* Fixing damaged ecosystems and communities forms the basis for the human enterprise, beyond the sustainable production and conservation of essential materials. Remaining wilderness and old-growth forests

all stay that way, agriculture being confined to existing cropland. Damaged lands and waters will be cleaned, re-planted, and rewilded. Reuse, recycling, and durability of goods replace an ethic of obsolescence, replacement, and waste. The air, water, quiet, and night sky are all sacro-sanct, with the burden of proof on potential polluters to show that their activities are harmless, and lighting and noise vastly reduced. The manufacture and use of synthetic chemicals become the rare exception rather than the rule. Farming is organic, small to modest in scale, and polycul-tural, in league with soils and organisms. Consumption emphasizes the local. Warfare and its weapons ultimately become irrelevant as the common struggle is realized and joined. Demilitarization must necessarily follow.

If Nature Matrix sounds utopian, it is actually a fairy tale. Lacking any practical corrective to greed and power, it equals the vaunted Earth Charter (2003) in its fond naiveté. I have no idea what sort of authority could possibly bring it about. A benevolent empire that saw the light and decided to impose these conditions could presumably do so only through totalitarian coercion, which is inimical to the whole concept. However, if such a vision were to be promulgated as a blueprint by organizations and successively approximated by various levels of authority, I can imagine that slow movement in this direction might be possible.

Nature Matrix could also arise in adaptive response to the aftermath of some level of ecological and civil collapse. If all of the important community and conservation struggles underway now and in the future would begin to think more and more about reconnection on a truly Leopoldian level, they could lay the dis-persed groundwork for a kind of recovery based on a new way of

thinking. Like monasteries in the Dark Ages, they could preserve
the methods, the seeds, the knowledge, the vital texts, the honorable impulses. Then, if a critical mass of humanity survived,
along with enough of the earth to be worth living for, something
like Nature Matrix could conceivably evolve out of the rubble. If
this seems like cold comfort in perilous times, it may nonetheless
be something to hope for. Either way, reconnecting people with
nature—at least, reconnection worth the name—will best be accomplished after the old, corrupted relationship finds a whole new
face.

Of course, I would prefer to believe that we may succeed
through less drastic measures than environmental Armageddon.
If conservationists stay the course, perhaps we can. But time is
short. As Gus Speth wrote when dean of the Yale School of Forestry and Environmental Studies: "A great tragedy is fast unfold-
ing. More than 20 years ago, the alarm was sounded regarding
threats to the global environment, but the environmental deterio-
ration that stirred the international community then continues essentially unabated today. The steps that governments have taken
over these past two decades include the negotiations of numerous
international agreements and represent the first attempt at global
environmental governance. It is an experiment that has failed."
In echo comes "A Planetary Defeat: The Failure of Global Environmental Reform," John Bellamy Foster's informed assessment
of the current state of ecological affairs in 2003. "The first Earth
Summit in Rio de Janeiro, Brazil in 1992 generated hopes that
the world would at long last address its global ecological problems and introduce a process of sustainable development," wrote
Foster. "Now, with a second summit being held ten years later in
Johannesburg, that dream has to a large extent faded."

Nature Matrix imagines a fundamentally different dream,

with a new kind of environmental governance, one whereby humanity accedes its ambitions to natural limits. A place where, as John Hay, dean of American natural philosophers, wrote there may still be "a chance to live and let live, a chance ... to get rid of that terrible, isolating concept of man as the lord of creation" (*In Defense of Nature*, 1969). But Hay also wrote, "We have a great deal of exploring to do in order to find the place where we share our lives with other lives ..."

Ultimately, reconnecting people with nature is a nonsense phrase, for people and nature are not separate, and cannot be taken apart. The problem is, we haven't yet figured that out.

Note: See the Introduction, "Pyrex, Postcards, and Panzers—the Birth of Nature Matrix," for the story of how this idea, this essay, and this book came about. Clearly, it was written before climate change became the obvious driver of almost everything. That doesn't fundamentally change any of my conclusions or suggestions. It just makes them more urgent. Some of my worries seem almost quaint in today's context, when almost all the conditions I describe have only magnified since. For example, George W. Bush's environmental record—described as the worst since Ronald Reagan's—seems almost benign compared to the far worse conservation calamity of Donald J. Trump.

The Blind Teaching the Blind

THE ACADEMIC AS NATURALIST, OR NOT

I had just returned to Logan, Utah, from the Teton Science School in Wyoming's Grand Teton National Park. Though it was a Sunday in deep midwinter, I had a class to prepare for Monday, so I visited my cold office in the second story of the English department. The campus of Utah State University was deserted; a new storm had left three feet of snow on every surface, and more flakes were falling, like cabbage whites gone crazy in a cauliflower world. A different flicker of movement called my eyes away from the student manuscript claiming my attention. In a leaf-stripped hawthorn outside my window, a great flock of cedar waxwings had appeared. For the next hour, until the early darkness blotted both the snowfall and the birds, I got nothing done. Nothing, but to watch the silky gray waxwings grab haws with their sharp bills and swallow them, their waxen-tipped secondaries out-reddening the fruits and their yellow tail-ends flashing. How those masked and crested wonders made it through the Wasatch winter amazed me, but at least I knew how they would make it through the night.

There have been dozens of campuses in my life. Every one has been a distinct, physical, inhabited place, rich in encounters such as that with the waxwings. It is my condition that I need to situate myself and take account of the citizenry of any place I inhabit, however briefly—the airs, scents, colors, seasons, substrates, waters, plants, and animals, including humans. Most of all, what matters to me in a workplace is the ability to walk and to be surprised by what I find. I maintain that an acute visceral attention to the literal places where I work as a transient academic has made me who I am as a scholar and teacher, and has dramatically enhanced life for me and for my students. Furthermore, much in my writing and study depends directly upon the living details of these places. I doubt, however, that many campus denizens—even place-conscious scholars—pay this kind of attention to their professional surroundings. In fact, in my experience, it seems that most of my colleagues have been almost oblivious to that which makes the academical enterprise not only tolerable, but often delightful for me.

My physical introduction to colleges came as a youth at Colorado campuses for visits to see my coed sister in Greeley at Northern State, for an aunt-inspired speed-reading class at the University of Denver, and for track meets at the University of Colorado in Boulder and Colorado State University in Fort Collins. I liked the ersatz "olde" buildings and the park-like settings, whether for the crispy Norway maple leaves underfoot in autumn or the air redolent of Hopa crabapple blossoms on May nights. These visits set the pattern for a near-infinitude of campus explorations to come.

When I left dry Colorado for the moist and verdant University of Washington as a beginning undergraduate, I dived into site survey and discovery with a passionate thirst for new landscapes, plants, and weathers. My daily prowls of the Seattle campus, its marsh and arboretum, over seven years were part self-education in the stuff of place and part displacement activity. Deeply wishing to be studying ornithology instead of physical chemistry, I failed the latter while indulging the former and spotting one hundred species of birds in one hundred days: #99 was a black-sterned gadwall in Gadwall Cove, #100 a brilliant orange Bullock's oriole calling above the duck. After that I went on to tick one hundred species right there on campus in the first year, and again I made it on the last day, with a red-necked grebe and a Virginia rail. I came to know virtually every corner and thicket of the large campus and what could be found there in each season. This devotion both saved and radicalized me. Harry W. Higman and Earl J. Larrison's book *Union Bay: The Life of a City Marsh* showed me what these habitats were like before the university leased them to the city for a landfill; my own explorations showed me what was left and committed me to helping to save it.

In clear danger of flunking out altogether, I found academic salvation by making up a 1960s-style curriculum based largely on the natural history I found around me, with the assistance of a remarkable group of professors hanging on before the purge of the naturalists from the biology departments became complete. When the campus wetlands, already compromised by a dump, were threatened with paving over, I led a band of students, faculty, and staff on a march to save them. While others took over the administration building and demanded peace and justice, we took over the marsh and landfill, demanding topsoil and trees, which we got. Our actions as student conservationists went far beyond campus, and we protested the Vietnam War as well. But the Union Bay Life-After-Death Resurrection Plant-In Life Park colored all that followed in my life as an activist. And when, after Nixon's Cambodian invasion, thousands of students faced off against hundreds of riot police before the student union, I sought the infinite sanity of the evening grosbeaks thronging the elms in front of old Denny Hall.

Coming to know my western college precincts so well made graduate school in the East both exciting and intimidating in its utter novelty. New Haven is an old industrial city, but the traprock ridges known as East and West Rocks loomed within easy reach of the Yale School of Forestry and Environmental Studies, and Atlantic shores lapped close to campus. The mature groves of hardwoods that graced the older colleges and cemeteries not only introduced me to the resplendent eastern autumn without having to go farther afield in New England, but also stood ready to receive the warbler waves when they appeared in April and May. Ailanthus trees along railroad cuttings were hung with cynthia moth cocoons like Christmas balls. Architecture and natural history merged as I took to seeking out the academic owls of Yale— stone carvings, wooden effigies, copper weathervanes—tallying in three years more than seventy-five "species."

Self-consciously Oxbridgean Yale was bracketed by the real thing, as I spent several years in and near Cambridge as a Fulbright Scholar and postdoctoral consultant. Wicken Fen, where Darwin collected beetles while skipping classes, was some distance from campus. But the college Backs, spattered with celandine and crocuses in early spring, opened onto the River Cam (or Granta), whose towpath could take you into fen, field, or forest, not to mention pub. I found ways to walk from my digs to my lab, three miles, entirely on footpaths, never on a road. I knew what nettle patch was most likely to offer up small tortoiseshells coming out of hibernation and which water meadows echoed with the rising and falling skylarks. Another season, I lived a block from Virginia Woolf's one-time residence, in Newnham, on a lane ending at a nature reserve known as Owlstone Close, where tawny owls really did wail at night. Blue tits and English robins haunted Little St. Mary's churchyard, swifts zipped open the ancient air between the Cavendish Laboratory and the Free Press Public House. It wasn't the Selborne of Gilbert White, but much of England's familiar natural history could be found in and around Cambridge's colleges.

Since then, as an independent scholar, I have been the guest of scores of academies. Most frequently, Evergreen State College, with its deep woods and long shoreline on southernmost Puget Sound; the urban enclave of Portland State; and a department store magnate's erstwhile estate at Lewis & Clark College, where poet William Stafford once had the right to glean fruit from campus trees written into his contract. I have watched a red vole skitter among gardens at the Saarbrucken University; confirmed global warming by giant mauve pasqueflowers blooming in April at the University of Alaska in Fairbanks, where I'd been promised dog-sledding and found bare-chested Frisbee throwers instead; and marveled at a lemon-and-heliotrope imperial moth hanging beneath a midnight archway in College Park, Maryland. At Thomas Jefferson's "academical village," the University of Virginia, I've watched pairs of cardinals (a big deal to a western birder) courting among old pines and a weathered and crocketed spire imported from Oxford in one of the many walled gardens. At a little college on Florida's west coast, wood storks stalked the lawn, while across the state, alligators cruised campus waters at the University of Florida in Gainesville. Recently, walking the shore path along Lake Mendota at the University of Wisconsin in Madison,

I reveled in the chartreuse explosions of fireflies (another biggie for westerners) in the campus bosque called Muir Woods after the esteemed naturalist and alumnus. One lampyrid beetle, plucked from a spiderweb, flashed on and off in my hand for half an hour. I can't think of a college or university I have visited without taking home some such sharp image of its living placehood.

Since I have never assumed a full-time faculty position for long, I have not (since Washington) had to contend with the daily reality of a particular academic locus for year on year, day in, day out. As an itinerant don, I have not had to face committees and quotidian life and the strains they impose. No doubt this has made it easier for me to view every appointment as a longer or shorter field trip.

Even so, I fully believe that, had I satisfied my original objective of a long-term professorship, I would have treated whatever campus on which I went to ground in exactly the same manner: as a habitat, to be known more and more intimately for all it might provide in the way of teaching, placement, and pleasure. If anything, such a relationship with one's place of employment ought to be a balm for the more tedious and difficult demands of the profession.

The closest I've come was as a visiting professor of creative writing at Utah State in Logan, the place of the waxwings in the snow. I designed and taught undergraduate and graduate courses in environmental writing for spring semester 2002. This furnished the opportunity to get to know a particular academy's locality in greater detail than those I might call upon for only an afternoon or a week. Normally a habitué of a rainforest that does have its seasons but that drips between them almost insensibly, I was struck by my first opportunity since childhood to experience a Rocky Mountain winter and its abrupt morphing into full-blown spring. It seemed that one week I was snowshoeing in the Wellsville Mountains west of town, the next hiking among balsamroot blooming in the Wasatch foothills to the east. The campus itself had suffered major disruption for new steam tunnels and was in any case fairly manicured. But one side of its hill dropped directly into the mouth of semi-wild Logan Canyon, and another fell away toward town through a squirrel-haunted arboretum. Pollination biologists and botanists in other departments steered me toward rare plants, such as the magenta Maguire's primrose, which bloomed in Logan Canyon when the naturalized violets spread their mauvy carpet across every unsprayed lawn in town. Two of my students were good naturalists active in the local Audubon chapter, and together we found the best local wetlands for waterfowl. Most of the others, though from small Mormon towns and farms, were not much oriented toward the voluntary out-of-doors. But through writing invitations and field trips, I got them out, sharing my discoveries and reminding them of things they had forgotten to remember.

But the most vivid memory of emplacement I took away from Utah State had to do with an alien invasion of the English department. Actually, the invaders were native; the students, staff, and faculty who noticed their invasion were the aliens. At least since the late Pleistocene, bright fire-engine-red-and-black insects known as box-elder bugs (*Leptocoris trivittatus*) have frequented the canyons of the Rockies. They lay their eggs in the bark of box elder trees (*Acer negundo*), a kind of maple, in the early spring. By fall, millions of adult box-elder bugs descend from the mountains seeking shelter in caves and hollow trees at lower elevations. When people erect big, heated buildings—the kind that campuses commonly consist of—within box-elder bug range, they should not be surprised when the bugs treat them as nice warm caves.

Yet people repeatedly express shock and indignation when their domiciles and workplaces are chosen for winter quarters by thousands of bright little bugs. And this was the case at Utah State, the winter I arrived.

I'd been enjoying the box-elder bugs all term, as they clustered in corners over the ineffectual radiator in my office. As the days began to warm, they flew about the hallways like bright little ingots, seeking egress. Occasionally, I witnessed common varieties of entomophobia or mild irritation as box-elder bugs flew into someone's careful coif or circled someone else's spectacles. But the first I knew that anyone was seriously disturbed by them was when a memo came around announcing that an exterminating firm had been engaged to spray the English building, as well as Old Main and the library. Apparently, some students and staff had become much distressed by the abundance of box-elder bugs, especially in the computer room, where they congregated in special abundance, sometimes damaging the hardware, other times dissuading users from even coming in.

I was disturbed by the bad biology of the plan, as well as the decision to subject workers to toxins without their assent or knowledge of the agents to be used (there were already several cancers in the department). Especially worrisome was the company's assurance that they would monitor for the bugs a month after application—by which date the insects would naturally have dispersed in any case! Between the opportunism of the exterminator and the entomological naiveté of everyone else, a bad situation had developed. Fortunately, many members of the faculty were incensed about the planned poisoning of their workplace for dubious reasons. As I wrote in a return memo, vacuums would do the job just fine where numbers of bugs constituted a real problem, and the bugs would soon evacuate the premises regardless of what we did—and, it was important to note, be back again next fall. The only way to prevent the annual influx would be to air-seal the building or to eradicate box elder trees from the canyons. Furthermore, the bugs were fascinating and quite beautiful, observed closely. Live with them, I advised my colleagues; even enjoy them. Vacuum them if you must.

At least that spring, we forestalled the spray. But I was sure the issue would arise again, after I was long gone. At least my colleagues would be better informed next time The whole episode illustrated the disconnection many people feel with regard to their nonhuman neighbors, a trait that too often distances academic employees from their workplaces.

As a matter of fact, many academies go to lengths to eradicate or damp down the experience of the more-than-human on campus. For example, sprays are not limited to controlling unwanted residents in college buildings. Too many campuses suffer heavy exposure to chemicals applied to their lawns and gardens. Driven by some administrator's floraphobic dictate that greenswards be pure bluegrass monocultures, grounds and facilities crews regularly spray the grass with herbicides and insecticides. When the snow melted and the grass greened in Logan, I was distressed to see work-study students employed to broadcast toxins here and there, completely free from protective equipment. I have also watched kids in shorts and sandals spraying herbicides at Albertson College in Idaho. This scene is repeated annually at many colleges and universities across the country. Recently, I watched wide-eyed as an agricultural rig suited for a Midwest cornfield, with ten nozzles on a boom, sprayed the very swards where students routinely bask, nap, study, and make out at the University of Maryland. At the same time, soccer and softball camps were in progress. The little yellow warning flags were invisible over most of the expansive lawns. Many of the most commonly used biocides have been linked to lymphomas and an array of reproductive ills for young women and men, and growing numbers of chemically sensitive people react badly to any sprays. How sad to think that the blandishments of going barefoot may lead to bodily harm for trusting scholars. Not to mention to boring lawns that might otherwise host an attractive and interesting array of clovers, veronicas, violets, English daisies, native grasses, and their attendant pollinators.

I reserve special disdain for another, nearly ubiquitous abomination on the campus scene: the leaf blower. Is it not ironic that the very ideal of collegiate tranquility, the much-vaunted and beloved grove of academe, where the din and fumes of the hurly-burly mercantile world are left behind in favor of the serene life of the mind, is the very place where one can almost be assured of hearing damnable leaf blowers every autumn? Many is the lovely campus where I have experienced the shriek of two-stroke gasoline engines shattering the contemplative calm, never worse than one perfect afternoon at Lewis & Clark College in Portland, Oregon. Couched as a labor issue by landscape foremen who call the shots, the displacement of the soft sough of rakes by earsplitting and calm-wrecking leaf blowers and weed eaters can be considered at worst nothing less than a certain sign of the decline of the academy in a deeply philistine land. At best, poisons and machines serve to further displace campus residents of ours and other species.

Not that academicians need any further disincentives. In my experience, few campus habitués—whether students, staff, or faculty—attend to the actual place of their college homes with much care. Even those who live much out-of-doors tend to flee the campus as soon as possible for the trails, beaches, kayak waters, and climbing rocks far away. This is perfectly understandable, when the less-exciting campus claims so much of their time already. But while they must be present, I maintain, there is no reason not to be more attentive to their surroundings.

I have known a few academics who exercised mindfulness toward their workplace. Not surprisingly, some of these were the relictual naturalists with whom I studied as an undergraduate in Seattle. The great botanist Arthur Kruckeberg, still situated at Washington after half a century, knows its every tree and shrub; he and Estella Leopold, another botany professor and daughter of Aldo Leopold, once chained themselves to a special South African tree at risk from a UW paving project, and saved it. Kruckeberg's friend and late colleague, mammalogist and ornithologist Frank Richardson, taught me how the eastern gray and fox squirrels partitioned their adopted homes between the campus and the arboretum, a convenient moat and bridge in between. One of the keenest such devotions was evidenced by my philosophy professor, John Chambless. While a resident of old, postwar faculty housing beside the landfill, he crossed the remnant marsh on foot daily to get to classes, bird-watching all the while. He became an astute birder, often presenting his introductory philosophy course in terms of local ornithological experiences and metaphors. This made Plato, Berkeley, and Descartes go down much easier for me, and I suspect for others, too.

Likewise, my mentor at Yale, Charles Remington, always knew what was happening outside his rooms in lab and museum. Sometimes, inside and outside merged seamlessly. I recall him lecturing on wasps of the genus *Vespula* one spring day when, as if on call, a big queen yellow jacket flew in the open window. "Yes, just like that one," he said with a flourish. "Thank you very much." The wasp took one more turn around the room and flew out again the way she had come in. That lesson was not forgotten; nor was the professor's power over his subjects.

It is not surprising that some of the academics who have most closely noticed their surroundings have been literary writers. Writer-biologists such as E. O. Wilson, Bernd Heinrich, Lynn Margulis, May Berenbaum, and Vincent Dethier quite naturally pepper their texts with observations from their home institutions as well as from distant settings. The genre of academically based fiction is also rich in examples. Vladimir Nabokov, smarting from leaving the wilds of Saint Petersburg's hinterlands, paid little attention to tame Cambridge while there, apart from boating, dating, and playing soccer. But his mordant and hilarious parody of a confused émigré professor, *Pnin*, deftly catches details of the campuses where Nabokov taught in this country, especially Cornell. In one scene, he even gives himself a cameo appearance, when Pnin disturbs a puddle-club of celestial blue butterflies: " 'Pity Vladimir Vladimirovich is not here,' remarked Chateau. 'He would have told us all about these enchanting insects.' " They were, of course, the famous Karner blue, now a conservation cause célèbre, originally given its scientific name and description by Nabokov.

In Jane Smiley's *Moo*, we see the big ag campus in intimate detail between an obsolete horticulturist character and a protagonist pig whose lone mad dash finally gains it brief freedom. Jon Hassler's several novels set in a small college in the upper Midwest dwell upon the physical setting with such loving depth that there is no perceptible separation between people, building, river, and geological substrate (e.g., *The Dean's List*). David Lodge's collegiate comedies, while hardly natural history, closely observe the airy Californian campuses and smothering redbrick English universities he loves to contrast. And in an inspired touch, his novel *Small World* apotheosizes the Two Cultures by placing the arts at one end of an expansive, new greenfield university, the sciences at the other, their planned bridging abandoned due to budget cuts that leave the intervening miles a wilderness both real and metaphorical.

The antithesis of Lodge's bicameral campus is Nabokov's High Ridge: "Does there not exist," he asks, "a high ridge where the mountainside of 'scientific' knowledge meets the opposite slope of 'artistic' imagination?" A recent appointment of mine was posited directly on the existence of such a meeting place. The sixty-five-thousand-acre H. J. Andrews Experimental Forest, a joint enterprise of the Willamette National Forest and Oregon State University, has advanced our knowledge of Cascade Range forests and streams for more than half a century through a program known as Long-Term Ecological Research. A recent initiative of the U.S. Forest Service and the Spring Creek Project of the OSU Department of Philosophy, spearheaded by ecologist Fred Swanson and writer-philosopher Kathleen Dean Moore, launched a parallel program to be known as the Long-Term Ecological Reflections. One of the first efforts I know of anywhere to attempt a left brain/right brain bridge based on place, the ecological reflection scheme is precisely an exercise in placing the academy. I was fortunate to be appointed to the first residency for this enlightened notion, subtitled "the Continuum Project." Subsequent residents have included poets Pattiann Rogers, Alison Hawthorne Deming, and Jane Hirshfield, essayists Scott Russell Sanders and Kim Stafford, and ecocritic Scott Slovic.

Drafting these thoughts while situated among deep wilderness, surrounded by massive Douglas-firs and Pacific yews slung with boas of lichens and moss, I was literally bringing the academy to the wild. I found that my habit of peering closely into each of my successive domains had prepared me to extend my view beyond the actual H. J. Andrews campus and into the old-growth territory beyond. Of course, as an ecologist and a writer, I had an advantage over one whose biology was less embedded. On the other hand, the experience of a scientific naïf, while less informed, might be more revealing for its freshness of view. What one would need for such an experience to be successful is the inherent or cultivated habit of close observation of external detail—for it is the details that make the place, whether or not one possesses names or facts to attach to them.

As stimulating as the H. J. Andrews immersion might be, it would be a mistake to imagine that genuine emplacement requires wilderness in the strict sense. Fortunate is the nature lover situated at Williams or Middlebury colleges, backing up to the Berkshire and Green mountains as they do. Yet when I visited Columbia University last spring, in its hyper-urban Manhattan setting, I saw that it not only possesses its own green space, but that it abuts the close of the Cathedral of St. John the Divine, which runs into relatively bucolic Morningside Park, which is a block from Central Park, where I had watched hermit thrushes, white-crowned sparrows, and brown creepers that very March morning.

Nor are we talking strictly about native species. Ornamentals, cultivars, weeds, and the animal life they support all add to the diversity of any scene. Just because most campuses are wildly mixed montages resembling no particular ecosystem to be found in the wild does not make them any less arresting to the eye and the mind. In fact, gardening, if not applied as a sort of ethnic cleansing against all things uninvited, may actually increase the overall diversity of a site over what one might find in that region and season in a more "natural" setting. This was true of the medicinal herb garden I frequented at the University of Washington, where many nectariferous plants and attending insects absent from adjacent woods could be found.

True placement should always lead one *out*, beyond the pale of the ivory tower, into the profane precincts beyond, crossing ecotones and back again like every other creature. We are, after all, the only species (and this may be the one thing that truly differentiates humanity from other beings) that has forsaken its animal vigilance and ecological adeptness for comfort and security, such as it is.

Ah, so how to get some of that back? By being a better naturalist, day by day, regardless of one's academic discipline. This is not a matter of becoming a dedicated birder or botanist, carrying around a Roger Tory Peterson as an inseparable text (though that can't be a bad thing, for any scholar interested in place). Rather, it is an openness toward gradual acquaintance, a willingness to get to know neighbors outside our species, let alone our departments. Most of all, it is an active resistance to that anti-intellectual, anti-communitarian quality that John Fowles has beautifully described as "contempt from ignorance." I am again and again taken aback by otherwise bright people who, in their lack of familiarity with the so-called natural world, exhibit actual contempt for it or for those who pay it much attention. In his 1977 novel *Daniel Martin*, a Fowles character tellingly asks, "Why isn't it enough that I just love it here? That I don't want to know all the names and the frightfully scientific words." The title character answers, "Because you shouldn't justify contempt from ignorance. In anything." That gets it just about right.

To place yourself in your academy, nothing serves better than walking. Walking, in the Thoreauvian sense from his essay by that name, means sauntering with few expectations other than being surprised—not dashing madly to class while shouting into a cell phone or trying to remember if you brought your lecture notes or what's for dinner. It means dedicating otherwise unchallenged time to perambulation of your immediate environs, again and again, through the changing seasons, and then following up on some of the questions that invariably arise. What were those huge pigeons in the deodar cedars? Are these madhouse squirrels native or introduced? Those mushrooms behind the greenhouse—were they palatable, poisonous, or psychoactive? This kind of looking and asking can lead not only to extra-departmental conversation, but to the occasional lyric impulse or connective insight.

I take special pleasure in long night walks on campuses, when sounds and smells are especially vivid and human bustle almost absent. On my lengthy noctivagation of UW Madison one recent summer, I watched Boston ivy ruffle in the breeze on the side of the carillon tower as if it were green waves, just before the bells rang eleven. College-gothic shadows, bits of stained glass, greenhouse palms, and premating primates all showed as they never would have by day, and a lean, feral black cat spotted not far from a small cottontail at graze predicted either a short food chain or a close call. I readily admit to a nocturnal advantage as a large male animal. Even so, company, if not overly loquacious, does not necessarily spoil such dark rambles. Nocturnal outings may also be indulged on wheels, in fact more and more so on our post-ADA campuses.

In the end, placing the academy means, to me, paying true attention to one's academic surrounds. I am both saddened and disturbed by how few seem to do so. Strangely, I have known few less versed in natural history than some of those who style themselves "deep ecologists." Doubtless these thinkers give good seminars, but most could no more lead an informed nature walk in their own home precincts than they could survive a month in the wild. Likewise, many ecocritics, ecofeminists, ecophilosophers, and ecohistorians of my acquaintance tend to neglect their own backyards. I have known professors of place-based disciplines, not to mention molecular biologists, who couldn't name five native plants or animals outside their offices.

I do not intend this charge as an indictment as much as an invitation. Of course, our jobs seldom demand or reward intimacy with the grounds outside Old Main, nor have we any call to go forth into the wilderness naked for a month (as former University of Washington professor of anthropology Monty West once did in order to perceive the plight of the unequipped aboriginal; he survived, barely). What, then, is lost through the failure to attend? Just this: anyone who is concerned with the literature or meaning of place, yet who ignores the physical and living details of the very place where she or he works, is forsaking a vast reservoir of inspiration, grounding, instruction, authority, tranquility, consolation, physical and intellectual stimulation, spiritual succor, fun, and sometimes ecstasy, but above all, *interest* in the real world. When you care about your own place, what you have to say about place in general is certain to mean, and matter, much more. If my experience is any measure, getting to know the campus *sensu stricto* can dramatically affect one's teaching, research, writing, engagement, and well-being.

Finally, I do not think it out of order to suggest that intellectual workers whose subjects of study impinge on place (and I can scarcely imagine a field that does not) bear a certain responsibility to know something about the locality in which they live, study, and teach. The aunts of Frank Lloyd Wright interviewed prospective teachers for their Hillside Home School based on their knowledge of the local flora and fauna. While we are unlikely to return to such an Arcady, there is something in that view of pedagogic qualification that still rings true. Would it be too much to ask of our academics that they make an effort to know their nonhuman neighbors as well as their colleagues and students? For me, doing so has been nothing but a pleasure. And when I arrived in Missoula not long ago for an appointment at the University of Montana and found a bill tacked to a telephone post a block from my apartment urging everyone to be watchful for the local black bear, I knew I was in for another adventure in campus creatures.

One recent year, I had cause to return repeatedly to the University of Washington, during a successful course of chemotherapy for my wife, Thea. These occasions gave me the opportunity to revisit many of the crannies and corners I'd known so well some thirty years before. Picking my way among new buildings since sprung up in the rich fertilizer of Gates and Allen cash, I sought the old haunts. The skyline and footprints of university buildings had grown radically, becoming more an academical city than village. Unaltered habitats had equally shrunk, one of my favorite bird groves having disappeared beneath the new law school, for example. But I found that much remained—from much-attenuated madrona patch to revivified herb garden. The route of the then-railroad—now the many-mile Burke-Gilman Trail girdling Seattle's midsection—took me round the campus when it was painted by autumn. In winter rain I found the immense graduate reading room of Suzzallo Library, though recently earthquake-proofed, still one of the finest rooms I know anywhere, and the mauve stained-glass chipmunk still guarded a secret stairway nearby.

Come spring, I circumnavigated the shore of Portage Bay, from Montlake Bridge to University Bridge, past marsh and freeway, past houseboat and dorm, past salmon spawning pool and birch grove, past Fisheries and Oceanography and Early

Childhood Development. Coots and spotted sandpipers still frequented bay and beach, marsh wrens the cattail patch, and Anna's hummingbird rose to the peak of his molten-throated courtship arc. As I returned to the hospital through the early dusk, the powerful seashore stink of *Cornus mas* displaced the diesel fumes of the day; and when I left Thea to her healing rest, the thick sweet scent of *Daphne odora* welcomed me back outdoors, back to campus.

Note: When my colleague in the English Department of Utah State University, Jennifer Sinor, asked me to contribute an essay to her edited book *Placing the Academy* (Utah State University Press, 2007), I gladly wrote this. I had long been wanting to conjure on my experiences as a naturalist in academia, and this was the perfect opportunity. My subsequent experiences as Kittredge Visiting Writer at the University of Montana in Missoula could have contributed a footnote as long again as the whole rest of the piece.

The most dramatic example of my own utter beguilement by campus creatures, just as utterly ignored by everyone else around me, took place on the campus of the University of Western Australia in Perth. The trees not far above our heads teemed with both rainbow lorikeets and pink-breasted, dove-backed galahs, two of the most beautiful of all parrots. I couldn't take my eyes off them, but almost every other set of eyes in the plaza was locked onto a telephone screen, the ground below, or straight ahead. I understand about familiarity and contempt, but still . . . !

Most recently, I explored Pacific University's old campus in Forest Grove, Oregon. Beneath massive Garry oaks and Douglas-firs stood a petrified stump, a memorial, that was thronged with invertebrates. I was enthralled and could have watched for weeks. Then came the leaf blowers!

It Was All About the Beavers

JOHN JACOB ASTOR I
AND THE RAPE OF THE WEST

The north wind carried my cap out into the river as I walked the shoreline toward the bridge. Little beaches of polished pebbles broke the tideline between washed rocks and waterlogged wood. Ring-billed gulls and dark geese, in singletons and pairs, worked the baylets out of the worst of the wind. An enormous green bridge loomed overhead, spanning the expanse of cold, gray water and whirring with morning traffic heading in and out of Astoria. So far, so familiar. I tugged my collar higher and swiveled back into March's harsh breath, scanning the opposite shoreline. What met my watering eyes was not the Willapa Hills of Washington State but the brown jumbled skyline of Harlem housing projects. Far to my left, I made out not Cape Disappointment, but the pointy stump of the Empire State Building. A second, graceful old bridge paralleled the first, just upstream. The pebbles were broken glass—blue, green, brown, and milky—rounded by the decades. And the geese? Atlantic brant.

I was in Astoria, all right—Astoria, Queens, about to fly home from nearby LaGuardia Airport. The most intimate of the three main air terminals serving Manhattan and greater New York City, LaGuardia Airport sits between Long Island and Astoria. I wanted to glimpse a fleeting expression on the face of this neighborhood that shares its name with Oregon's oldest city. By spending my last night in a marginal airport motel, I had just enough time before my flight. After a fine green-pepper-and-onion omelet at the Airport Diner, I caught the Q19 bus opposite immense St. Michael's Cemetery and rode it along Astoria Boulevard to Astoria Park. There, sweet gums and sere grass lined the shoreline between the Triborough Bridge and smaller, trains-only Hell Gate Bridge, a span of purple iron arches and white limestone pillars named for a once-treacherous channel of the East River.

Leaving the waterfront, I wended back through the edge of downtown Astoria. Away from the river, the similarity between this scene and its Pacific counterpart diminished. A white onion dome topped a triangular brick building with a Chinese kitchen on its ground floor. Nearby, a famous Czech beer garden awaited summer's steamy evenings. The visual jumble of vibrant streets crowded with many small shops let me know for sure I was in an old ethnic East Coast community—largely Greek, overlaid with Slavic and Asian. No surprise was the abundance of familiar Victoriana here, just as back home, considering that both Astorias shared much of the nineteenth century's exuberance on their respective shores. But smells, sounds, and cultural clutter foreign to my Northwest Astoria overtook any superficial resemblance.

Not that Astoria, Queens, is any older than Astoria, Oregon. The New York City neighborhood was named in 1839, while the West Coast fur fort that spawned Astoria, Oregon, was established in 1811. But the former, platted on old Dutch and English farms and subject to more diverse influences, developed much faster than the latter, grafted precariously into the wilderness. After all, the eastern Astoria lay just a river's-width away from the young country's major metropolis, while its western namesake was hung out to soak in the rain a continent apart from all the action. It was here, at the narrows called Hell Gate, where an immigrant-made-good established his country retreat, and where his houseguest and hired scribe, Washington Irving, wrote *Astoria*—the chronicle not of Astoria, Queens, but of Astoria, Oregon.

The commonality that struck me that chilly morning transcends the Victorian facades and the vague likeness of all big rivers with bridges near estuaries. Though three thousand miles apart, the two Astorias carry the same man's name, and both owe their existence to his extraordinary reach, vision, mercantile zeal, commercial acumen, and sheer cupidity. Yet something greater than a mere continent's width sets these two cities' tales apart. While the early development of Hell Gate was inevitable, given its position near the hub of human affairs in America, no such certainty lay at the mouth of the Columbia. That distant reach could well have escaped white settlement for decades to come. As things went, it was a close call for the first city in the new Northwest. Had Astor's master plan gone just a little more wildly awry than it did, there might be no West Coast Astoria at all.

John Jacob Astor I, unlike his descendants, was not born to wealth. He came forth on July 17, 1763, in Walldorf, at the edge of the Black Forest in Baden, then one of hundreds of German city-states. His father, Johann Jakob Astor, descended of Italian Protestants, was town butcher; his mother, Maria Magdalena Volfelder, gave birth to four surviving sons and a daughter. The last son, also christened Johann Jakob, proved a quick study, good with numbers and manual skills, but also a reader. He soon learned the butcher's trade, adeptly and with neither complaint nor affection. Brothers Georg and Heinrich both emigrated and anglicized their names. George worked for an uncle making musical instruments in London, while Henry sailed to New York, where he set up his own butcher's business. Johann envied them, but his father needed him in the Walldorf butcher shop, so he remained there, cutting and selling meat. But Johann Jr. had acquired admirers and advocates in a local schoolmaster and pastor. They finally prevailed upon the elder Astor to allow his youngest son to join George in England. There Johann, now John Jacob, learned flute making and selling at Astor & Broadwood, and in 1778 the new firm of George and John Astor opened. But it wasn't long until he wanted to see if brother Henry was making out as well as he boasted in America. With a load of flutes in his trunk, he sailed west in November 1783; and after a sixty-six day crossing and an ice-bound delay on Chesapeake Bay, he landed in Baltimore in late March of 1784. Three weeks later, having consigned and sold some flutes, he caught a coach for New York with his first American-made cash in his pocket.

It didn't take long in the hurly-burly of New York for John to realize that he didn't want to be a butcher there any more than at home, so he turned down his brother's offer of a job and went to work for a baker. His next job was moth-beater for a furrier called Quaker Browne. Thus began John Jacob's lifelong infatuation with fur. He also took out newspaper ads for his instruments, and found that he could sell them at a suitable gain. He invested his first intoxicating profits in more flutes from his brother George and in skins for which he bargained on the docks. In many ways, his course was set then and there; and with it, Astoria's.

Only a year and a half after arriving in New York, John Jacob returned to London to sell his first consignment of furs, restock with Henry's musical instruments, and acquire a franchise to import English pianos. Transatlantic trade proved still more intoxicating. In spring 1786, he established his own music shop. His horizon was expanding. John Jacob was never a dreamer in the artistic sense, but he was ambitious from the start. What dreams he entertained settled on business, and how business could grow, when conducted with vigor and aggressive imagination. There was money to be made in this new land. And then there was Sarah.

Sarah Todd was the daughter of Astor's landlady. When they married on September 19, 1785, he acquired an excellent business partner, friend, and mother to his children. She would bear him Magdalena, John Jacob Jr., William Backhouse, Dorothea, Henry, Eliza, and another son and daughter who did not survive. The couple set up housekeeping comfortably if simply in lodgings at the rear of Mrs. Todd's house, where the music store occupied the front. Then Astor booked passage on the Hudson River, in pursuit of pelts in the near north. The newlyweds plunged into the business, and as John Upton Terrell put it in *Furs by Astor* (1963), "furs overflowed into the woodshed and the Todd stable, and the general odor was not that of a florist's shop."

To learn more about this lucrative frontier traffic (then known as "peltries") and how it might be made to work for him, Astor traveled farther afield to the St. Lawrence River and west to Montreal. He befriended French and English agents and investigated the modi operandi of the rival North West and Hudson's Bay fur companies. Occasionally, to ingratiate himself with Indians and the ditty-loving French Canadians, he would take out a flute in village or frontier saloon. He took bales of beaver, martin, mink, and other skins back downriver, sold them for the London trade, and invested the return in his adopted city. He recognized that his greatest opportunity lay in furs, where profits might easily exceed 900 percent. Astor's plans grew with his experience. Even though the fur trade in the East and the "Old Northwest" was already spoken for, and the furbearers were diminishing in those regions, it was a big country, and the sky was the limit for anyone who would push harder, farther.

Fast-forward to 1806. Astor has invested in real estate all over Manhattan and has become the richest man in America and its first millionaire. But his passion for pelts remained. With the piles of pelts, trading houses, and sailing ships long gone, you have to look deeper for its evidences today. Down in the subway, for example. Entering the West Side subway station at 81st Street, I passed a long montage of natural history subjects emblazoned on the ceramic tiles of the tunnel wall. The panel included several furbearers. A quick and thundering trip swept me downtown for a meeting with my literary agent, situated at Number 10, Astor Place. When I left the train at the Astor Place station, I was met by colonies of terra-cotta beavers on the platform walls. What better emblem? As much as anything other than the ground itself, the Astor fortune was built on the backs of beavers, relieved of their pelts at the pleasure of profit.

At that time, the powerful North West Company, with four thousand employees in the field, controlled much of the fur trade in Upper Missouri, and would continue to do so for a third of a century. This private British powerhouse had a formidable competitor in the royally chartered Hudson's Bay Company, which took over in Canada after the French were unseated. In attempting to break into the cartel, a group of Montreal merchants formed the Mackinac Company at the neck between Lakes Michigan and Huron. In 1810, John Astor entered as a partner. The Canadian-American alliance, to be known as the Southwest Fur

Company, hoped to push the trade beyond the Rockies. Astor was now well positioned to spread his fingers through the peltries of the continent.

If I needed a reminder of Astor's eventual reach among the furbearers, it came on a visit to Green Bay, Wisconsin, where I lodged in the Astor House Bed & Breakfast, a restored mansion south of the city center in a nationally registered neighborhood known as "the Astor District." It makes up the southern half of a township first platted as the Town of Astor in 1837 by John Jacob Astor, at the height of his American Fur Company. If there hadn't been two of them already, would Green Bay have become yet another Astoria, giving a certain football team an entirely different image? By any name, this trading hub on the river carried the Astor empire deep into the region that later would become Ohio, Indiana, Illinois, Michigan, Wisconsin, and part of Minnesota. Now Astor I had his foothold firmly set in the Old Northwest.

Rivalries abounded among the big fur companies, especially the North West and Hudson's Bay, but also American outfits trapping and trading out of St. Louis, including the calculating Manuel Lisa's Missouri Fur Company and William Ashley's Rocky Mountain Fur Company. The easily accessible peltries were overexploited and jealously defended. If Astor was going to make inroads into the continent's fur supply, he would have to ply new territory. Thomas Jefferson's Louisiana Purchase opened the Mississippi, but jurisdiction was far from settled, and competition along the main stem was already thick. What about the western wilderness, even the Pacific? So in 1809, with several partners and a $400,000 investment, Astor established the Pacific Fur Company.

For some years, a small number of trading vessels had visited the West Coast and trafficked with the Indians. Prominent

among them were Captain Robert Gray, in 1792 the first to cross
the Columbia River bar in a sailing vessel, and George Vancouver, whose ship went farther upriver but a critical few weeks later.
Like Gray, a number of other Boston-based merchantmen sailed
around South America, up the Pacific Coast, to trade manufactured goods for sea otter pelts. These they took to China to trade
for silks, spices, and teas, convertible for profit back in Boston. By
this route Gray became the first American to circumnavigate the
globe.

Ten years later, by the time Astor was outfitting his nascent
empire with ships and cargoes bound for Canton, the feat was
almost commonplace. Astor found the China trade more profit-
able than the continental fur trade, and he wondered if the two
might be combined. This idea gave rise to the concept of a great
fur fort at the mouth of the Columbia. To grasp this fundamental
point, visit the Astoria Column in Astoria, Oregon, and examine
the historic friezes that grace its stucco walls. Lewis and Clark
are there, of course, and Gray, and Astor, and other characters
including the local Indians who received them all. If you look
closely, near the base, you'll see the artist's portrait of the town's
real raison d'être: beavers. They may be the funniest beavers
you'll ever see, giving no great confidence that the Italian artist
ever saw the animal in person. But beavers they are, and in their
quiet, long-suffering way, they say *fur*, and they signify John Jacob
Astor's dream: to control the peltries of the Far West, linking his
Manhattan, Great Lakes, and Asian interests into one great circle
of commerce and gain.

So Astor dispatched two expeditions, one by land, one by sea,
to claim the Far Northwest peltries. Thus began the ultimately disastrous chain of events leading up to the founding of Astoria, Oregon. For a full account of the almost incredibly ill-fated panorama

of (in Zorba the Greek's immortal words) "the full catastrophe," read one—or better yet, all three—of these sources: *Astoria*, by Washington Irving (1836, still in print in several editions); *Astoria*, by Peter Stark (HarperCollins, 2014); or my expanded version of this essay, "John Jacob Astor I: A Most Excellent Man?" in *Eminent Astorians* (Oregon State University Press, 2011). Stark's excellent *Astoria* might be the more reliable of the books by that title, but Irving's is more fun to read. My essay is much longer than this one, but much shorter than either book. By any telling, compared to the Astorians' ordeals, coming and going, Lewis and Clark's worst trials look like a cakewalk. Instead of recounting that whole tortuous, two-headed chimera, I offer here the super-concise verse rendition that I wrote for a collection of Lower Columbia River poems with photographs by Judy Vandermaten (*The Tidewater Reach*, Columbia River Reader Press, 2020):

In the Fort George Taproom

So what did they expect?
Mr. Astor wanted to corner all the furs
of the Far Northwest—last of the unclaimed peltries.
So he sent both a ship and a party by land,
in the near wake of Lewis and Clark.
But lacking Jefferson's hiring skills, Astor chose
a strict Navy man to command an unruly crew
of French-Canadian *voyageurs*,
each his own man, around the Horn.
They nearly mutinied the first night out!
And when the *Tonquin* finally made the mouth
of the Great River of the West? Fed up
with them all, Captain Thorn ordered boat

after ship's boat across the stormy bar,
and of course they died.

After offloading most of the others
on the Oregon side, Thorn scooted north
into hostile waters, eager to trade for pelts,
but absent any manners, or respect. When he kicked
their furs into their faces, the Indians took out
their knives. The sole surviving white hid in the hold
and blew up the powder magazines, killing
all aboard. And who would have wondered?

Astor's expedition by land fared almost as badly,
thanks to the Sioux and the winter. When they joined
the ragged remainder at Fort Clatsop, it was hard to say
which of them was worse off. So many casualties—
John Day and all the rest. And then came the war
of 1812, and Astoria, such as it was, became Fort George.
Afterward, Mr. Astor got some beaver, but had to share
with the Hudson Bay Company after all.

The sheer fact is, between bad choices and bad luck,
it's amazing to think that Astoria ever happened at all.
Now, sitting here at ease, out of all danger except
that which accompanies every day alive, we sip,
and we ask: so what did they really expect?
Of course the beavers finally bit back.

For, of course, though a tragicomedy told in human lives,
it was really all about the beavers. Even the relief ship that was
supposed to save the Astorians was called the *Beaver*. When it

was greatly delayed, Astor's ill-chosen and traitorous Scots commander McDougal gave up the shop to the British-Canadian North West Company, on the bluff that a coming British warship would be accompanied by a frigate and two sloops of war. The ultimate arrangement held very poor terms for Mr. Astor's Pacific Fur Company. On November 30, 1813, not the expected armada, but the single British sloop *Raccoon*, rounded Cape Disappointment. Had the Astorians stood up to the Royal Navy, with the aid of friendly Chief Comcomly, they quite likely could have resisted successfully. On December 12, the Union Jack rose over the little settlement, which the Nor'Westers promptly rechristened Fort George.

On his fiftieth birthday, Astor sought, through his indebted friend Albert Gallatin, the Secretary of the Treasury, to beg Secretary of State James Monroe to provide naval protection for Astoria. Monroe agreed in principle, but that didn't work out. As historian Axel Madsen put it, "Lost, for lack of a frigate, was 614,000 square miles of the West—a domain larger than the thirteen original colonies." Lost, by the way, to a mere sloop bearing the name of one of the lesser furbearers.

At the end of the British war in 1814, under terms of the Treaty of Ghent, the Pacific Fur Company regained its ownership of Astoria. On October 6, 1818, at Astor's behest, Monroe sent Captain James Biddle in the sloop-of-war *Ontario* to reclaim the mouth of the Columbia, and the American flag rose there once again. In theory, Astor could reoccupy Astoria. But in practice, by then the North West Company was firmly in charge of the Columbia peltries, and for the next twenty years a treaty allowed equal access to western waters for both American and British traders. There was no one to kick the Nor'Westers out—at least not until they merged, most unwillingly, with the Hudson's Bay

Company in 1821. Hudson's Bay was a formidable presence up-river, not easily dislodged or outcompeted. So, although he had earlier pledged that "while I breathe and so long as I have a dollar to spend I'll pursue a course to have our injuries repaired," Astor eventually had to let it go. All the dollars he possessed were not enough to recover the dream, or to bring back the sixty-one men lost in its pursuit, as tabulated by company clerk Alexander Ross. "How vain are the pursuits of man," he wrote. "That undertaking which but yesterday promised such mighty things is today no more."

The loss of Astoria was its eponymous founder's greatest reversal, costing a fortune, his pride, and deep disappointment, not to mention all those lives. But if many human lives were lost, just think of the other animals.

As a boy growing up in Colorado, I gobbled up old books on mountain men and trappers, gifts from my historian grandmother. I was entranced by ads in the back of *Boy's Life*: "Become a government trapper, live a life of free adventure in the great outdoors." I sent away for free pamphlets on Colorado's furbearers and instructions for trapping muskrats and skunks. And I wore out my faux coonskin cap, à la Davy Crockett (who once stayed in the Waldorf Astoria). But at my first sight of a beaver in a mountain marsh, fascination with the animals themselves eclipsed my romantic view of trappers. I came to understand what traps actually did, and that animals' pelts more properly belonged on their own backs. Now, when we think of John Jacob Astor and his guild, we should not forget the millions of creatures killed miserably in leg-hold traps and snares on his behalf. Not that this haunting debt is uniquely Astorian: furs were the frontier currency of the time.

After the breakup of his Pacific Fur Company, Astor and his son, William Backhouse, beefed up the American Fur Company, which would dominate the trade for decades. Ramsay Crooks, having survived his hellish walk to Astoria and back, managed the northern section from Michilimackinac, a fur-trading post on the southern side of the strait separating Lakes Huron and Michigan. Many of their affairs are summarized in three big red buckram books housed at the New York Historical Society. They contain the Calendar of American Fur Company Papers—typed abstracts of 18,181 letters written between 1831 and 1849. Riffling through them, I found many accounts like this: "The season is unfavorable for the sale of buffalo robes," and "All Lake Superior skins have arrived. Northern returns are short in beaver, otters, and muskrats but have an excess of martins and lynxes." As inviting as they were from the outside, I searched in vain among these tomes for anything of Astor's heart. Even the traces pertaining to his nearest and dearest are merely fiscal, as cold as stones, or gold ingots. More passion is to be found in the reports of the peltries, the ups and downs of deer skins and buffalo robes, beavers and martins, lynxes and mink, than for any of his loved ones.

But Astor could see the twilight of the peltries looming. Silk was replacing felted beaver for men's top hats. Beaver were thinning out, and the mountain men were thinning on top. The buffalo herds would not last long, the passenger pigeons would no longer darken the skies, sea otters and condors were already checking in absent at the Columbia. The Indian nations themselves were unraveling under the stresses of disease, alcohol, guns, and the whites. Steamboats chugged and belched where the voyageurs once dipped their silent paddles. The wilds were getting crowded, and the profits were spread too thin. John Jacob Astor, his fur dreams done, sold the northern operations of the American Fur Company to Ramsay Crooks in 1834, and the southern branch to Choteau & Co. in St. Louis.

After the fur business, John Jacob enjoyed a long, comfortable denouement, filled with family and an active business life well into old age. He carried, and exercised, great influence over presidents and anyone else he wished to sway. He subsidized the government on more than one occasion, and if he played both ends against the middle by lending money to the British as well as the Americans during the War of 1812, well, that was business. He couldn't be charged with treason because Madison owed him a personal loan. Favors, licenses, competitive advantages, and all manner of indulgences could be bought or leveraged, and few called it corrupt outright. Astor's image, romanized, appeared on coins for use on the frontier, to be presented like Lewis and Clark's Jefferson medals to impress the Indians. Astor was the only American businessman ever commemorated in coinage, the direct result of exerting his influence with Lewis Cass, Secretary of the War Department.

But Astor suffered losses as well as victories, and not just in business. A favorite grandson drowned during a European visit. His beloved daughter Magdalena twice married badly and died too young. His greatest loss was that of his wife and lifelong partner Sarah, who died while John was returning from Europe in the early 1830s. No wonder he broke up his million-dollar fur empire soon thereafter. His heart wasn't in it after that. As he left more and more of the business to William, he forsook his city mansion for his country house at Hell Gate, where he indulged his old love of music and surrounded himself with literati. Two respected poets, Fitz-Greene Halleck and Joseph Green Cogswell, came often to Hell Gate. Halleck became Astor's resident secretary.

But none of this distraction effaced Astoria from his mind, and what it might have been, versus what actually happened. Though the Astoria story could be seen as Astor's greatest speculative business loss, he wanted the story told, and told to his advantage. So he prevailed upon the best-known writer of the day, Washington Irving, to come to Hell Gate and write the book that would become *Astoria, or Anecdotes of an Enterprise Beyond the Rocky Mountains.* Irving agreed, on condition that the book would not be a mere puff-piece for the boss. He had no desire to be Astor's flack. Still, James Fenimore Cooper, uninvited to Astor's literary soirees, was spiteful in his dismissal of Irving as Astor's creature. He predicted that Irving would present Astor as greater than Columbus.

I was disappointed to learn that Irving himself never actually visited Astoria. He did travel as far as Montreal and Missouri, where he saw the inner edges of the fur trade on the near frontier. He drew on this experience, and on journals, letters, interviews, and published and unpublished accounts of the Astor expeditions and the peltries in general. His sources included John Bradbury and Thomas Nuttall, naturalists along on the front end of the expedition by land; the memoirs of Astorians Gabriel Franchère and Ross Cox; Hunt's and Crooks's letters; and Robert Stuart's eyewitness account. Irving worked at Hell Gate through the fall and winter of 1835, and *Astoria* was published in October 1836. Irving said he wrote more in a month than he had ever done before, and found the experience revivifying. Astor loved the literary energy that pervaded the place, and was well pleased with the outcome.

Yet, with greater generosity than strictly required, Irving took pains to unreel the full chain of unintended consequences—the almost Shakespearean sequence of screwups and bad luck—that added up to what he called, with perfect pitch, "the tissue of misadventures" that doomed the Astorian project. Irving's account, carefully read, implicates Astor at every turn.

Irving can be as fine a writer to our ears today as he was considered in the days of *Knickerbocker Tales*, as in this lovely sentence, which would stand anywhere, anytime: "It is in this way that small knots of trappers and hunters are distributed about the wilderness by the fur companies, and like cranes and bitterns, haunt its solitary streams." Besides tracing the essential birthing story of Astoria, this thrilling, sweeping book gives a devastating and deeply affecting portrait of the continent at the very moment of its violation, a volatile time in a violent history.

Arthur Howden Smith, in 1929, wrote that Astor was "simply the product of a period and an environment . . . How he would have hated himself had he been able to view some of his acts objectively, as we can, through the perspective of time!" Such regrettable acts might include Astor's lubricious maneuvers to evade Jefferson's embargo on overseas shipping; opportunism, influence trading, and coercion with Madison, Monroe, Gallatin, and other elected and appointed officials; playing both ends against the middle in the War of 1812; flying chameleon flags on his vessels; and opium running. Some of his least handsome behavior related to Native Americans, in spite of his ignored instructions to Captain Thorn to always treat them kindly. He wasn't overtly genocidal— far from it. Rather, as Howden Smith put it, he was "prey to a moral blindness which was instinctive rather than reasoned." So, as Madsen charged, Astor was "never happier than when surrounded by his grandchildren," but "was also a slumlord, a war profiteer, and a ruthless jobber who shipped opium to China, and sold liquor to Indians knowing the devastating consequences."

Native Americans devastated by alcohol, firearms, and disease might be enough. Yet another legacy that does not appear in the executors' minutes books, but can readily be found in the business ledgers, includes countless other lives sacrificed to Astor's Big Business: 390,000 bison and 375,000 beavers just from 1815 to 1830, as well as all the other species. Astor's mining of the peltries caused boundless cruelty to furbearers while devastating populations. Astor alone was not responsible; he was just doing what everyone else was doing, which was his oft-stated rationale. But he did much more of it, and more energetically, than almost anyone else.

Astor was the first great American preview of the baleful consequences of rapacious power mixed with unlimited capital expansion for its own sake: a worthy instrument of Manifest Destiny, the grand conceit of his benefactor, James Monroe. He was a suitable precursor for all the takers: the Buffalo Bills, the James Hills, all the Carnegies and Rockefellers and Kennecotts and Halliburtons and Trumps to come. By the measure of a country in love with laissez-faire and the self-made man on the make or the take, Astor was indeed "a most excellent man," as Thomas Jefferson once called him. But by modern standards we might want to emulate—generosity, humanitarianism, mercy, sustainability, restraint, wanting less and conserving more—maybe not so much.

Not that the man was without merit. As Howden Smith wrote, "In his features you might trace meditation, courage, and masterful resolve—and coldness, indifference, and acquisitiveness. But never brutality, intolerance, or stupidity . . . And add this for him: at his most detestable, he was no hypocrite." An astonishing array of the notable people of his era had truck with him or his people: Jefferson, Madison, Monroe, Gallatin, Hamilton, Burr, various Napoleons, Kamehameha, Comcomly, Daniel Boone, John Colter, John Day, Kit Carson, Thomas Nuttall, Audubon, Irving, and on and on. No one can say that Astor, apart from being the first major plutocrat in the country, failed to touch its people, and sometimes for the good.

In *Furs by Astor,* John Terrell suggested that Astor never forgave McDougal for selling out Astoria. Yet he retained pride over his project on the Pacific. "When everything else he had accomplished was long forgotten," Terrell wrote, "Astoria would stand as an indestructible monument to his memory." In various ways, his impact extends beyond the city's founding. When John Jacob Astor V, Baron Astor of Hever, came to Astoria with Lady Violet and their son Gavin in 1961 for the town's sesquicentennial, he left behind a check for $100,000 for the city's betterment. It broke the fundraising logjam for that fine little library that bears his family name. Though this gift was one-fifth of what his ancestor left for the other Astor Library, and the facility it helped to build is not a hundredth part of the massive one on Fifth Avenue, it enriches the lives of all Astorians no less than the edifice behind the lions uplifts New Yorkers.

John Jacob Astor I was arguably the most eminent Astorian of all, though he never beheld his fort, and though Astoria arose in spite of his overreaching grasp and ultimately violent failure. Does the city deserve his name? The word "Astoria" falls pleasantly on the ear. And like its unofficial sister city in Queens, this Astoria is an amenable, stimulating, and lively place. But as a town known for its strong communitarian, conservationist, and traditional working- and middle-class values, its nomenclatural debt to the founder of the Astor dynasty might be seen as ironic, even embarrassing.

Today, if you perch on any available dock or waterside bench, the town you see is very much more than it was when Astor died in 1848, but less than he might have imagined or what some still picture as possible. On an Indian summer pre-sunset eve on the veranda of the Wet Dog Saloon, I watched cormorants and gulls bobbing off a still-open stretch of shore between a fish market and a dental office with the best view ever. Across the three miles of river, past two ruby-hulled freighters at anchor, lay the subtle hills of Willapa in Washington, where I live. Upriver, sea lions oinked on the mooring basin slips. A school of small boats testified to a strong run of summer Chinooks. Toward the sun, beyond the crab plant and a boomer couple mounting their classic Harley, stretched the longest bridge on the West Coast. Its traffic was mostly RVs and show-bound hot rods, instead of commuters.

Most of the Astoria-Megler Bridge is flat like something out of the Florida Keys. The part I could see was the elevated south end over the shipping channel: a green steel fretwork of triangles, other angles, and curves. It too has pebbled shores beneath, but of siltstone instead of the glassy burden of the other Astoria's beach; and brant in winter, but the black brant of the Pacific. The only tug in sight was the little green-and-white pilot boat returning from a freighter loaded with the carcasses of a couple of thousand local trees, bound for Japan. The eve was still mellow and warm, a rarity at the mouth of the river. It felt a million miles from the high green bridge of Astoria, Queens, in the stiff March wind; light-years from the veranda at Hell Gate, where Irving penned *Astoria*. Yet the elements are much the same: river, bridge, and waterbirds, and a name that sounds like a flower, but rhymes with a dollar sign.

We should turn from the river, look back up the hill to the Column with its beavers at the base, and remember what they stand for. If the nature of this place changes wholesale in ways that presently threaten—with big money crowding out affordable housing, high-rise hotels and condos erasing the public shoreline, and profit-chasing, carbon-based big industry endangering the river's health and security—then the city's namesake could be all too suitable.

In another vision of this estuarine enclave, where beavers

once again thrive, and where the air and water and room to move are the envy of a crowded nation, we could choose to embrace its vicarious founder's name in a different way: as a reminder of what we have, how it could all be lost to greed and hubris, and how it must jealously be cherished. Now, every time I see those funny beavers at the base of the Astoria Column, I thank them for the reminder, and remember: it was always all about the beavers.

——————————————

Note: Steve Forrester, former editor and publisher of *The Daily Astorian* in Astoria, Oregon, concocted the book *Eminent Astorians* to commemorate some of the most important people in the city's past, and to mark Astoria's bicentennial. When he asked me to contribute a profile, I asked who was left. "Only Comcomly and Astor," he said. Knowing that various people in my county claim descent from Chief Comcomly and that nothing I said could get it right for all of them, I passed on that tinderbox and asked for Astor, about whom I knew very little. I enjoyed the research and reading, both in Oregon and New York, very much. I even found a signature of Washington Irving among Astor's estate papers that the librarians at the New York Historical Society didn't knew they had, a way to repay their many kindnesses. The resulting essay, "John Jacob Astor I: A Most Excellent Man?" came out novella-length. So I recast it in much briefer form here, highlighting the beavers and their relevance to Astor's impact—and those for whom he opened the way—on the young West, and on the chances for survival of our complicated green world.

In his wonderful new book *Eager: The Surprising, Secret Life of Beavers and Why They Matter* (Chelsea Green, 2018), Ben Goldfarb gives an enthralling picture of the massive significance beavers held for the North American landscape and its cultures, how the purposeful stripping of their numbers and creation of a beaver desert devastated the land and the people, and how beaver restoration is just the ticket for a wide array of conservation challenges today.

Swift and Underwing, Boulderfield and Bog

NABOKOV'S INDIVIDUATING DETAILS

Everywhere the details leap like fish

—JANE HIRSHFIELD,

"The Stone of Heaven"

In the year 2005, I taught place-based writing to instructors and students from several universities in Tajikistan, Kyrgyzstan, and Kazakhstan. This took place in Dushanbe, the Tajik capital, sponsored by the Aga Khan Humanities Project. English skills varied widely, the only *lingua franca* among the participating writers being Russian. Much of the workshop was presented in English, translated into Russian, and the responses and writings then translated back again—sometimes with Kyrgyz, Tajik, or Kazakh detours along the way. There were many moments of levity and mystery, and sometimes deep connection. But as for true transcendence—that moment when everyone present completely melded—nothing matched the recording of Vladimir Nabokov reading his poem "The Swift," first in English and then in his native Russian, on a cassette tape. The listeners liked the English version well enough, but when I played back the Russian reading, in his own sonorous, accented voice, my students were proudly transfixed.

"The Swift" describes a moment of high romantic tension, when the appearance of a certain swift over a misty bridge cements the moment "forever" in the minds of the young lovers. What captured that instant, the poet and his love, and the hearts and minds of my students, was the extraordinary attention given to one small *detail* of the physical world, at that precise time and place. I believe it is this same, almost preternatural attention to detail that informed Nabokov's remarkable visual art, his literary work throughout, and ultimately, his science as well.

In *Nabokov's Butterflies*, Brian Boyd and I did not include "The Swift," since it is an ornithological reference (though a thin case can be made that it is also a sneaky lepidopteran allusion: see below). But another short bit that we missed definitely refers to a moth. Merely a snippet in the *News* of the Lepidopterists' Society about *Catocala fraxini* feeding on dead fish in Russia, it was attributed to Nabokov by the editor, Charles Lee Remington, when they were both at Harvard's Museum of Comparative Zoology in 1947. This "beautiful Palearctic species," in Remington's words, is commonly known as the Clifden nonpareil. It belongs to a group of owlet moths whose forewings match the bark of trees, but whose alarming hindwings ("underwings") are usually banded with scarlet, pink, or orange, like bright petticoats peeking out beneath a dull cloak. On this species alone, the bands are palest blue. In *Sky Time in Gray's River*, I described the similar white underwing (*Catocala relicta*), a visitor to autumn porch lights in North America, as "a big gray delta nearly two inches to a side [with] fox-gray fur, the pile deepest on the thorax, lightened into a silvery pelt knitted with black-and-white bars, spots, and zigzags across the wings." Nabokov speaks to the Clifden nonpareil in a rhyme of Fyodor's in *The Gift*: "Your blue stripe, Catocalid, shows from under its gray lid." While he never drew it, to my knowledge, he caught a similar chalky pallor, gray striations, and cool bluish shades in several of his illustrations of his favorite blue butterflies, drawn with a fine nib and wash to catch the subtle hues of a blue's scales.

That Nabokov would take notice of such a thing, while it would fly right over most people's attention, is not unusual. He spoke often of the importance he placed in what he called "the individuating detail." As much as any other element of his output, scientific or literary or combined (for he *did* combine them), it is this extreme attention to exactly which elements distinguish one thing from another that so enlivens his fiction, ennobles both his poetry and his science (even unto its latter-day vindication), and elevates his drawings from doodles to art. Maybe the very fact that the world he sees and describes is largely invisible to his readers helps to render their thrall so complete.

Nabokov did, indeed, discover the individuating details everywhere he went, and by no means always pretty ones. On weekend collecting trips away from Cambridge or Ithaca he was as likely to be put off by the stench of a rancid clam-fry shack as entranced by early hairstreaks on the wing. When traveling in the West, between moments in motels or on the road that would later find their way into *Lolita*, he could not help but notice the low notes: "I visited a remarkably repulsive-looking willow-bog, full of cowmerds and barbed wire," he reported in a 1953 *Lepidopterists' News* note entitled "Collecting in Wyoming."

No one's poems, essays, stories, and novels are more richly dressed in nuance than those of Nabokov, who exalted "the individuating detail" in service to his art: as Humbert and Lolita passed through all those motor courts, the American landscape rolled by in the first-person particular, trained under the same microscope that the author brought to bear upon butterfly scales and genitalia. It was this extreme sensitivity to detail that allowed Nabokov to pick out one blue from hundreds he encountered in the Alps one summer; and though it turned out to be a hybrid between two species rather than the new species he initially suspected, its subtle distinction was enough to catch his eye, later to be celebrated in both a scientific paper and the often-quoted poem "On Discovering a Butterfly." It was this same acute perceptivity that allowed him to spot subtle likenesses and distinctions between specimens in his drawers and on his microscope slides, and to deduce real relationships between North and South American blues and those in the Holarctic, in spite of precious little material at hand.

By that same "good eye," as the old lepidopterists admiringly called such a subtle talent, he plucked particularity from every object or setting that engaged his interest, and frequently hung his writing raiment on those pegs. For example, in his poem "Lines Written in Oregon," he notices not only the pale, saprophytic phantom orchids in the forest, but also "peacock moth on picnic table." The phantom orchid is a real plant (*Cephalanthera austiniae*). The "peacock moth" may have been a silver-marked plusiine that reminded him of a related moth he thought he had discovered anew as a boy, but had been gazumped by another lepidopterist long before. Nabokov got his own back in *Laughter in the Dark* by naming a blind man Kretschmar, after "his" moth's original namer. He may have evoked that moth in the poem, also, in the phrase "Esmeralda, *immer, immer*"—because the closest thing to "his" moth in the main handbook and checklist of the time was then called *Chrysoptera moneta esmeralda*. If I am right about that (and it is mere conjecture), then from this moment "in the bewitched and blest / Mountain forests of the West," Nabokov penned a haunting lyric that both evoked a sharp disappointment of childhood and inspired extensive debate as to the (maybe multiple) ID of "Esmeralda"—all because he *noticed* a random moth on a picnic table. Taking extreme notice is just what he did.

When I visited the Berg Collection at the New York Public Library while working on *Nabokov's Butterflies*, and confronted the extensive body of drawings archived in the mostly unworked area labeled, at the time, "Leppy Stuff," I was struck by Nabokov's ability to transfer his attention to detail into graphic as well as verbal form. I was already well acquainted, of course, with the *Lycaeides* scale-row drawings from his scientific papers, and with the commemorative fancies he contrived for certain inscribed copies of his books, several of which I had examined at Wellesley College and elsewhere. But I had no idea of the breadth, range, or number of the drawings he had done. I was especially taken with a coppery-green rendition of remarkably anthropoid-looking male genitalia. Not only was the drawing beautiful, but it showed certain distinctive features of this minute structure that prompted Nabokov to conclude the close connection between the blue genera *Scolitantides* and *Glaucopsyche*.

Another drawing that struck home for me was that of a related European blue, *Lycaeides ismenias*. It brings to mind, in its shape and shimmery dark coloration, the unrelated *Erebia magdalena*. The Magdalena (or rockslide) alpine is a denizen of the high alpine talus slopes in the Rocky Mountains. This ebony-black butterfly pops up in a botched story related by Nabokov's first biographer

Andrew Field; and in the corrected and fleshed-out version, told humorously by John Downey (Nabokov's legatee for his work on the blues), in an oral history transcribed in our *Nabokov's Butterflies*. The butterfly also reappears in a poem written by a character in his novel *Look at the Harlequins!* In between, Nabokov actually encountered the Magdalena alpine during a summer in which he often felt, as he wrote Edmund Wilson, "some part of me must have been born in Colorado, for I am constantly recognizing things with a delicious pang."

Nabokov's meeting with Magdalena took place in the summer of 1947, when he and Véra spent a month collecting out of Columbine Lodge, situated along the Peak to Peak Highway between Estes Park and Nederland in the Colorado Front Range. Columbine Lodge is just south of Longs Peak Lodge, built and formerly run by the famous nature writer and early national park advocate, Enos Mills. (Today, Columbine Lodge is a retreat owned by the Salvation Army, known as High Peaks.) There, on the morning of July 13, the Nabokovs met up with Charles Remington, a PhD student he knew from Harvard, where Nabokov curated the Lepidoptera. It was Remington whom Nabokov would later refer to as his "fellow sufferer" at the Museum of Comparative Zoology. As Remington described the day to Harry Clench in a letter archived at Yale's Peabody Museum of Natural History, he left the University of Colorado's Science Lodge near Ward, then "drove over to Estes Park and picked up Nabokov and his son and wife and took them on a jaunt to Tolland, the famous locality for *Brenthis*."

The party drove south to Rollinsville, then west beside the railroad tracks toward the East Portal of the well-known Moffat Tunnel. There they entered Tolland Bog, the type locality for *Boloria selene tollandensis* (then known as *Brenthis myrina*). "We had a very pleasant day and excellent collecting," wrote Remington.

"Nabokov and his son are both skillful net wielders." This butter-fly is the Rocky Mountain subspecies of the silver-bordered frit-illary, a species Nabokov knew in the bogs of Vyra as a youth in Russia. It was likely the one referred to when he "stooped with a grunt of delight to snuff out the life of some silver-studded lep-idopteron throbbing in the folds of my net," in the stilling, time-traveling, penultimate paragraph of chapter 6 of *Speak, Memory*.

That Tolland outing with Remington took Nabokov back to his boyhood bogs and their smells and sights. But his actual encounter with that most mysterious of alpines, Magdalena, al-most certainly took place right near Columbine Lodge itself. The cabins back right up to Mount Meeker, a southeastern arm off Longs Peak in Rocky Mountain National Park and an impres-sive 13,911-foot peak in its own right. The entire front of Mount Meeker consists of perfect Magdalena habitat, so much so that I have rechristened it "Magdalena Mountain" in a novel by that name. It is likely that Nabokov climbed the scree behind the lodge to collect this butterfly. No account of this event seems to survive. However, we know that he saw it just a little to the north, in the lap of Longs Peak itself. Concrete evidence of this encounter ap-pears in another work of fiction: Nabokov's novel *Look at the Har-lequins!*, where the character Vadim relates a visit to Longs Peak with his daughter Bel:

> From Lupine Lodge, Estes Park, where we spent a whole month, a path margined with blue flowers led through aspen groves to what Bel drolly called The Foot of the Face. There was also the Thumb of the Face, at its southern corner. I have a large photograph taken by William Garrell, who was the first, I think, to reach The Thumb, in 1940 or thereabouts, showing the East Face of Longs Peak with the checkered lines of ascent

superimposed in a loopy design upon it. On the back of this picture—and as immortal in its own little right as the picture's subject—a poem by Bel, neatly copied in violet ink, is dedicated to Addie Alexander, "First woman on Peak, eighty years ago." It commemorates our own modest hikes:

Longs' Peacock Lake

the Hut and its Old Marmot;
Boulderfield and its Black Butterfly;
And the intelligent trail.

In the context of Nabokov as a visual artist of words, what this shows me is his capacity for *deep refraction*: to skate from a moment's attentive encounter with pure physical detail, across the broad rink of reality and time, to arrive at the critical creative moment several removes away. A profound expression of what I mean arose from another high place with butterflies. Such rarefied redoubts in thin, clear air held a powerful claim on Nabokov's affections. Again and again he sought the alpine haunts—in Russia, the Crimea, the Rockies, the Alps. It was in one such montane locale where he achieved two of his greatest summits—one scientific, the other artistic, both wrought of the same stuff, and both sprung from the same details that he had not failed to notice. And happily, it is the Magdalena alpine once again whose broad black wings carry us to that very locale. In a footnote to "On a Book Entitled *Lolita*," Nabokov wrote that "the locality labels pinned under these butterflies will be a boon to some twenty-first-century scholar with a taste for recondite biography." Well, here goes, because a pin label for a specimen of *Erebia magdalena* I saw at Cornell University reads: "**Telluride, COLO.**/Alt. 10,000 ft./

July 15, 1951/V. Nabokov"—and this locality label connects us directly to *Lolita*.

Since well before he'd met John Downey in a canyon above Alta, Utah, Nabokov had been engaged in parsing the systematics and geographic plasticity of the scintillated, orange-bordered blues in the genus *Lycaeides*. Many of his drawings of scale rows and genitalia concern this group, as do his longest, most detailed scientific papers. He managed to deduce major relationships and biogeographically iconoclastic (but correct) conclusions for these and other groups of Nearctic and neotropical blues, based on relatively little pinned material. He also correctly separated out the taxon *Lycaeides samuelis* from the bunch, now known as the Karner blue, which has become a conservation cause célèbre that drives a great deal of Midwest land management (and which has finally been elevated to full species status, as he suspected it someday would). Yet his large series and extensive field studies of western *Lycaeides* left him flummoxed as to some of the evolutionary directions involved (or as flummoxed as Nabokov ever allowed himself to be). As he wrote about a particularly challenging tangency of these blues: "in the Jackson Lake region such an intergradation actually does occur, apparently within the same colony or array of connected colonies. At this point of its development *argyrognomon* does turn into *melissa* (from which, however, only 300 miles to the west, it is sharply separated in all characters). That it wavers here at the crossroads of evolution and may select another course, is proved by the *ismenias*-like genitalia of the paratypes."

One of his most persistent personal challenges was to find the previously undiscovered female of *Lycaeides argyrognomon* (now *idas*, as he also suspected) subspecies *sublivens*, which he had described as a new taxon from the male. In July of 1951, he wrote, "I bungled my family's vacation, but I got what I wanted." When he did, it was just where he expected it to be: in southwest Colorado's San Juan Mountains, above the (then) small mining town of Telluride—where he also found the Magdalena that now resides in a specimen cabinet at Cornell University.

"The colony I found was restricted to one very steep slope reaching from about 10,500 to a ridge at 11,000 feet and towering over Tomboy Road between 'Social Tunnel' and 'Bullion Mine,'" he wrote in a paper describing the female of *Lycaeides argyrognomon sublivens*. "The livid tones of the butterflies' undersides nicely matched the tint" of their lupine host plants, he wrote, on which they rested during the frequent dull and wet weather with which both butterfly and collector had to contend. And in a letter to his sister Elena that fall, he wrote, "It will not be hard for you to understand what a joy it was for me to find at last my exceedingly rare god-daughter, on a sheer mountainside covered with violet lupine, in the sky-high, snow-scented silence."

But it wasn't all silent up there above Tomboy Road, as we know from another letter Nabokov sent to Edmund Wilson about the same time. What he revealed in that letter proved in advance something Nabokov would write one year later: "Does there not exist a high ridge where the mountainside of 'scientific knowledge' joins the opposite slope of 'artistic imagination'?"

If Nabokov's discovery of his "exceedingly rare god-daughter" were not enough in itself to demonstrate Nabokov's balancing act on that high ridge (literal, in this instance), there is one particular detail of that day that ties it deeply to his best-known work of literature. For when Nabokov discovered the missing female of what came to be known as Nabokov's blue—a linchpin in his science—he also discovered perhaps the most important scene in what many consider to be his most important book.

It happened like this: as Nabokov scaled the stony, flower-flecked habitat of the Marshall Basin, which feeds the San Miguel River, and that the Dolores River, and finally the Colorado River, he noticed many details. Among them, a plenitude of blue: Colorado blue columbine, the western Jacob's ladder known as sky pilot, alpine forget-me-nots, a sea of lupine, and bursts of blue butterflies: Boisduval's (for which he had erected the genus *Icaricia*), arctic, silvery, and greenish blues among them. It was on the lupines where Véra first spotted the brilliant blue male, and then, at last, *mirabile dictu*, Nabokov netted the heretofore unknown female of *Lycaeides idas sublivens*: "rather peculiar, smooth, weak brown, with an olivaceous cast . . . more or less dusted with cinder-blue scales." Of course, he knew her on sight, because he had taken notice, exquisitely so, of her exquisite details. It had been fifty years since the male's discovery by a collector in Telluride, and three years since Nabokov had described it, based on eight specimens that he had found in the Harvard collection. Now, at last, he knew it as a living creature.

But the blues, the lupines, and the troublesome weather were not the only specifics he noticed up there above Telluride, under a sky of columbine and cloud, that rainy and windy summer month of 1951. For here is what he wrote to Edmund Wilson about the experience:

"I went to Telluride (*awful* roads, but then—endless charm, an old-fashioned, absolutely touristless mining town full of most helpful, charming people—and when you hike from there, which is 9000', to 10,000', with the town and its tin roofs and self-conscious poplars lying toylike at the flat bottom of a *cul-de-sac* valley running into giant granite mountains, all you hear are the voices of children playing in the streets—delightful!" And that is the exact detail of the scene that enables the climacteric of *Lolita*, in the sixth paragraph from the end of the novel, when Humbert

Humbert, bereft, wretched, and sick, high on a mountain road, hears "a melodious unity of sounds rising like a vapor from a small mining town that lay at my feet, in the fold of the valley." "Reader!" he says. "What I heard was but the melody of children at play, nothing but that . . . and then I knew that the hopelessly poignant thing was not Lolita's absence from my side, but the absence of her voice from that concord."

This is the very moment where Humbert Humbert acknowledges the enormity of his crime, the nature of his monstrosity. Martin Amis, in a reconsideration of the novel *Lolita*, wrote that "it has often been suggested that the 'morality' of *Lolita* is not inherent but something tacked on at the end." His essay shows why such an assumption is exactly wrong. It takes a careful reading to see why *Lolita* may be the greatest moral statement we have on pedophilia: a subject rendered almost banal today through its ubiquity in the news, but undiscussed in 1956, even unmentionable. "Even sophisticated readers," wrote Amis, "still think that Nabokov had something to feel guilty about."

For a writer of such a story at that time, or at any time, to leave the moral payoff until the very end of a long book was an astonishing artistic risk to take. Yet it pans out: as Amis wrote, "in Nabokov, art itself provides the reproach and the punishment." In that one alpine wail of a sentence about the voices of the children at play, any careful reader who has suspended his or her judgment thus far is bound to hear the judgment meted out to Humbert as intended, and to grasp the inherent morality of *Lolita*. This paragraph is the most heartbreaking thing I've read, and ties only with Darwin's final paragraph in *On the Origin of Species* as the most beautiful and affecting passage I know in the language. It is "Humbert on the hillside begging forgiveness of Lolita and the

American landscape," in Amis's words, and it "can still make the present reader shed tears as hot as Humbert's." This reader, too.

All this, because the author pursued a little butterfly up this particular high ridge, "somewhere between climb and cloud," as he put it, and brought back something else: something that he had not expected, but that he certainly figured out how to use. Gary Snyder, in a poem called "What You Should Know to Be a Poet," enjoined writers to follow "your own six senses, with a watchful and elegant mind." This exactly describes Nabokov's artistic sensibility.

When he wrote about "The Swift" that captured the young lovers' momentary attention on the bridge at sunset, Nabokov might have actually *meant* a swift, or a swallow, or even a moth. The swift in question is commonly assumed to be the bird of that name (*Apus apus*, family Apodidae). But in the original Russian version, it is called "*lastochka*," which is better translated as "swallow" (family Hirundinidae), "swift" in Russian being "*strizh*." In Nabokov's translation of *The Gift* (where the poem first appeared) into English, the bird became the unrelated but similar swift, and so it is called in the collection and recording referred to above. Yet in an interview, in which Nabokov refers to this verse as "probably my favorite Russian poem," he calls the creatures *swallows*. More than likely, the author's taxonomic flip-flop was a tactical, artistic decision involving scansion—"*lastochka*" working better in the Russian, "swift" in English. I like to think that in switching to swift, Nabokov was also punning on the moths of the family Hepialidae, known in Europe as "the swifts." The swift (or ghost) moths appear at dusk, with a phantasmal shimmer that is difficult to forget. No matter. Whether Nabokov had in mind one bird or the other, a moth, or all three, the point is the same: even when his subject's biological identity is fluid in this arch-taxonomist's mind, its role as a particular atom of experience is unequivocal. As he explained it to the interviewer, "the boy turns to the girl and says to her, 'Tell me, will you always remember *that* swallow?—not any kind of swallow, not those swallows, there, but that particular swallow that skimmed by?' And she says, 'Of course I will,' and they both burst into tears."

Individuating details: they are what Vladimir Nabokov mined, from which to build both his science and his art—often exploiting the same ore deposit for both endeavors. His fine lines, the pen-strokes that made his drawings, were just one more medium he employed. Maybe even more directly than the poems and the papers, the drawings cut to the heart of the beholder. Both bodies of Nabokov's work, his words and his images, display the breadth of his super-acute vision, in every sense—his "good eye." Taken together, they tell us how he rebuilt the world—Terra, Antiterra, Telluride, all of it—out of its own delicious yet all too often overlooked details.

Note: When Stephen H. Blackwell and Kurt Johnson asked me to contribute to *Fine Lines: Vladimir Nabokov's Scientific Art* (Yale University Press, 2016), there was no question in my mind what tack I should take. Nabokov's concept of "individuating details" has always been hugely important to me. The surprising convergence of my novel *Magdalena Mountain* with Nabokov's own experience of *Erebia magdalena* in the same place, and the remarkable linkage with *Lolita* in the Colorado high country, cinched the deal.

Real Wilderness:
Extinct in the Wild?

Conundrum Hot Springs bubble out of a slice of alpine faerie-land in Colorado's Maroon Bells–Snowmass Wilderness Area. These modest-sized hot springs, nested in the lap of high meadows thick with magenta paintbrush and Colorado blue columbines, are situated 11,200 feet above sea level, a good stiff hike from any trailhead. When I got to know Conundrum in the mid-1970s, hiking from the Rocky Mountain Biological Laboratory at Gothic to Aspen, it was in good shape and never very crowded with the naked soakers who came to supplicate its powers. That changed with popularity, as more and more weekend sybarites made the long trek up from Aspen. Internet images now show Conundrum still pretty, not entirely spoiled, but sometimes bank-to-bank with bodies, as if it were the Blue Lagoon in Iceland. The U.S. Forest Service has had to impose various controls on numbers and camping, in order to protect the sensitive site.

Conundrum Hot Springs is, relatively speaking, still wild. But it has grown less Wild.

What do I mean by that? The words *wild* and *wilderness* have different meanings for different people. They can stand for anything you love, anything you don't understand but are trying to, or anything you long for, fear, resent, or rejoice in; any state you wish to elevate or derogate, praise or blame, inveigh against or agitate for. It would seem that these words can mean almost anything you want them to. Are they therefore useless as words? As ideals, or as realities? I don't think so. But I believe we should be at great pains to be clear when we discuss them; and even more so when we seek to apply them on the land. The chief conundrum here, as I see it in the context of our ravenous contemporary culture, is this: to what extent can the wild and the Wilderness include our own species; and how? Since conundrums by definition are unanswerable, this riddle may be too. But given how many people care passionately about what they consider the wild, this wild riddle is at least worth talking about.

Conundrum Hot Springs are no different from thousands of special places that have become more and more trodden with population and recreational growth. But were it not for the springs' lucky inclusion within a federal wilderness area, they would likely be utterly overrun by crowds come to enjoy them via jeep and truck and dirt bike, not on foot. Indeed, a couple of watersheds away, around the glorious Cumberland Pass, ATVs ravage the arctic-alpine tundra that lies outside a designated wilderness area. Wilderness designation is often questioned because it excludes humans except as visitors, while what we consider wilderness was often human habitat in earlier eras, to a degree only recently realized. For example, James Benedict discovered abundant, never-dreamt-of evidence of native occupation of the high country in the Indian Peaks Wilderness (across the Continental Divide from Conundrum). This wilderness too was surely well used by humans before, in their seasonal, altitudinal migrations, which must have included medicinal stop-offs at Conundrum. But those humans, and their pre-ATV level of impact, are long gone. So now I have to ask, is it better to toss the distant wild to the wolves, and just occasional humans; or to all the people, with all their modern engines and appetites?

Happily, it needn't come to such a stark either/or for most of the land. The national forests, by design and slogan, are "the land of many uses." The formal wilderness areas are just one of those many uses, and humans are abundantly accommodated in all the other zones. Nor is the wild entirely absent from them, whether logged, mined, grazed, or drilled. In fact the wild goes down much deeper than that: all the way to the cracks in the city sidewalks. For here's the big secret: it's not a matter of wild or non-wild—wildness (in the sense of that which takes us out of ourselves) exists all along a great big continuum—a sliding scale, graduated not in numbers but in degrees of differentiation from the human quotidian. And why should this surprise us? We have come to learn that many qualities once seen in black-or-white, either/or terms—character, art vs. craft, sociopathy, race, beauty and ugliness, certainly gender—are actually present as continuums. Upon honest examination, most dualisms and dichotomies blur.

My own sense of the wild gradient began with a beguiling stump on the corner, and traveled from there along an actual, physical continuum: a ditch. But first, that stump: walking to kindergarten, my mother and I stopped beside it daily to poke for beetles. I was inconsolable when it was removed. As long as I was still too small to roam, our backyard contained my multitudes.

Soon I graduated to the High Line Canal, an irrigation ditch coursing the altitudinal contours across the landscapes of Greater Denver, carrying Platte River water from its mouth at the edge of the Rockies out onto the plains near the present Denver International Airport. I first met it as a young boy in love with, but too far from, the mountains. Living on the east side of Denver, I might as well have been in Kansas, for all the access I had to the Rockies. However, I found that I could escape my raw suburban tract by traipsing off to the old ditch, and along it as far as my short legs and the long days would allow. I learned my butterflies there, the wood nymphs and admirals, coppers and skippers, and how mountain species would come down to the plains along the green corridor of the canal, and vice versa. I also learned that the farther west I roamed, beyond the city, toward the foothills, the wilder and more diverse in species things grew. And when eventually the butterflies drew me beyond the hogback and up into the Indian Peaks for myself, I learned what real Wilderness really was.

In the same year as the passage of the Wilderness Act, I gained the mobility to reach the high wilds that the Act set out to protect. Not long after that I went to college, read Roderick Frazier Nash's *Wilderness and the American Mind*, and understood why I'd felt what I had; and that I would always fight to preserve Wilderness in the world. I also read Leopold, the Muries, and Robert Marshall. Over the next half century, I sought deep wilderness from Mount Bierstadt in the Colorado Front Range to the Brooks Range of Alaska; from the High Sierra to the Himalaya, the Pennines to the Pamir, the Dolomites to the Dark Divide; from the Astrolabe Range of Papua New Guinea to the Qinling Mountains of Shaanxi, China, to the Vatnajökull of southeast Iceland, and many other places in between and along the way: all *Wild* with a capital W, some occupied by my own species, some not. And after it all, I still believed (and believe) Thoreau, when he wrote, "We can never have enough of nature. We need to witness our own limits transgressed, and some life pasturing freely where we never wander."

Yet I never lost my feel for the wild in its most compressed, contained, and essential forms: the moss and blossom in a sidewalk crack; that raggedy old ditch on the backside of Denver; the marsh-*cum*-dump on my college campus, which we young conservationists saved along the way while we were also campaigning for North Cascades National Park. When Justice William O. Douglas accepted our invitation to come march with us to protect the Glacier Peak Wilderness Area from Kennecott Copper, it gave me the same thrill as leading a few hundred marchers with trees in hand down to the campus landfill, to occupy it and declare its destiny to be the habitat it once was, instead of the parking lots it was intended to become. And all these things came to pass— the mountain fastness, the urban wetland, and so much more in between: the whole great panoply of wildness, seeking a future among our species' unslakable demands.

Having learned the love of damaged lands from the High Line Canal and the beat-up old fields-becoming-suburbs of Denver's hinterlands, I eventually made my home in the several-times-logged-off lands of the Willapa Hills. And now I've lived more than half my life in a sparsely populated rural county among manhandled forests and fields, finding beauty and, yes, wildness among the clearcuts of Willapa, when I cannot make it up to the Olympic Wilderness in the north. In some ways am I right back where I started: fascinated by a stump on the corner.

Now that we understand that the general condition of wildness lives along a string that stretches from the back alleys of Gotham to the far peaks of Shangri-La (and I have hiked in a place called just that, in Diqing Tibetan Autonomous Prefecture, Yunnan), we can ask what to call the knots along that elastic string. I don't really worry much about *wild*. It's one of those ambidextrous words, like the Irish *craic* or the German *Gemütlichkeit*, that is difficult to define but you know it when you feel it. *Wildland* goes a bit beyond, and indicates places that retain some notable degree of wildness despite their history: I called my book about my old ditch in Colorado *The Thunder Tree: Lessons from an Urban Wildland*, and that's not really an oxymoron. But then there is *wilderness*, or even more so, *Wilderness*. Here I draw upon others. Thoreau: "life pasturing freely." Dr. Johnson: "a tract of solitude and savegeness." Bob Marshall: "possesses no possibility of conveyance by any mechanical means and is sufficiently spacious that a person in crossing it must have the experience of sleeping out." Aldo Leopold: "an antidote to the biotic arrogance." Or how about this, from Shann Ray's novel *American Copper*: "the wilderness, where she could be alone in great tracts of land, inviolable and fierce of their own accord." Many commentators speak of the wild as being "self-organized." I'm not entirely sure what that really means. But I do understand "inviolable and fierce of their own accord," and it is a way to denote that far end of the continuum, the Big Wild, the Real Wilderness.

When I was a graduate student in forestry at the University of Washington, I took a course in wilderness studies from Forest Service scientist John C. Hendee. In one exercise, we took a test that was supposed to measure our position on a scale of *wildernism*. As a passionate advocate for wilderness, I was appalled and embarrassed when I came out as a *weak wildernist*. The reason? I had checked that I enjoy driving on small forest roads. Well, I still do . . . very much. Yet I also enjoy walking in the Big Wild, the

Deep Wild. And I still don't find the two pleasures to be at odds. They're some distance apart on the continuum, but they both take one into greater contact with the extra-human. I firmly support road-ripping to increase the size of roadless areas, and I would always oppose a new road into a designated or de facto roadless area; but I would also, always, take that bowered lane ahead in my small old car, with zeal. And then, I hope, park it and walk beyond the ruts, tank traps, or gates. Walking the wild gradient.

In 1990, I spent much of an autumn in Washington State's largest (55,000 acres) de facto but undesignated wilderness, the Dark Divide, in connection with my book *Where Bigfoot Walks: Crossing the Dark Divide.* The Dark Divide is so chopped about and entered on its edges that the U.S. Forest Service used to refer to it as Amoeba. The experiences I had convinced me that motorcycles need to be eliminated from its ancient trails, a road or two ripped, and its forests protected beyond the vulnerable provisions of the Clinton Forest Plan. Those goals will be accomplished only by inclusion in the national wilderness protection system. However, the Third Congressional District in Washington State, through gerrymandering, has become a virtual sinecure for the party that never originates, seldom supports, and often blocks new wilderness areas.

Apart from obvious commercial considerations, what is it about wilderness opponents, such as our congresswoman, that so engages their animus? Very often it has to do with the exclusion of human uses (such as dirt bikes, mountain bikes, and ORVs) from wilderness areas. In many a wilderness hearing, discussion, or reading, I have heard the charge that wilderness protection is somehow elitist. This goes back to at least 1926, when forester Howard W. Flint, in an article entitled "Wasted Wilderness," attacked Aldo Leopold's wilderness advocacy as being for the "elect few." Many writers since, including Peter H. Kahn Jr., J. Baird Callicott, and Peter Sutter, have considered the elitist charge at length, and generally found it self-interested. Maybe there are ways that a true elite has employed the idea of wilderness in its favor—such as the Rockefellers buying up Jackson Hole to protect their neighborhood—but would anyone wish to give up their gift to the nation of Grand Teton National Park today?

One unfortunate legacy of wilderness debate in recent years has been to render *wild* just a four-letter word in some people's vocabularies (many of them in Congress), and to give sanction to the re-demonizing of Wilderness. Once demonized by the superstitious who were simply afraid of the sublime wild (sometimes with good reason); then largely tamed, then valued, cherished, embraced as a vital legacy, and protected in its lingering margins by the force of law; only to be damned all over again as elitist! That simply won't do. We knew better, even as dumb college kids: anyone with a pair of boots or sneakers and a crappy knapsack and a canteen knew that he or she could head to the hills with friends, by bus or hitchhiking if necessary, and walk into a federal wilderness area, and keep walking, for *free*. The wilderness, to the young conservationists with whom I came of age, was—and still is—the antithesis of elitist. Unless that elite includes all the plants and animals that live there, and every cash-strapped kid or working stiff who can put one foot in front of another on a trail. I do not know a more democratic ideal than that of Wilderness, *sensu* 1964.

Now, as regards human beings—the upright primate species designated *Homo sapiens* (*wise man* in Latin or *all the same and wise* in Greek—my, what an optimist Linnaeus really was! Let us hope we someday deserve the name), in or out of the wild, let's get a couple of things straight. First, we are just another species of primate, and everything we manufacture or perform is a product of an evolved species of upright hominoid ape. Ergo, all of us and all of our productions are part of nature, if nature is everything, which in my view it patently is. As John Steinbeck and Ed Ricketts put it in *Log from the Sea of Cortez*: "most of the feeling we call religious" is an "attempt to say that man is related to ... all reality ... all things are one thing and that one thing is all things."

So far, we're good: No one who understands that humans and nature are indivisible, parts of one continuum, could sanction the Alberta tar sands crimes against the taiga and its people, or mountaintop removal in West Virginia. If people are part of nature and the wild lies out there in nature, then the wild dwells within, as poet Gary Snyder, author of *Practice of the Wild*, has shown us. But Thoreau also wrote, "We are aware of an animal within us." And Steinbeck and Ricketts also asked, "Why do we so dread to think of our species as a species, our eyes the nebulae, universes in our cells?" Why indeed? Antipathy to Wilderness must often be rooted in this question.

Here's another fact that might help us to weasel in a little deeper. Wilderness existed for billions of years prior to the advent of humans, and will exist forever, at least until Earth's molecules are assimilated elsewhere, and then it will continue to exist somewhere else. Humans have coexisted with the wild (been part of it, and vice versa) for the tiniest fraction of that time—maybe 1/5,000th of it, so far. Further, the time will come when we humans will be extinct, for that fate befalls all species. That is, unless technology conjures a means of extinction avoidance; in which case, we might actually move beyond biology: maybe *extant* in some cyborg form, but *extinct in the wild*, nonetheless. There is no telling *when* we might go extinct, although sensible bets among anyone conscious of natural limits to growth might well wager on sooner rather than later, given our present proclivities. But however long we manage to forestall the inevitable, the fact remains that the wild was here for a long time before us, and will continue for a long time after us. That basic understanding tends to place many of our views as wild-thinkers in a rather different light, and should encourage us to take a longer view of our actions.

The thing is, we are not constrained to love only one part of the relative wild, to hold fast to just one concept of what we should talk about when we talk about wildness. Nor do we need to oppose our conceptions against one another for ideological, intellectual, or political reasons. The world is big and great enough to have and to hold all faces of the relative wild—but only if we continue to work as the activists of old, to allow the world to do so, in the face of boundless human cupidity and insupportable excess. Why should we work with one hand tied behind our backs, one arrow in our quiver? Can we not have the ever-present wild and Wilderness too? Is it beyond our powers at this late date to maintain the entire blessed continuum?

Which brings us back to people on the land. Heaven knows that outrages have taken place against indigenous or latter-day native people in the name of wildland conservation. Examples are rife on the world scene, and in historic times in North America, and it still happens today. Some forms of traditional occupation of the land can foster (not create, but support) native plants, animals, and the whole ecological community. One such example is the acequia culture of the desert Southwest. This is not a mystery: water concentrates life in arid lands, including old, human-dug, well-managed watercourses no less (and sometimes more) than rivers and streams. I knew this from an early age, by becoming a near-full-time denizen of a prairie ditch myself, and studying its butterflies and plants. Now that the farms are gone and Denver

Water has shut all the head gates, dewatering the High Line Canal, the butterflies are in trouble, along with the old cottonwoods and the people who love them. And when the acequias and their keepers are ejected from their valleys, the result can be not only cultural genocide but also a net loss of natural diversity. For example, Gary Paul Nabhan, in *The Desert Smells Like Rain*, heartbreakingly documents the removal of Tohono O'odham people from Quitobaquito Springs when Organ Pipe Cactus National Monument was established, and the subsequent loss of diversity from their oasis. (Now Trump's border wall is wrecking what's left.)

When my own ditch-studies led me to England to learn more about butterfly conservation, my eyes opened wide to learn how British orchids and insects, primroses and bluebells, have adapted to ancient forms of grassland and woodland management, and languish without it. And after Common Market and Thatcher-era "improvements" had done their worst, my colleagues were finally able to say with documented certainty that *every instance of butterfly endangerment in the U.K. can be directly attributed to disruption of traditional agriculture.* At least in the case of the extinct English large blue, reestablishment of the old grassland management has allowed the butterfly (reintroduced from Sweden) to thrive once again.

Speaking of reintroduced British goshawks, in her book *H Is for Hawk*, Helen Macdonald writes: "Their existence gives the lie to the thought that the wild is always something untouched by human hearts and hands. The wild can be human work." Surely we should fight for husbandry that returns to such a mutualism, even as we fight to expand wilderness areas and corridors.

So, can the wild persist, is the wild sometimes even *enhanced*, by human occupation, in both senses of the word? Of course. And that's not mysterious either: human farmers, cattle, and sheep coevolved with native plants and animals in the British Isles since Day One after glacial retreat, for more than ten thousand years. Acequia culture in the Southwest may be just as old, or older. And there are endless other examples of humans coexisting and coevolving with the rest of the wildland community in a manner that seems beneficial, or at least largely benign, for both. There are notable instances where National Park Service tolerance of established uses seems to work, as I have seen in the Wrangell Mountains of Alaska. But when old, sustainable forms of land and water use are trashed by authority, such as the policy of both Washington and Oregon fish and wildlife commissions to eliminate salmon gillnetters from the mainstem Columbia River (on the pretense of conservation, but many believe actually for greater sport fishing revenue), the result can be both socially repugnant and personally tragic. Sometimes, it can even redound to the detriment of native plants and animals. And yes, these things have happened in the name of saving the Wild. As a former Nature Conservancy land steward, I have felt a similar sense of transgression (if on a smaller scale) when the organization takes down tree forts, sometimes used by generations of children getting *out there*.

When human uses respect and sweeten the wild, let's recognize and celebrate them, and preserve them when we can. But let's acknowledge the opposite, too—Pleistocene overkill of North American megafauna, the cedars of Lebanon, Steller's sea cow, the great auk and dodo. Sometimes humans, ancient and modern, have done anything but enhance the integrity of the wild. Or what about when traditional human occupation has long been absent from a wildland, and present (or threatened) use—mining, logging, off-road vehicles, shooting, any number of other modern manifestations and infestations—is far from consistent with the well-being of native ecosystems and their constituent species?

This has been much more often the case in the establishment of American wilderness areas than the kicking out of sustainable residents. Because we are capable of recognizing the injustices that sometimes occur in the establishment of protected areas cannot mean that we must also forswear the tool of strict land zoning, when such legal measures are what the facts indicate and what our consciences require. Sometimes you only need a hoe; sometimes, a hammer.

In the spring of 2014, I attended a wonderful party thrown by the Polly Dyer Cascadia Broadband of the Great Old Broads for Wilderness, to celebrate the fiftieth anniversary of the passage of the Wilderness Act. The Broads brought in poets to speak the liturgy. Bill Yake, dressed in period garb, spoke the words of Henry David Thoreau in character: "In wildness is the preservation . . ." I read six poems of early wilderness encounter, all describing incidents in the 1960s, the decade of the Act's passage. And the poet Clem Starck read the essential text of the Wilderness Act itself, crafted largely by Howard Zahniser, perhaps the most beautifully written measure in American legislative history. It spoke of saving for all Americans, and all people, the kind of land "where the earth and its community of life are untrammeled by man, where man himself is a visitor who does not remain." Or, as Thoreau had it, where we can "witness our own limits transgressed, and some life pasturing freely where we never wander." Or seldom wander, but where we earnestly hope we someday may. And what is wrong with that?

Was the Act blindered to the people who had once been there, and sometimes still were? Perhaps, but not entirely. Hunting is allowed in wilderness areas, as is grazing—if they are outside national parks, as most of them are. But had the Wilderness Act and its proponents not been as single-minded as they were, that remarkable moment would have passed, Aldo Leopold's roadless area groundwork might all have been wasted, and many of our finest wilderness areas would have been rendered entirely unsuitable for the purpose by now. Just scan the horizon of gas, oil, and coal development across the West today to get a sense of my meaning. Are there still abuses? Sure—the very difficult task of managing the blessed public lands in a bloated mercantile country such as ours is bound to lead to abuses and bad decisions. But these are no reason not to celebrate one of the most forward-looking laws in the world annals of conservation.

However overused, acid-rained, climate-changed, or otherwise compromised from their pre-contact condition, the wilderness areas will continue to define one end of that great continuum we can call the Relative Wild. Many other points along that sliding scale may easily be found by anyone who sets wet foot out the door, in the mud, off the path. Each of us will continue to express our love, concern, and energy toward the varieties and expressions of wildness with which we most identify. And I suspect that for most of us, that will mean more than one, maybe many, notches on the wild dial. I know that for my part, my tastes and loyalties range over the whole spectrum, from end to end: I shall go on loving my local stumps and sidewalk cracks, the moss-rich masonry of a city wall, my dried-up and scruffy old ditch, the barbered timberlands that support my human community, and my grandchildren's backyards—even as I long for, celebrate, work to protect, and sometimes even visit actual Wilderness.

I will also continue to haul my sorry old ass up into the more and less wild parts of the Gifford Pinchot National Forest, by both car and foot, where I am welcome to swing my butterfly net and learn new things, every chance I get. The Klickitat are long gone from the Indian Racetrack in Indian Heaven Wilderness Area, but several tribes continue to set up berry camps in autumn just to the north. I will try to honor their once and future lifeways when I venture up there. And my own personal keenest devotion in my life as a conservationist will remain the eventual establishment of a Dark Divide Wilderness Area, to protect the heart of the land where Bigfoot walks from the dirt bikes that bedevil its trails and meadows today, and from the threat of the chainsaw, the dam, the mine, the road, or as Zorba put it, "the full catastrophe."

Then, if ever as a people, as a world, we get past the catastrophe, at least there will still be a few places that we chose not to waste along the way. After all, maybe our utterly unsustainable capitalist economy will somehow moderate such as to allow one or another vision of working with the wild to take, and we will enter a brighter time, with greater capacity and amplitude for coexistence among ourselves and all the other species. If so, we will be glad for the options we have preserved, by setting aside some slices of Wilderness. And if not? Well, then at least we will have preserved the best possible building blocks for evolution's next iteration: banks of genetic diversity, to give natural selection another chance. This is why I say the Wilderness Act is so forward-looking: because of all the laws by which we live, it is almost alone in looking to the good it can do even beyond human existence.

Sometimes I conjure on the phrase Extinct in the Wild. From an early age, I found that phrase heartrending. I remember reading it in one of the nature stories that made up most of my earliest diet as a reader, and how I recoiled from its implications. *"Extinct in the wild?"* I worked it out and understood what it meant—that I could never, ever, go *out there* and find it, whatever it was. So, I suppose, the word *wild* and the idea of *out there* came to mean one and the same thing to me. To a large degree, they still do.

On a recent trip to the Scottish Highlands, my friend Florence and I came to a place called Borgie Glen. Standing there, gazing off into the high purple heather hills, we noticed a small sign pointing toward a dark forest of Scots pine, deep in a receding crease of the Cairngorms: THE UNKNOWN, it read. And there I realized: *that's* what I most want out of this slippery word *wild*. I don't want to live in a world become so relative, that The Unknown itself is Extinct in the Wild.

Note: In 2014, my friends Gavin Van Horn (of the Center for Humans & Nature in Chicago) and John Hausdoerffer (of Western Colorado University) convened a gathering of writers and activists in Crested Butte, Colorado. The topic was "The Relative Wild," and the proposed outcome was a book by that name. They asked me to write the introduction. But I wrote much more than that and my piece turned out to be the only one about real, legal, Big Wilderness, so it became the opening chapter instead, entitled "Conundrum and Continuum: One Man's Wilderness, from a Ditch to the Dark Divide." The book, a fine and thoughtful compendium, came out as *Wildness: Relations of People and Place* (University of Chicago Press, 2017). The best book I have read in years on the strict wild is William E. Glassley's *A Wilder Time: Notes from a Geologist at the Edge of the Greenland Ice* (Bloomsbury Literary Press, 2018), winner of the 2019 John Burroughs Medal.

The Extinction of Experience Revisited

EVERYBODY'S DITCH STILL MATTERS

As Amtrak Cascades Train #8 hurtles northbound, it passes its sister southbound at 4:21, just north of Winlock, Washington. The compression of their nearly meeting noses whams the air aside. I can hear the *whomp!* it makes right through the window. A line of oil cars sits on a siding that dead-ends into a marsh outside Chehalis. Golden ash trees ring the scene, glinting back this purely sun-bound October day.

A little farther north, past Olympia and over the Nisqually River, we will leave the Puget Trough behind in favor of the Puget Sound shoreline. From there to Tacoma, we will limn that coast so closely that the great blue herons, bald eagles, crows, and cormorants haunting the pebble beaches no longer pay any attention to the passing trains. We will roar by the Steilacoom dock for the small ferries to small islands, and then roll right beneath the Tacoma Narrows Bridge before entering the city of Tacoma.

As it happens, this may be the last rail journey I'll make

along this gorgeous shore. For sometime soon Amtrak's Cascades line will shift inland to a not unpleasant but vastly less stimulating route. The ostensible reason for the change is to diminish congestion on the line, reduce conflicts for rail-space with freights, and to save ten minutes on the Eugene–Seattle run. Ten minutes! Yo, Amtrak—what are you thinking, dude? Your biggest selling point is scenery, and this stretch of coast is one of the most blatantly scenic on the entire nationwide route system. Furthermore, this change has already cost human life. On December 18, 2017, on what was to be its maiden voyage, the train took a thirty-mile-per-hour curve at eighty and flew off the overpass. Three people were killed and dozens more badly injured. What a false economy this change obviously is! We have a reprieve only until Positive Train Control can be installed for the route, which would have prevented the accident; but it will come.

Meanwhile, as we cross the Nisqually and lean into the curve over I-5 and around the vast Nisqually National Wildlife Refuge, the fall colors are fabulous, chiefly big-leaf maples. And now, here's the shore. Little spits, dogs running out on them to harass the basking gulls. Old pilings, silver in the afternoon sun. The panoply of islands small and smaller. A scuttle of scoters, a cluster of cormorants, a group of grebes. Every park and shingle alive with Sounders snatching the tail end of this sun-gift before the winter rains reassert themselves over the Maritime Northwest. Parti-colored hoops of brambles briefly frame each watery scene as viewed through the train windows. Across the waters, the Olympics. Whistle through a bohemian beach hamlet, past Narrows Brewery, and now beneath the bridge itself, once called "Galloping Gertie" when it took its big bucking ride and collapsed into the Sound on November 7, 1940, now a pair of gigantic modern spans not going anywhere but Gig Harbor and points west. And finally, a big black tunnel.

Which is about all that many of the passengers see: curtains drawn, turned away, burrowed into their devices like lugworms in a piling. So why bother to take the train? Never mind; to each her own. But when the route change comes, for everyone who does care, all this will be gone: exchanged for more reed canary grass, asphalt, post-ag, semi-industrial, edge-of-urban fields, suburbs, warehouses, and scrapes. We'll look out onto I-5 instead of a wild beach. Not boring, maybe, but far from this lovely shore, and vastly less diverse to the attentive eye. In other words, just one more unnecessary example of what I call the extinction of experience.

Way back in 1975, my professor, Charles Lee Remington of the Yale Biology Department, asked me to take his place on a panel at the American Association for the Advancement of Science (AAAS) meeting in Boston. The subject was "Wildlife in the Year 2000." I decided to speak about the local extinctions I'd already witnessed—butterflies found and lost on the edge of my native Aurora, along the High Line Canal, in the Platte River watershed. The rise and fall of the painted crescentspot following the great flood of 1965. The disappearance of the Olympia marblewings from fields displaced by my own junior high school. The general fraying of a butterfly fauna that had nurtured me as a young naturalist.

In thinking of this presentation for the AAAS, I realized that I would be speaking about the loss of the *experiences* that made me, as well as about that of the butterflies themselves, and the term popped into my head: *the Extinction of Experience*. I gave the talk and noticed many heads nodding. I was asked to write it up for *Horticulture* magazine, whose editor, Paul Trachtman, was in the audience that day. Later I fleshed it out in *The Thunder Tree*, my portrait of that landscape in which I'd grown up. The extinction of experience would become my most frequently anthologized, quoted, cited, and repeated phrase, idea, and essay, in all of my work. Often it was attributed to me, as it was by Richard Louv, who has generously acknowledged its influence on his concept of nature-deficit disorder. Other times it is used anonymously, which pleases me too, as it suggests that the concept is entering the lexicon of conservation. Many have riffed on it, alongside the diminished baseline, landscape capability, biophilia, nature-deficit disorder, and other related ideas. All this grown out of that long-ago pinch-hitting talk for Professor Remington. But it really came from those lost butterflies and their hand-me-down habitats in the backyard of my youth.

The loss of neighborhood species endangers our experience of nature. If a species becomes extinct within our own radius of reach (smaller for the very old, very young, disabled, and poor), it might as well be gone altogether, in one important sense. To those whose access suffers by it, local extinction has much the same result as global eradication.

The extinction of experience also implies a cycle of disaffection that can have disastrous consequences. As cities and metastasizing suburbs forsake their natural diversity, and their citizens grow more removed from personal contact with nature, awareness and appreciation retreat. This breeds apathy toward environmental concerns and, inevitably, further degradation of the common habitat.

So it goes, on and on, the extinction of experience sucking the life from the land, the intimacy from our connections. This is how the passing of otherwise common species can be as significant as the total loss of rarities. People who care, conserve; people who don't know, don't care. What is the extinction of the condor to a child who has never known a wren?

So, how does this idea hold up, four decades farther on? All too well, I'm sorry to say. I wish I could say it was merely a young man's jeremiad, hyperbole borne of callow zeal, or even just overstated. Sadly, that's not at all the case.

Even if we look at only butterflies, the losses of elements of diversity have only accelerated. Comparing cities with various published data baselines and follow-ups, I demonstrated radical declines in butterfly diversity in Staten Island, New York, Orange County in the Los Angeles Basin, San Francisco, and Aurora, Colorado, the steepest decline having taken place in Aurora. I posited a method to quantify the extinction of experience through a derived indication of the degree of natural change (which I called ΔN). This showed a strong likelihood that, insofar as local butterfly extinctions could represent it, the opportunity for children and others to encounter natural diversity on home ground has been greatly reduced in these places.

As I put it in another essay: "Factoring in the high proportion of biologists, conservationists, and other resource professionals who gained their initial inspiration through contact with insects, ΔN as indicated by urban butterfly extinction may be considered a reliable index of the extinction of experience in action and a predictor of its effects. While it is not possible to demonstrate that environmental leaders will no longer arise from the streets of contemporary Aurora, it seems reasonable to conclude that the likelihood that young Aurorans will become avid naturalists and conservation voters has been reduced in proportion with the town's butterflies and the diversity they represent."

In recent years, several widely published studies have confirmed even greater butterfly diminishment, amounting to the regional collapse of large parts of entire faunas. Arthur Shapiro's thirty-five years of biweekly butterfly monitoring surveys in several sites, when critically analyzed, showed what he and his coauthors describe as "pervasive declines in California's low-elevation butterfly fauna." The granddaddy of all butterfly-recording programs, the U.K. Butterfly Monitoring Scheme, in their 2015 paper on "The State of British Butterflies," reported that "the new analyses provide further evidence of the serious, long-term and ongoing decline of U.K. butterflies, with 70% of species declining in occurrence and 57% declining in abundance since 1976." And a very recent statistical analysis of a 27-year, 1,600-site butterfly monitoring program in Ohio, as reported by Tyson Wepprich at Oregon State University, has revealed a 25 percent drop in overall abundance, 34 percent if the cabbage white is included. And it's not just butterflies: Recent issues of both *Science* and *Scientific American* have published inquiries into why scientists all over the world are reporting major declines of insect populations and diversity, which some call "insect Armageddon." And I suspect that many readers will have read or at least been sent the more recent, viral article by Brooke Jarvis in *The New York Times* entitled "Insect Apocalypse."

These piled-on studies are concerned not only with a decline in *diversity*, but very much with *abundance* as well. Michael McCarthy's 2015 book, *The Moth Snowstorm: Nature and Joy* describes the author's memory of moths so thick in the English evenings of his youth that they resembled a snowstorm in the family automobile's headlights. No more. He goes on to document in excruciating detail, and to pick apart the causes of, a dramatic decline of life in Britain and elsewhere. Most of the diminution (as had been shown for the British butterflies) derives from changes in traditional forms of agriculture, especially intensification of farming and chemicals.

So it is *not* the case that humans and diversity and abundance are inherently antithetical. The Britons, their husbandry and tillage, coevolved with wild and domestic species since glacial retreat. Ancient British grasslands rich in chalk wildflowers, orchids, butterflies, and much else, yet productive for cattle and sheep, occurred commonly until World War II, and declined radically thereafter. Greater and more intensive production, under the Common Market and Margaret Thatcher, did the deed in large part. Similar patterns have been replicated on the Continent and elsewhere in the Global North. And of course tropical biology has shriveled under its own sets of extractive stresses, all around the equator.

Now, of course, we perch on the rim of the much-discussed sixth extinction event, even as we name a new geologic era for ourselves with overweening hubris. The climate news grows worse by the month if not day, and does anyone still believe we can—or *will*—get a handle on it? For while many creatures decline, one species resolutely gains in abundance: our own. Not that we're the only winner. As numbers and variety decline on the whole, some species expand their ranges and proliferate as never before: sea salps, for example, planktonic tunicates that some marine biologists feel will take over the oceans, ruining nets and shutting down power plants. Even certain butterflies will advance and increase with climate warming, such as annual northward immigrants like painted ladies. But the winners tend to be already-common generalists, while the rarer specialists have always dropped out first.

Yet, as the big butterfly studies have shown, even many commoner species are suffering the crunch. In fact, our long-term annual counts of High Line Canal butterflies have sadly tailed off in recent years, for sheer lack of butterflies to count. So it's not just the painted crescentspots and the Olympia marblewings anymore, but much of the whole checklist, that I fear is gone. I recorded a tenth of the butterfly fauna of the United States along the High Line Canal between 1959 and 1970. I'm not sure I even want to know how many are there now.

So the extinction of experience proceeds apace, faster and ever faster. And every electronic device that distracts a child's attention from the real physical details of the actual world only exacerbates the condition. When life is largely gamed, we self-impose the extinction of experience upon ourselves. In the face of all the different pathways to loss, what to do?

Good, old-time conservation is what. A term popular in the Nature Conservancy when I worked there an eon ago, when it was a different animal and so was I, was this: "Removing land from the development stream." This act, whenever and wherever it can be done, and the concomitant management to maintain its elements of diversity, is still worth doing. And here is why I think so:

1. If it is the case that a catastrophic extinction event is upon us, then everything we can do now to hold back the flood of loss will mean a richer reservoir of recolonization for the next evolutionary iteration. In other words, all we can accomplish now will mean a better start for the next time around.

2. If human mercantile and technological culture as we know it is to collapse, as I think it must sometime if we continue

to grow and to undermine many of the species that hold it up, then the surviving clusters of low-tech humans will have more to work with for another try at cohabitation. Perhaps a post-tech, postapocalyptic world could be neither dystopia nor utopia, but a rough version of what, in the optimistic 1970s, author Ernest Callenbach dubbed *Ecotopia*. And where better to expect survivorship to take hold and settle in than city neighborhoods—the ones that have nurtured caring neighbors, skills with plants, and humane green spaces in their midst?

3. More immediately and perhaps more cheerfully: every scrap of beauty and biological richness we can save now will serve as possible antidote to the extinction of experience for those who still go about with open eyes to the world around them. As Costa Rican ecologist and writer Alexander Skutch wrote: "Those who care greatly because they appreciate greatly have no more sacred obligation than to do everything in their power to preserve the kind of world that will nourish appreciative minds for countless generations. Appreciative, cherishing minds are the world's best hope."

If Skutch was right, and there is actual hope to be found in appreciative, cherishing minds, then it is up to those of us who care greatly to furnish the fodder for such minds to come.

Even now, I still wonder what the condor's extinction would mean to a child who'd never even known a wren. But I do know this: as legendary Portland urban ecologist Mike Houck recently wrote me, "Kids especially should have access to nature within their 'immediate radius of reach' ... adults too!" Right on, Houck. And I know this as well: when I see the reflection of a wren in a child's eye, I am still capable of sensing something that feels quite a lot like hope.

And I should say this: there have been gains, as well as losses. Certain rare species and biomes have come back spectacularly under informed and enlightened stewardship, including the California condor. Many of these have been realized along watercourses, the natural magnets and nurseries of life. If the cultural and biological ravages of the extinction of experience are to be withstood, it will be accomplished at the watershed level: for what unit is more ecologically indivisible?

Salvation, what there is of it to be had, lies in places like my old ditch, the High Line Canal. I even hold high hopes for rebuilding something of that cottonwood corridor's former glory as a young naturalist's Valhalla, with all the good, cherishing work going on there now by the High Line Canal Conservancy and others. These initiatives have counterparts everywhere, and many of them are succeeding in their limited, but interconnected, spheres. For all of their local, even parochial ambit, they will have real consequence. For how we conserve, manage, and, ultimately, *love* our secondhand lands within our own radii of reach may make all the difference to the kind of world that goes forward from here.

Yes! Everybody's ditch *does* still matter.

Note: These days, for all the bad news, there seems to be a perceptible uptick in the number of folks whose ditch (or equivalent) is still intact, or under restoration, or the target of a bond issue or other conservation measure. Certainly I have heard "the extinction of experience" on many lips and read it in various papers, books, and articles, and seen the hopeful responses. But that's just in the U.S. Traveling in some of the wilder parts of China in 2012, and then witnessing the virtual absence of any such leftover lands in Beijing, Shanghai, and others of the several cities over twenty million, gave me pause. These people are clearly surviving, even thriving economically, under an almost complete extirpation of biological experience in their neighborhoods. So is it really as important as I've thought? Or maybe just a "first-world problem"? But then I regarded the filthy air and the black water and the inhumane concrete dwellings, all adding up to a clearly unsustainable state, and I thought, Oh, yes—it's even more important than I ever thought.

The Semiotics of Sasquatch

O n a recent book tour for the new Counterpoint Press edition of *Where Bigfoot Walks: Crossing the Dark Divide*, I encountered many diverse attitudes about the Big Galoot. Not the rarest of these was the fear that what I had to say might deprive the listener of his or her heartfelt hope that Bigfoot walks as an actual flesh-and-blood animal.

During this tour, all around the Pacific Northwest, I was reading (who knows why now, at last) Umberto Eco's *The Name of the Rose*. So it was with delight that I came across the following exchange between the protagonists, Brother William of Baskerville, a Franciscan, and Adso of Melk, a Benedictine novice under William's tutelage. The two are investigating the magnificent but secret library of a mythic fortress monastery in medieval Italy, when monks start dropping off in a series of bizarre apparent murders. As they examine a fine illuminated bestiary in the scriptorium, young Adso is distressed to learn from his worldly mentor that unicorns might not actually exist outside the imaginations of the chroniclers, or might have been metamorphosed into existence over time from reports of actual rhinoceroses. William explains to Adso that "books are not made to be believed, but to be subjected to inquiry." He continues, "The unicorn, as these books speak of him, embodies a moral truth, or allegorical, or analogical . . . one that remains true," though not necessarily the literal truth.

"Then higher truths can be expressed while the letter is lying," replies Adso. "Still, it grieves me to think this unicorn doesn't exist, or never existed, or cannot exist one day."

William rescues the moment, and Adso's feelings, like this: "It is not licit to impose confines on divine omnipotence, and if God so willed, unicorns could also exist. But console yourself, *they exist in these books, which, if they do not speak of real existence, speak of possible existence.*" (Emphasis mine.)

I was pleased to read this because it expresses exactly what I would like readers to take away from *Where Bigfoot Walks*. Personally, I feel the observed facts suggest that we would be foolish to dismiss the actual occurrence of unnamed hominoid apes in North America as fantasy, hoax, or solely a metaphor. My own experience with tracks and calls, detailed in the book, allowed me to conclude my studies with an open mind on the question, which I consider a great gift. (Jane Goodall, as quoted on the back cover, told me she finds the evidence overwhelming.) However, I cannot in honesty or with scientific rigor say that the existence of Bigfoot should be "believed" based on my book, as I have never seen one, and that wasn't the point of the book in any case. Rather, I can say that what I present should be subjected to inquiry—that *if it does not speak of real existence, it speaks of possible existence.*

Reading Eco also reacquainted me with a term that I had once learned but, like most jargon from lit crit, I'd gone on to misplace:

semiotics. Umberto Eco is one of the leading semioticians. It sounds forbidding, but like his books (by which I was long intimidated), it's really not that hard. Semiotics, in its simplest, purest form, is the study of signs (deriving from the Greek σημειωτικός, *sē-meiōtikos,* "observant of signs"). According to the wiki, semiosis (or *semeiosis*) is "the process that forms meaning from any organism's apprehension of the world through signs," and this is the area of semiotics in which Eco largely worked.

I bring it up here because of something that happened half a century ago. On October 20, 1967, two cowboys from Yakima, Washington, claim to have encountered a female Bigfoot on Bluff Creek, in the Six Rivers National Forest of northwestern California. The footage they took, on a 16-mm movie camera rented from a drugstore, became the famous Patterson-Gimlin Film— still the linchpin in the argument for Bigfoot as an actual animal in our midst. It has never been debunked, no one has been able to figure out how it could have been hoaxed, and modern digital analyses only back up its likely status as genuine. This fact has left Roger Patterson and Robert Gimlin in a curious position, rather like that of the monkish copyists in *The Name of the Rose*: their famous film cannot prove the real existence of Sasquatch, but it does "speak to its possible existence"—which is no small thing.

Roger Patterson is long gone, to a premature death from ALS. But Bob Gimlin is still with us, finally basking in the affection and respect of the Bigfoot community, after nearly forty years underground. I've had the pleasure of getting to know him in recent years. In the book, I wrote this: "Now past eighty-five, he is still lean and handsome in his cowboy hat, bandana, and silver Fu Manchu . . . sitting around a campfire with him, hearing his unaffected voice and watching his bright rider's eyes, I cannot believe that he was lying. He could no more have taken part in faking the famous film (even if anyone could figure out how it could have been faked, which they can't), than to mistreat his horse. Which he could not do."

But this isn't really about Robert Gimlin and Roger Patterson. I mean to speak here of Patty, the creature who is the subject of the film, named of course for "Patterson." Demonstrably female, her pendulous breasts sway with their heft as she half-turns to look back, crossing the stream (in a good copy, you also see the fluid movement of the muscles in the thigh, the flexure of the foot, and other anatomical details that have swayed sophisticated analysts toward her authenticity). Now, few words have become as clichéd in recent years as "iconic": if you've seen something as much as twice, it all of a sudden becomes somehow "iconic." But Patty was an icon, a real one, before that word was ever devalued. That image of Patty striding across the stream—that single frame in the public domain that we all know, of her looking toward Patterson, one arm raised ahead, one behind, legs in stride—is blazoned on brains all over the world, five decades after Gimlin held the bucking horses and Patterson dismounted to get the shot that would be seen around the world.

Roger Patterson never managed to make much of a buck on his movie before he got sick, but if he had received a royalty on every use of the image he made famous, he could have funded an institute for the study and cure of the pernicious disease that took him. You can find Patty decorating air fresheners, bumper stickers, road signs, lunch boxes, tee shirts, garden stakes, tattoos, jewelry, and any number of other commercial objects, including my own book jacket. I've even seen Patty, in red, striding across the TV screen in a BBC America trailer on rented DVDs. In short, it is my contention that Patty represents one of the most universally recognized signs/symbols/images in the world today. Another word that has been so overused since its fairly prescriptive beginnings as to have almost no remaining meaning is *meme*. But if a meme is "a virally-transmitted cultural symbol or social idea," as Paul Gill has defined it, Patty certainly qualifies. And this is where we get back to semiotics: because in my opinion, Patty's stance and features represent one of the truly indelible signs in all the history of iconography. All from one afternoon's encounter on a small stream in the Trinity Alps of California, fifty years ago.

But just what, we finally have to ask, does the sign of the Sasquatch really say to people? What "social idea" follows from the symbol? Clearly, to many, it's just a joke—the more out of place, the better. That's the point of Patty pacing behind the British bobby in the BBC clip: a visual non sequitur. To some, the whole proposition of Sasquatch is preposterous, so the sign of the animal connotes mere silliness. To others, members of the large class of people who are interested and hopeful that such a thing might walk in the world, Patty conveys just that—hope—and a friendly reminder of something they recognize, always a welcome waypost as we attempt to situate ourselves on solid ground. For the true believers, obsessives, and cognoscenti, the meme of Patty can go either way: she can bring a smile of pride in how deeply this phenomenon has penetrated the common culture, or a sneer of condescension for those stuck on that simple level of awareness, well outside the inner circle of initiates. And it goes from there.

I am not interested, for the moment, in parsing the sign language bestowed upon us by Patterson and Gimlin any deeper than that. What I *would* like to do is to tell what the image means to me, and what I would like it to mean to others. Much of the point of the book was to press for the long-term protection of the

Dark Divide (Washington's largest unprotected roadless area) as a federal wilderness area. I am as interested as the next person in Bigfoot as possible member of our fauna, perhaps more than most, as one of the few biologists who have written about it with seriousness of purpose. But I am also deeply engaged by the giant hairy ape's metaphorical power, another area of semiotics. The power to speak of wildness, to represent the "something" out there beyond the campfire that we all seem so dearly to need.

As much as I wanted to console modern counterparts of Adso with the *possibility* of Bigfoot's existence (if not unicorns), I wanted to put readers in mind of *wildness*. I want people to think the word *WILD* every time they see Patty on an air freshener, a beer coaster, or as a fleeting shade in a forest. In *Where Bigfoot Walks*, I put it like this:

> Most of all, Bigfoot shows what could have been and what still could be, if only we treated the land as if it were really there. For the very wildness from which the Bigfoot myth emanates is disappearing fast. The struggle for the leavings—the roadless zones, the old growth—is vigorous and current.
>
> If we manage to hang on to a sizable hunk of Bigfoot habitat, we will at least have a fragment of the greatest green treasure the temperate world has ever known. If we do not, Bigfoot, real or imagined, will vanish; and with its shadow will flee the others who dwell in that world.
>
> Looking at that tangled land, one can just about accept that Sasquatch could coexist with towns and loggers and hunters and hikers, all in proportion. But when the topography is finally tamed outright, no one will anymore imagine that giants are abroad on the land.

And so it is. If the ubiquitous sign of Patty in full stride across Bluff Creek means anything, it should mean this: just like peace, justice, and other long shots, such things are possible—but only if we hang on to what's left of a world in which they *seem* possible. Let go of that, and let go of hope.

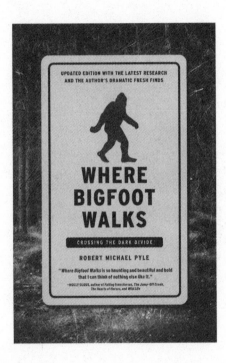

Epistemology of the Big Year

Certain American birders have for many years prostrated themselves before a particularly demanding idol: the Big Year. In this tersely but grandly named exercise, the aspirant goes forth upon the American and Canadian landscape in search of as many species of birds that can be confidently identified within one calendar year. Why do such a thing?

One of the first North American (north of Mexico) Big Year counts to be published was not even undertaken as such. It grew out of the arch-birdwatcher Roger Tory Peterson and his British buddy James Fisher's extended outing to experience the continent's wildlands in the year 1953. Fisher had shared many European wild places and birding hot spots with Peterson over the years, and Peterson wanted to reciprocate. So that year, Fisher came over and they set out in an old Ford station wagon to do just that. Fueled by cheap gas and nickel Cokes, they drove many thousands of miles from one corner of the continent to the other three. Those were different times: they described Orlando, Florida, as a "charming inland town." Their gambit resulted in the exquisite, funny, and timeless book *Wild America*, published by Houghton Mifflin in 1955 and never out of print since.

Peterson and Fisher had not set out to do a Big Year, and in fact their wild circuit lasted just one hundred days, but their tally of 532 species beat any previous Big Year count. Peterson went on to tally 572 for the whole year—and thus, set the record to break. Another Brit, Stuart Keith, followed their route in 1956, reaching 598 species. Slowly it inched up over 600. In 1973, at the age of sixteen, Kenn Kaufman set out to challenge the record. Ultimately Peterson's legatee as the next great field guide series author and editor, Kenn was then a high school kid and utter ornithological devotee. With his parents' blessing, more or less, he dropped out of school to travel the continent and find birds. His mother asked him only to please not hitchhike; but how else is a poor kid to get around? So he hitchhiked only about 75,000 miles. Spending just a thousand dollars, he slept on the ground and on floors and wherever, ate kibbles on the trail, and sort of fell in love here and there. Got to remote islands he had to reach to have a chance, was taken under the wing, as it were, by seasoned chasers, and racked up the birds. Discovered well into his year that another birder, Floyd Murdoch, was also chasing the record. For a while he worried about it, birded side by side with him on pelagic expeditions, and finally said the heck with it, because something else became more important to him than the numbers. The resulting book, *Kingbird Highway: The Biggest Year in the Life of an Extreme Birder* (1997), also published by Houghton Mifflin and still in print, is a masterpiece.

The next big step in Big Years was Mark Obmascik's very popular 2003 book *The Big Year: A Tale of Man, Nature, and Fowl*

Obsession, documenting an epic Big Year battle among three contenders. A fine read but a very different one from Kaufman's, the book is drenched in all the effusions and exudates of Male Competition. *The Big Year* was made into an entertaining 2011 movie by the same name, starring—no lie—Steve Martin, Jack Black, and Owen Wilson as obsessed birders. In real life, the very first Big Year aspirant who managed to tally 700 species of birds was Benton Basham, in the mid-1980s. The record now stands at an astonishing 836, set by John Weigel of Australia in 2016.

Birding Big Years have become commonplace. But there had never been a Butterfly Big Year. So, inspired by both Peterson/ Fisher and Kaufman, I essayed the first Butterfly Big Year in 2008. I even stayed with Benton Basham in his trailer in the Lower Rio Grande Valley for a spell. Having gone over to butterflies after a stroke (we call them "birders gone bad"), he was the best of guides and encouragers for that crucial listing region, where one can tally species available nowhere else north of Mexico. My adventures, high and low, led to the book *Mariposa Road*: also published by Houghton Mifflin, and still in print, but with Yale University Press. Suffice it to say that it was the grandest field trip of my life, even counting my 1996 following of migrating monarchs across the West (*Chasing Monarchs: Migrating with the Butterflies of Passage*, also Houghton Mifflin/Yale University Press), which led to a new model for the western migration.

Ten years later, feeling as if I'd like to do another Big Year— but not *that* big!—I decided to do a Washington Butterfly Big Year in 2017–2018, between my seventieth and seventy-first birthdays. I saw no reason to do it from January 1 to December 31, as a calendar-year butterfly hunt in the North is bound to be pretty boring (at least for butterflies) at both the front and back ends. And unlike my national Big Year, this time I had a Sancho Panza along: Dr. David Branch, my former dentist and good field buddy. We try to have at least one memorable field trip per year (he calls them our "soirees"), and we decided to make this an extended one, consisting of several soirees, or sorties.

The Big Year idea didn't come immediately. This was a big birthday, so I thought why not try to do it up big? You don't enter your eighth decade, your seventh of being a lepidopterist, just every day. It seemed only right to play it for all it was worth. Not inclined to bungee-jump or have hot ink stuck under my skin, I opted for the field—because any birthday spent out-of-doors is better than almost any day spent otherwise. At first, I was inclined toward a great big wilderness hike, as I had done for my fiftieth and sixtieth birthdays. I planned to backpack into Horseshoe Basin to try to see the far northern Labrador sulphur, a butterfly I'd never encountered. But as the date approached, the daunting logistics, the fact that this area is already rather well known, and concern over wildfires and smoke inclined me in a different direction: how about visiting a number of under-sampled parts of the state instead, where I could really make a contribution in terms of new dots on the map? My chief scientific interest in butterflies is their biogeography, ecology, and conservation. The dots on the map are essential for understanding why they're here and not there, and sometimes what must be done to conserve them. So that became the plan.

My late wife Thea and I, on our last big field trip together in 2012, had rambled the southern part of the North Kettle Range, above Rogers Pass. The part of the range still farther north, adjacent to the Canadian border, has seldom been visited with butterflies in mind. So that seemed a good place to begin. And then I had one more thought: Why don't David and I try to see seventy species in a month—one for each year on

Pan's Green Earth that I'd be celebrating? So that's what we set
out to attempt in the first place. But having found well over a
third of the 153 Washington butterflies in our first week in northeast Washington, David and I (over a glass or two of single malt
whiskey) rashly decided to undertake the first Washington Butterfly Big Year. Why not? That left around 100 species to find, including some very difficult and challenging species, which should
make, we reckoned, for some great soirees afield.

The Big Day itself, my LXXth birthday, turned out to be just
that. We chose to sample Mount Annie, Okanogan County, east
of Tonasket, new territory as far as we knew. Beautiful if close-
cropped green and moist spring meadows on the way up were
more inviting to us than to butterflies. From the end of the road
we hiked nearly to the top, where the larch forest closed in. The
day gave forth only sixteen species, but they included the gorgeous
Christina's sulphur, Boisduval's blue, and Edith's checkerspot, as
well as an absolutely brilliant and giant red admirable. Then,
coming back down late in the day, on a thistle, I spotted from
afar (then caught) a variegated fritillary! It was the first Washington specimen ever netted, after two prior probable sight records.
What a birthday present—I'd been seeking this widely vicariant
visitor from the South in the state for forty years. We still had
time to explore around the top of Bonaparte Lake and across to
the pioneer mining hamlets of Chesaw and Molson. The former
offered steak and beer in a great old cowboy tavern, and the latter
a poignant border sunset. Back at the Red Apple Motel in Tonasket, that bottle of fifteen-year-old The Macallan came out for my
other fine birthday present, with which to toast the fritillary and
the whole coming enterprise. We would surely see the day's other
species again, so we decided to begin the Big Year with that mo-
mentous encounter, at four in the afternoon.

And so it went for the next 364 days. Not all of them were spent afield, of course, nor as thrilling. A full account would be another hefty book, if not the 574 pages of *Mariposa Road*. My point here is not to document the whole caper, but to ask, why even *do* such a thing? What can be learned from it? So just to get a whiff of what a lucky Big Year can provide, here are a few representative images selected from that long litany of butterfly rendezvous.

July 21: Two Colville Indian moms watching their kids frolic in a reservation lake, not a man-made device in sight. Also in attendance, Oregon swallowtails, Becker's whites, purplish coppers, and a Melissa blue sipping salts at the lakeside gravel.

July 24: Walking the Pacific Crest Trail to Government Meadows, a vast green expanse of high wet meadow where four counties meet. Fast little brass pellets shooting over the soggy turf were the Sonora skippers I was hoping for. Then at the top of Chinook Pass, galaxies of glacier lilies and a single silvery blue.

July 25: Way up Strawberry Mountain, just northeast of Mount St. Helens, snowberry checkerspots abounded, no surprise. But also a robust colony of mountain parnassians at road's end. Snow-white, spotted with cherry and coal, they made a significant southwestern range extension from the nearest known colony on Jumbo Mountain in the Dark Divide: new news!

August 8–9: With my grandson Francis here for our annual Grandpa Camp, we ventured up Radar Hill, a bare prominence over the Naselle River estuary into Willapa Bay. There we found a bright rowdy mob of anise swallowtails hilltopping, and hydaspe fritillaries drunk on thistles. The next day Lorquin's admiral glided over the North River, and Francis found late Clodius parnassians on the watershed divide to Brooklyn, deep in the Willapa Hills. A good prelude to oysters at Bay Center, which he likes best as shooters, backed by hot chocolate; I took mine pan-fried, with IPA.

August 15: Once more into the breach, over the Cascades to Yakama country. Little Tieton Pond was rife with the bright wings of summer, such as acmon blues mobbing pink knotweed blooming around the shore. Walking a little bower between alders and willows along the north shore, I had just said, "what a good place for a cloak," when a big, bright, summer mourning cloak flew out and circled my head. If only it were ever thus. I camped at Stonehenge near Maryhill, drifting off to the warm breeze and train whistles in the gorge below.

August 21: I spent the total solar eclipse studying the behavior of the abundant woodland skippers around my rural home during totality. They behaved!—ceasing flight and nectaring and returning to roost trees when the temperature and illumination dropped, then coming back out as the moon gave back the day. I got some actual data, and published a tidy little scientific note about it.

September 1: The morning of September came thick and grim with smoke, with a Level 2 evacuation warning for the Jolly Mountain Fire too close to David Branch's house in Roslyn. I'd rejoined my boon companion and Ur-lepidopterist Jonathan Pelham to seek the Mormon metalmark, my last autumn-emergent butterfly as yet unfound: this would be my one chance. The thick smoke all around cooled the day and put our success in doubt. As we three, plus Loke the Butterfly Dog, headed out, we hoped there would still be a home to return to.

The thing with a Butterfly Big Year is that you have to be attentive to the passing seasons and their fading faunas, because they will not be back again until your year has come and gone.

But no worries. We no sooner got to Reecer Canyon and stepped out into the sere, smoky, desiccated landscape than the little metalmarks popped up all around, like so many new pennies.

I left the boys to it and headed south and east down to the Columbia, hoping to avoid the smoke blanketing the Cascades. It was hot and still, and I stopped for a Fudgsicle in the Mexican American town of Mattawa. There I beheld the greatest butterfly spectacle I've seen since I was last among the monarchs in Mexico: tens of thousands of orange and clouded sulphurs circling, rising, flirting, and falling among the pre-harvest fields of alfalfa. The day closed out under Vernita Bridge, with a fine spectacle of both monarchs and viceroys thronging the brilliant nectar banks of purple loosestrife: a troublesome invasive weed in wetlands, but one that has perversely become an essential nectar source for migrating monarchs in Washington.

September 2: Escape the smoke I did not. The fires were region-wide, and as I westered down the Columbia Gorge after sunset, the skies only seemed to thicken toward Mount Hood. What followed was a truly hellish trip home through the margins of the devastating Eagle Creek Fire, which had just blown up across the river in Oregon. I plowed through the worst traffic imaginable, as all of I-84 was detoured onto little, two-lane SR-14 on the Washington side. Between the raging red inferno on my left, the chaos of the insufficient road, and fiery brands falling around us, I wasn't at sure my 1982 Honda with her 432,000 miles, Powdermilk, would make it home at all. That was one of the most shocking nights of my life. Good thing we got the metalmarks.

April 18, 2018: The winter went by, and La Niña made for crappy conditions week after week on the dry side of the Cascades as well as in rainy western Washington. Crappy, that is, if your object is finding butterflies. Which mine was. So I missed a couple of the butterflies that one really should haunt the sagebrush steppe in March or April to find. When a genuinely clear, warm day came, I couldn't stand it, and had to get out into my local hills. At the end of Eden Valley's pastoral green slot, a gated logging road continues northeasterly into the private timberland. This stretch hadn't been logged for a while, so the roadside vegetation was in good condition, including loads of spring beauty. When there had been so few warm days for chrysalides to cook, it was just too early for the new species I sought. However, brilliant blue echo azures (Frost's "sky-flakes down in flurry on flurry") abounded as mint-fresh males, and buttery-linen margined whites glided up and down the road in their dozens. Both butterflies visited the spring beauties and little spots of birdlime on rocks of the road, as many as seven to a cluster. So, while tallying nothing new, Big Year—wise, I got a splendid butterfly hit to launch me out of the drizzly doldrums, into spring.

April 22: In Rock Creek Canyon, Klickitat County, the first swallowtails flashed the same yellow and black as the many meadowlarks piping into the crisp cool morning air. A minute, pale yellow female of Julia's orangetip apparated by the roadside, no bigger than a dainty sulphur. At the Rock Creek Longhouse of the Klickitat/Yakama people, many families had gathered for their big spring powwow. All morning and afternoon Native American people continued to pour down the road from the north, as I headed up in search of butterflies. Their own powwow, a swallowtail soiree at a long puddle by the edge of the dusty road, included dozens of anise and Indra swallowtails. Later I would find even larger puddle clubs of pale, western, and two-tailed tigers by various muddy banks of hot canyons.

May Day: Over the crest with Jon Pelham again, and young David Droppers. What a different scene now at Reecer Creek—all

green, rampant with spring wildflowers, and no smoke! It was a
relief to find Sheridan's green hairstreaks, as I'd missed them in
the desert earlier. Altogether it was to be a four-elfin day, with
pine and Moss's at Reecer, and brown at Umtanum Canyon in
the afternoon, plus that Sheridan's green elfin like some escapee
from Oz.

May 12: My next youthful companion was Caitlin LaBar, my
coauthor for a new field guide to the region's butterflies. She took
me into the heart of Skamania County, where Columbia blues hit
on buckwheat below Dog Mountain, and Grassy Knoll flickered
with bramble green hairstreaks and other spring specials. At the
end of the day, we found Juba skippers going to roost in firs above
high Peterson Prairie, not long free from snow and not a green
blade of grass yet in sight.

Mid-May: Hoary elfins on Kinnikinnick prairies at the edge
of the Olympics. Icy-blue Lucia blues in Cowiche Canyon near
Yakima, shimmering all around the footbridge. And then the
most trying drive of the year: a vertical rock-pit of a road, the
most evil I ever hope to face, to the summit of Umtanum Ridge,
the classic locale for the Nevada skipper. My shattered frame (and
my auto's) had just about had it when, on top (after 7:00 p.m.!), up
popped the first Nevada I'd ever seen in Washington, followed by
half a dozen brighter-than-Brillo western green hairstreaks. So I
thought it was worth it, even if got there by a route that I would
never recommend to anyone I actually like. But later, rats!—when
Jon Pelham took a look, he declared my voucher specimen to be
a male Juba skipper. So I almost destroyed Thea's old Subaru for
a Juba. (Powdermilk was sidelined.) Next time I'm going to make
Pelham take me up there himself to find Nevada, in his Jeep!

May 28: My first of three visits to fabled Satus Pass for the
year. Butterflies abounded, and I met with five new ones: great

arctics, western sulphurs, dreamy duskywings, lots of the usually uncommon northern cloudy wings, and a Great Basin checkerspot. When I returned on **June 14**, I would add northern checkerspot, and on **June 27**, Hoffman's checkerspot: so I found all three of our *Chlosyne* checkers in the vicinity of Satus Pass, last accomplished by E. J. Newcomer in the 1960s. On the middle visit, one Satus streamside mud puddle hosted sixteen species.

June 15: An epic day afield with lepidopterist David James, to the upper and lower reaches of the crazy-long, off-and-on watercourse known as Crab Creek, which cuts across much of the Columbia Basin. Not far from Ritzville, we walked a tiny perched wetland among silver-bordered fritillaries, northern crescentspots, garita skipperlings, and a big, bright arrowhead blue. That afternoon, and many miles southwest almost to the Columbia, we found the hoped-for ruddy coppers, my first ever in Washington. Next day in the Klickitat River Gorge, just a few blossoms supped dozens of sylvan and California hairstreaks.

June 27: Following a failed spring attempt to reach a storied high meadowland known among the Yakama people as the Lakebeds, when I was nearly stuck in a giant snowmelt mudhole where I might still be, I tried again from the south. A Yakama gate stopped me a couple of miles from the Lakebeds, but in trying, I did find the thickest concentration of butterflies of the year, in the Simcoe Mountains: forty-two species, a few of them new, and thousands of individuals. It was a butterfly jamboree.

July 1+: With my time running down, I set out on a three-week field trip to finish off the year with a bang. David Branch again joined me for much of it. Independence Day found us meeting Caitlin LaBar in her long-term study locale of the Sinlahekin Wildlife Area in upper Okanogan County, along with her mentor, retired manager Dale Swedberg. We found the gold nuggets of

Behr's hairstreaks on bitterbrush and Canadian tiger swallowtails, but fire and flood nixed the pale crescentspot habitats. When
we got to the Long Swamp on Toats Coulee for Freija fritillaries,
it was 39 degrees and snowing. But next day it was warmer, and
we found both Vidler's and Butler's alpines, rich chocolaty with
cinnamon and butterscotch notes.

Thence to Slate Peak above Mazama. It was still spring at
this famous and (only) drivable arctic-alpine height, and devilish
windy. None of the high-country specialists were present except
anicia checkers and a lone arctic blue hunkering in the lee. Yet on
the summit, where male butterflies hilltop in their dozens when
the airs are more temperate, David managed to pull an astonishing capture out of the gale: a female coral hairstreak, an uncommon butterfly even in its accustomed lowlands. We had no
explanation whatever for that anomaly, but there it was.

David had to head back to the city, so I carried on alone. In
quick succession, I found a single big golden Yuma skipper among
the sparse great reeds in its sole known Washington colony, Sun
Lakes; and then shot back to Omak, camped near Conconully, hit
Lone Frank Pass in the morning, and finally spotted *Boloria freija*.
I'd been seeking Freija's fritillary in Washington for fifty years,
and she was one of my greatest desiderata. A lone chryxus arctic
found me up there too.

And then it was time for the Great Northeast! Up to Disautel,
the Colville Reservation, and Moses and Tiger meadows. I was
seeking various uncommon skippers, and managed to find one I
didn't expect instead: the long dash, an Okanogan county record.
Butterfliers love to record new county records, and they're not
that easy anymore, especially in well-collected Okanogan. There
were lots of a recent introduction, the European skipperling, in
the vast meadows, and both Atlantis and northwest fritillaries

near the dark forest edges. The next day, finding the Pend Oreille Selkirks east of Sullivan Lake sparse for butterflies, and with only a few days to go, I shot all the way down the state to the Blue Mountains.

Across the beautiful Chewelah highlands and the parched, heated lowlands I flew, pausing only for a quick look at Sprague Lake, a longtime study site of Thea's and mine. Not a lot there. But a single showy milkweed that I reversed for was covered with dark wedges—half a dozen or so bright male coral hairstreaks! A real spectacle for this thoroughly unpredictable butterfly, and a much more sensible place for them to be found than the top of Slate Peak in gale.

But it was late that afternoon when an even greater spectacle struck. The road ran straight from Sprague to Steptoe, as it left the Channeled Scablands and entered the Palouse on the way to the Blues. So I took a short detour to the summit of Steptoe Butte, that high volcanic plug poking up through the loess prairies, where I'd seen painted ladies hilltopping in the past. This time, with the brilliant green-and-gold Palouse spreading its broad checkered apron of wheat fields below and just a narrow hem of natural habitat protected around the Butte, the tip-top was aswirl with hilltoppers: Oregon swallowtails, common wood nymphs, western whites, Colorado skippers, and very pale little callippe fritillaries, among others. When they all went to bed around six, the ladies came out: the first one was the rarest, a big-eyed American lady (*Vanessa virginiensis*), alighting right beside me on the asphalt. The second, landing right next to it, was the other one I still sought, the West Coast lady (*Vanessa annabella*)—I couldn't believe my luck. And then in succession came a couple of painted ladies (*Vanessa cardui*), followed at last by a red admirable (*Vanessa atalanta*)! By seven o'clock, several ladies of each species were dashing all around the top, each courting all the others, in a veritable carnival of color and action! This was my first-ever Four-Vanessa Day, including in Hawaii, which has one additional species, *Vanessa tameamea*. I will never forget it.

July 15+: Based at Wickiup Campground, I found the Blue Mountains to be better than the Selkirks, but not as rich as they can be; and to my disgruntlement, there wasn't an Edith's copper to be seen anywhere. But another Blue Mountain specialty did show. Between Mount Misery and Diamond Peak, Great Basin fritillaries (with their unusual baby-poop ground to the silver spots below) flew up from every wet spot.

Then all the way once more across the arid Basin and back up to Slate Peak, for another go at the high-country denizens. Less wind, later conditions, better results: Astarte and arctic fritillaries, and a mating pair of spring whites, right on the not-so-windy summit. On the way down toward Mazama, I paused to revel in one of the whole year's most memorable visions: some twenty Hoffman's checkerspots puddling in the late sun. Little did I know that a couple of days later a butterfly watchers' foray would find arctic skippers, which had eluded me all year, at nearby Whistler Meadows. I might have gotten there in time myself that afternoon to see them, had I hurried. But those checkers were worth lingering over. The numbers weren't everything.

But I was still chasing them, nonetheless. Now I had just one day left, and part of another. On **July 18**, I tried the other side of the North Cascades, the North Fork of the Nooksack, for Oreas anglewings and Compton tortoiseshells, without any luck. Then dashed for the shore, the ferry, and the Olympics, for the finish. I had defined the beginning of the Big Year as the moment I caught the first specimen of the variegated fritillary ever nabbed in Washington, at four in the afternoon of my seventieth birthday, July 19, 2017. So I had until that time on my seventy-first.

July 19: By 2:00 p.m., I had burst out of the marine layer clouds and reached the sunny summit of Blue Mountain above Deer Park in Olympic National Park. And there, on the very top, what should appear but what I sought: Hulbirt's branded skipper (*Hesperia comma hulbirti*), an Olympic endemic. Spring whites were still coursing the slopes way up here. Then I dropped back down into the cloud, sought a good seafood dinner and a celebratory glass in Port Angeles, and that was that: a year of passionate, all-out play, and 127 of Washington's 153 species—*finis!*

So why do a Big Year? After all, it takes a lot of planning, time, gas, and effort. One must organize life around this one goal, to do a proper job of it. It ain't easy. What's in it for you? And above all: What you can learn from it? What kind of knowledge? How secure and truthful? And how to trust it to change your life? This is the epistemology part.

For some, it is the draw of competition, breaking a record, and meeting a goal. You get a sense of that in the book and movie, *The Big Year*. For those who enjoy a good competitive game, I gave them something to shoot for: 486 (out of 800) species for the U.S. and Canada, when I did my Big-Big Year in 2008; 127 (out of 153) for Washington this time. Chris Tenney did the second continental Butterfly Big Year in 2015, topping me (as he certainly should have) with 523 species.

In 2008, I did my continental Big Year, as reported in the book *Mariposa Road*. It was the first one, and Chris Tenney's was the second. In 2017–2018, I did my Washington State Big Year. It is still the only one.

Who's to say that "mere" competition is shallow? My friend Benton Basham takes great glee in having been the first to see 700 birds in an American Big Year. It is a harmless pursuit, and cannot be any worse than golf, for which some claim great Zen value for concentration, beauty of the stroke, and attention to the moment. But I will decline to comment further, since competition did not apply to either of my Big Years. Since no one had done them before, I had none. The bar was zero. My only competitors were the calendar, the clock, and the clouds. And I made the rules.

For me, the greatest virtue of the Big Year is the accelerated learning curve for *actual physical details of the earth* that it both provides and demands. I learned so much on both of my Big Years that I can barely imagine my posture in the world before them. I know all these butterflies, their behavior, distribution, and ecology, better than I did before, and the same is true for many of their non-lepidopteran neighbors. Simply by being *outside* all that time, attentive to butterflies, yes, but also to everything that moves and the background it moves against, one cannot help storing up knowledge as well seeing something beautiful and wonderful every day. Though you don't *need* a Big Year in order to venture forth like this, being committed to one ensures that you get yourself out there into the field, probably more than you would otherwise—and the beautiful and wonderful part just follows as a matter of course.

As for the *nature* of the knowledge thus gained, it is the true and lasting knowledge, devoid of fashion or fad, that comes from the actual functioning of animals and plants as they have evolved in the context of their physical setting of weather, climate, and geology. Thoreau put it best: "Daily to be shown matter, to come in contact with it,—rocks, trees, wind on our cheeks! the *solid* earth! the *actual* world! the *common* sense! *Contact! Contact! Who* are we?

where are we?" The reliability of this sort of knowing is vouchsafed by impartial reality to be entire and unimpeachable, depending only on your own honesty and willingness to take it as it is given, free of the refractive personal filter. It cannot be faked except by a faker to himself. Do this kind of deep watching much and you are bound to experience and illuminate entirely new quanta of knowledge. Science itself flows from just the kind of observation so necessary to a good Big Year, strained through its own crisp and salient methods. In my experience, few things are more bracing than spotting, parsing, confirming, and sharing something that hasn't been known before—like that variegated fritillary, butterfly #1. Again, Thoreau: "How sweet is the perception of a new natural fact!" This is the kind of satisfying knowledge that makes such a rarefied devotion all worth it. As for its ability to change your life, well, that's up to you.

So this is the great gift of the Big Year. In putting everything else aside to the extent possible—quotidian cares, social demands, and, as far as possible, the so-called news in favor of extreme attention to certain living elements of the land—you invite the real world in all its texture, grit, and sublimity into your wholly attentive presence. Very good hunters will know what I mean.

Another boon for me was getting to know the nation and the state I live in, study, and love better than ever before. In 2017–2018, I drove Washington roads I'd never driven before (which are getting hard to find!), hiked trails I've never hiked (which is easier), and revisited beloved places not seen for a long time. Many of them brought back memorable trips I'd taken with Thea and other people dear to me, and their special encounters. I felt that I reconnected with Washington in a way I hadn't for years. And by being outdoors walking almost every day, gaining strength all along, I returned much healthier for having done it. All this also applied, on a much grander if coarser scale, to the continental Butterfly Big Year I had taken in 2008.

And then there is the just plain fun of it all. It certainly isn't worth doing if it isn't fun. Like that four-lady day atop Steptoe Butte, every species of *Vanessa* in the state swirling about me all together at sunset—now, *that* was fun! I don't know if there is an epistemology of fun, but I do know that a butterfly bonanza beats the insect apocalypse every time.

Of course it wasn't all a picnic. Weather, shifting flight periods with warming climate, drought, wind, flood, fire, washouts, et cetera, et cetera, let me down over and over. There was danger, and tedium, and disappointment. But while the rest of the world continues to go to hell, on a Big Year, hope simply has to spring eternal, or at least each morning. What will you find today? asks Hope. It could be good!

Note: I have since gotten to know Kenn Kaufman, and the man is the measure of his wonderful book. As he put that final thought of mine above, toward the end of *Kingbird Highway* (which may be one of the best book finishes ever), *"Any day could be a special day, and you just had to get outside, and see what the birds were doing . . ."*

Bright Lights, Big City *Is a Classic Nature Book!*

As a former guest professor and visiting writer at several colleges and universities where I was responsible for something called "Environmental Writing," and a many-time leader for workshops, classes, and seminars on "Nature Writing," as well as a person commonly labeled a "Nature Writer," I have come to an unswerving belief that there is no such thing. My objection is not that of some friends who feel marginalized by being described as practicing a form widely seen as a lesser genre of literature, although that certainly happens. Rather, my belief is based on the firm conviction, arrived at over half a century of writing and reading both natural history and many other shades of books, that these terms are simply redundant. "Environmental writing" and "nature writing" are, I contend, just superfluities, for they are exact synonyms for the simpler word, "writing." This is because I know of nothing—not one thing—one can write about that is not a part of the environment, a part of nature.

I understand that some people recognize, in their cosmos, a spiritual dimension or plane that they believe lies outside of "nature" as we know it. Many call this a "supernature" and refer to events or entities from that realm as "supernatural." I have never found nature wanting in any essential respect such as to require a supernature, and do not accept, in my cosmos, any such thing. To me, it is plain that another synonym for the noun *nature* is the verb *to be*. To exist is to be a part of nature. So how can the term "nature writing" be anything but repetitive?

Now, even many rationalists have trouble accepting this premise, I have found. They want, and perhaps need, there to be something called "unnatural" to account for "unnatural acts," for how can clear and abominable aberrations of behavior and norms be considered "natural"? For if *to be* = *nature*, then *everything* needs must be "natural." That's hard for people to take, as it was for me for many years.

I didn't come to this premise early. My younger writings show a considerable strain of wishful dualism, in service to my prejudices. But truly, how can anything in the physical universe, all produce of stardust evolved, be anything but natural? It's a big step to understand and accept that nuclear bombs are natural, because the reactions they are based on take place within stars, and an evolved species of upright hominoid ape manufactured them just as a beaver its dam. But there it is, and beyond logical argument.

All or almost all of what people consider "unnatural" comes from, is made by, or is enacted by their own species. Of course we wish to distance ourselves from serial killing or sexual predation or genocide or mountaintop removal or oil spills. But if we designate the perpetrators of all these as acting "unnaturally,"

then we are either omitting our own species from the fellow-
ship of life, or declaring only the norm to be natural, and where
do you draw the line? Then there is the moldy old "natural vs.
artificial" argument, which goes nowhere worthwhile. There is
an old fishing industry boiler in the Columbia River in Astoria, Oregon, whose rusted metal and eroded concrete run insensibly into the many species of land and water life that have
colonized it as it releases its constituent minerals. Moss, lichen,
algae, grass and sedge, barnacle, tubeworm, iron, rust, concrete, gravel, calcium carbonate, a blooming aster on top . . .
I challenge anyone to define where nature becomes artifice in
this constantly mutating tableau.

Or take the opening short chapter of my novel *Magdalena
Mountain* (Counterpoint Press, 2018):

> The yellow Karmann Ghia left the road at forty-five. Its tires
> never scored the soft tissue of the tundra. It simply flew over the
> edge, into the mountain abyss.
>
> A lookout marmot shrilled at the sight. A pair of pikas,
> young of the year, disappeared beneath their rockpile as the
> strange object passed overhead. Clearing the stony incline, the
> doomed auto glided over the rich mountain turf. Its shadow
> fell across a patch of alpine forget-me-nots, deepening their
> hue from sky to delft; then passed over a pink clump of moss
> campion. A black butterfly nectaring on the campion twitched
> at the momentary shading. Such a shift of light often signaled
> a coming storm, sending the alpine insects into hiding among
> the sod or stones. But this cloud passed quickly, so the sipping
> butterfly hunkered only briefly, then resumed its suck from the
> sweet-filled floret. A bigger black form took flight when the

bright intruder entered its territory. The raven charged the big yellow bird to chase the interloper out of its airspace, succeeded, and resettled.

As the slope fell away toward the canyon below, more than keeping pace with the glide path of the Ghia, so fell the yellow missile. Sky whooshed aside to make room for it, otherwise there was no sound but for three shrieks on the alpine air: a nutcracker's alarm scream; the whine of the engine, gunned by the foot glued to the Ghia's floorboard; and a third, muffled by the glass, growing into a hopeless wail.

The thin alpine air parted before the plummeting car, smelling of green musk, of the great high lawn that is the Colorado mountain tundra. The perfumes of a hundred alpine wildflowers filled the grille of the Ghia. Soon the sweet mingled scents would be overcome by the rank fumes of oil and gasoline mixing with the terpenes of torn evergreens, as the grille split against pine and stone. But the rider smelled nothing.

The air took on a chill as the projectile left the sunny upper reaches, crossed over timberline, and entered the shade of the upper forest. Never once had it touched down since takeoff, nor could it fly much farther. Gravity never ran out, but the earth rushed up at last to meet it. All the elements of the alpine earth—mineral soil, bare stone, grass, sedge, herb, shrub, and solid trunk of ancient limber pine—mingled with the yellow metal when the Ghia went to ground. Soft parts met hard. Granite tore rubber. Branches smashed glass and pierced the cloth upholstery. The engine block escaped its mounts and flew a little farther before shattering against a boulder and coming to rest as shiny shrapnel in the streambed far below. The blow that tore the motor free, ending its long scream, ripped the driver's door from its hinges. That other shriek was loosed into the general clamor. Then nothing.

Almost nothing remained from this unplanned event to disturb the day up above, where it began. The nutcracker returned to its snag, the marmot to its post, the raven to its rock. The black butterfly nectared on, then flew. The forget-me-nots still flowered low against the ground. Not even the green verge of the road betrayed anything amiss. Only a black rubber streak in the roadway gave away the launching spot. Even the golden-mantled ground squirrel whose mad dash across the asphalt had started it all lay not dead on the shoulder, but basking on a boulder nearby in the late summer sun, unabashed by her close call.

Of the steaming yellow mass among the trees and rocks a thousand feet below, no one knew a thing. Bumblebees investigating the yellow spatter on the slope found battered, barren steel instead of woolly sunflowers. The Karmann Ghia's aberrant track would never be repeated. And for all the difference it made to the mountain, it might never have happened at all.

What do you think—is it nature writing, or not? Nature or artifice? Where does nature begin and end? Thomas Hardy spends the first six pages of *The Return of the Native* describing the landscape-character of Egdon Heath, before a human being (the reddleman) even sets foot on the scene or the page. But I have never heard Hardy called (or dismissed as) a "nature writer."

And yet sensible people still want their dualistic universe: human vs. all the rest. I think I know why. Many folks tend to conflate the words *nature* and *natural* with words like *good, admirable, acceptable, okay,* or *desirable*—with *values*. Likewise, *unnatural* equates with *bad*. Just look how advertisers and the mercantile world exploit this notion: "It's NATURAL—buy it!" And buy we do.

But this equation is erroneous, because (in a rational society that does not actually accept tablets from on high) all values are human constructs, or conceits, that come about to try to prevent chaos and to promote order on the societal scene. "Good" and "bad," so far as we know, do not exist in the world outside their human parameters. Because we love the beauties of untrammeled nature, we like to consider nature, and the natural, as good (until we're faced with a man-eater, forest fire, tornado, or tsunami, or a cheetah eating a Thomson's gazelle on TV). But nature isn't good or bad; nature was amoral, until humans imposed morals on the world. We make ethical choices and laws for our own good in an imaginary moral framework. We decide what is good and bad for us as a community, a culture, a species, and then act on those decisions politically or religiously to try to mold behavior. In that way, we choose what we consider to be right or wrong, and we are likely to label choices that fall outside those rules "unnatural."

To call something "natural" in the sense I mean does *not* condone it. It does not exculpate antisocial, sociopathic, or psychopathic behavior. Because they are natural, they simply occur in Nature. And when we label the "right" choices "natural" and the "wrong" ones as "unnatural," we do a grave disservice to the more-than-human world, and potentially to ourselves. This mistaken identity has the unwonted power of real consequences, to which I will later return. For now, I'll just say that nature/human dualism is dangerous; very dangerous. It sets us apart. Robinson Jeffers enjoined us to love "the wholeness of life and things . . . / . . . not man / Apart from that . . ."

Which brings me to *Bright Lights, Big City*, Jay McInerney's slender blockbuster book published by Vintage in 1984, its title from a blues song by Jimmy Reed. John Barrett McInerney Jr., an educational product of Williams College and Syracuse University (where he studied with Raymond Carver), wrote this novel in his late twenties. Later he wrote the screenplay for the film, and it appeared as an Off-Broadway rock musical as well. The book was a sensation for its harsh, second-person account of a cocaine-driven life of misdirected love and heady yuppie clubbing by a hopeful New York writer, who eventually makes it out alive. Raymond Carver himself described it as "a rambunctious, deadly funny novel that goes right for the mark—the human heart." McInerney was dubbed a member of the "literary brat pack" of the eighties. A major figure in literary circles since, he later became wine critic for *The Wall Street Journal.*

I enjoyed the book and watched with interest as it became branded a beacon of the young and restless-for-the-next-sensation in Manhattan. Anyone would have assumed, and I'm sure it was both said and thought, that *Bright Lights, Big City* was the ultimate infra-urban book, and the living antithesis of "nature writing." (One well-known "nature writer" friend of mine used to like to say that it was the so-called nature books that should really be considered mainstream lit, and the "urban dysfunctional" tales like McInerney's that should be considered a subgenre. The critics never quite saw it that way.)

As a former urban naturalist, I was never comfortable with such a hard-and-fast distinction. For one thing, there is no reason that a Manhattan-based book should be, ipso facto, antithetical toward the natural world. Wonderful books of natural history have arisen from these streets (and parks, and marshes, and waters). Two of my favorite reads, some years back, were the great sportswriter John Kieran's lovely *Footnotes on Nature* and *A Natural History of New York City.* "For many years," Brooks Atkinson wrote

about Kieran, "he has been using the region of New York City as
if it were a wilderness, watered by river and sea, and he has been
plucking out the heart of its nature mystery as if he had no other
occupation." In later years, we have seen Marie Winn's affecting
Red-Tails in Love, and Leslie Day's wide-ranging *Field Guide to the
Natural World of New York City*. So the material is obviously there.
But none of these are yuppie novels. Where's the connection with
Bright Lights?

For a start, it seemed to me that with its plot dependent upon
coca, cannabis, and other plant-derived stimulants, *Bright Lights*
was every bit as much a nature book as Michael Pollan's popular *The Botany of Desire*, which told of the impact of the tulip,
potato, apple, and marijuana on society. I knew that McInerney
also spoke of the winds and waters around the island, some of
the urban animals if only rats and pigeons, and the geological
formations created by upright hominoid apes having mined and
reformed other, older geological formations. This line of reasoning amused me and I took to making the argument in public.
It struck a chord with initially resistant listeners, so I pursued it
further. Eventually I decided to conduct a full deconstruction of
Bright Lights to winkle out, so to speak, every natural history reference I could find in the blessedly short text (just 182 pages in my
Vintage paperback edition). It was still a much bigger job than I
had imagined, and I was gobsmacked by the results, which I present below. Here are all the references I found in *Bright Lights* to the
so-called "natural world":

Solar and Atmospheric: fire, rain, "the harsh, angling light
of morning," air, "the dawn's surly light," haze, glare, ice, water,
cloud, sunlight, snow, wind, spring, fall, precipitation, climate,
moon, "a blue, sunny day," "thermoclines between cool shadows

of tall buildings and brief regions of direct sunlight" (ergo, canyons), morning.

Geological and Geographical: anticline, Andean peaks, terrain, transcontinental, oil, islands, silver, dust, sidewalk sparkles (mica), crystal, volcano, ocean, "the broad expanse of the Hudson and its black, fetid water," river, pool, lake, flint, earthquake, tornado, diamonds, gold, stones, emerald, plains, ground, gravel, rock, cave, marble, lead, borax, red dirt, chemicals, neutrino, lithium, cobbles, asphalt.

Botanical: root, plants, tulip, banana, coca, cocoa, rye, wood, maple, seed, loofah, ginger, kudzu, oak, olive, ivy, tea, coffee, straw, mescal (agave), vodka (potatoes), cherry blossoms, beer (hops, yeast, barley), scotch (malted barley), reefer (cannabis), wine (grapes), honeysuckle, palm trees, wheat, smut, leaves, trees, weeds, beans, fruit, peach, vegetable, flowers, tomatoes, squash, oranges, basil, garlic, romaine lettuce, mannitol (seaweed).

Zoological: animal, birds, duck, pigeons, swallow, phoebe, eagle, finch, flicker, falcon, emperor penguin, lizard, "robin listening for worms," cricket, cockroach, "piranhas cruising your bloodstream," turtle, crane, carrion birds, cream, camel, shoat, pigs, horse, ass, ten-point buck, deer, lion, fur, bear, game animal, fox, ferret, mink, tarantulas, scallop, sharks, dragon, parrot, rabbit, roadrunner, "small furry and large scaly creatures," "a hive of rollers on her head," German shepherd, beagle, dachshund, trout, coyote, dog, wolf, screaming gulls, clams, cats, sheep, walrus, cattle, foal, mouse, monkeys, humans, peccary, swine, egg, chicken, fowl, malaria (mosquitoes, microbes), duck, rhizopods, sporozoans, gophers, rodents, ciliates, lobster, rats, flagellates, sulphur duns (dry fly), silk (moth), salmon flies, flies, piss-ant, fly-fishing, fish, Siamese fighting fish, blubber, cod, brown trout, rabies, bat.

Cosmic: comet trail, nature, life on other planets, environment, world.

This is a remarkable inventory of natural objects for a book generally considered to represent strictly a human, urban perspective. As every one of them is placed in context, can this be called anything other than nature writing? Unless, of course, one accepts that all writing is nature writing and nature writing is just writing.

Similar or even more dramatic results could be logged from the pages of many literary authors not considered nature writers: certainly some with biological training or inclination like Steinbeck, Fowles, and Kingsolver, who might even exceed this list with any of their books. But also authors you wouldn't even think of as nature lovers, like Updike, Conrad, or Welty. Even Kerouac is full of naive but beautifully observed natural history. And the poets: Wordsworth, Whitman, Frost, Snyder, Oliver, and Pattiann Rogers, of course; but also Heaney, Thomas, Langston Hughes, Van Morrison, and Bruce Springsteen. As for Shakespeare, George Eliot, T. S. Eliot, and Nabokov, forget it! You cannot separate them from their natural settings without doing them real violence. And not just *Midsummer Night's Dream*, with its botanical litanies. In *Henry V*, Act III, scene V, lines 18–20, where the Constable of France says

> Is not their climate foggy, raw, and dull,
> On whom, as in despite, the sun looks pale,
> Killing their fruit with frowns?

you know you are in the hands of one who was keenly aware of the world around him. As, I submit, was McInerney.

* * *

So let this little argument stand for literary ecumenism and inclusivity. As I said above, there are dangers inherent in dualism. When nature and non-nature are seen as genuinely separate, when it is generally believed that there exists an actual line between humans and the rest of nature, then our kind is free to call nature the Other, to objectify it, and to conquer it—or try to do so, exacting plenty of mischief along the way. The separation of humans and nature is the most dangerous idea in the world, because it licenses all manner of enormities against the systems that support, ennoble, and enlarge us.

I have no interest, by the way, in launching semantical reform along these lines. I am not going to try to change the names "nature writing" or "environmental writing" in the academies. I am quite happy to be called a "nature writer," because I know that by saying so people are respecting me as a naturalist. And these terms have a certain utility as shorthand. As I tell my students, they simply mean writing that pays more attention to other species besides ourselves than is usually done.

Very few works of literature with any heft or power of persuasion are devoid of the more-than-human natural world. I will continue to argue that good writing is good writing, and that all writing is nature writing, and vice versa. Our very future may depend upon the general comprehension that there is no clear distinction between our species and all the others. In the meantime, I'd be content to see *Bright Lights, Big City* receive due recognition as brilliant environmental writing. Not only does it serve as an elegant ethology of one species of upright hominoid ape under the influence of one species of plant in the contemporary canyonlands, but it does so in a very broad context of other species, formations, and elements.

Bright Lights, Big City is a classic nature book. And somehow, I think Jay McInerney might not be entirely surprised, or unhappy, to hear it.

Outro

ALLTHEISM (ALL IN ALL IS ALL WE ARE)

Tanager chips, dove hoots, young men chatter playing soccer. Lake Chapala, very high this spring, laps the shore. A
packed pelican roost shines to my right on a palmy little peninsula,
an egret heronry to my left in bare deciduous trees, both white as
Ivory soap. Coots and cormorants pepper the surface, plus plastic
bottles. One white pelican drifts past an old-style, high-bow fishing boat. A fisherman in a hoodie gathers in line and net by hand-
over-hand, tosses lake perch into the bottom of his boat.

Behind me, a long line of leaf-cutter ants, their route deeply
indented into the lawn, travels some thirty yards from upper
boughs of an acacia to a hole in the ground near the base of another acacia—why not mine that one? Insect Armageddon be
damned, these *Atta* ants are thriving here and across much of the
neotropics in their almost-incredible food and transport systems.
I could watch their parasol-lofting progress across bark and grass
and sidewalk and stick and leaf all day long. Back lakeside, an ibis

slips past like a sleeker, slimmer cormorant. All this in a busy city park, as the pelicans filter past from the early southern sunset side to the hazy east, training runners jog past, and there is no sign of any visible or palpable barrier between any two elements on the scene.

* * *

I had no religious upbringing as such. Some Methodism in the past, I gather. The first comer on my father's side married in the Church of England's Inner Temple Church in London in 1697. My mother's side were Pennsylvania Germans of a Protestant persuasion. Both sets of grandparents divorced in the 1920s, and there were no churchgoers among the Colorado branches of either family, as far as I know. A Christmas or Easter or two with some handy congregation, and I wore the terry-cloth bathrobe as a wise man for the Lutherans one yule. But that was about it, until my great-grandmother, Mary Winfrey Cannon (or Gimma), a Southern Baptist, came to live with us from Toledo. As no one else would, I took her to church a few times. But the oily call to be saved was not James Brown's version from the *Blues Brothers*, and I soon opted out. I couldn't see confessing to sins I had not yet properly enjoyed, and the gospel didn't jibe with the Charles Darwin I was carrying around in my back pocket at the time.

But my high school friends mostly went to church, so out of curiosity and attachment to various girls, I tried out the Jews, the Episcopalians, the Presbyterians, a few others; all of them were interesting, but took way too much of my precious weekend time, and only confused me with all their paradoxes and doxologies.

Then one Sunday in *The Denver Post*'s Religion column, I read a conservative Baptist preacher's rant inveighing against what he called "syncretism"—the taking of bits and pieces from various faiths and creeds and tacking them together into what he saw as a meaningless pastiche. He seemed to find this blending even more of a threat to Christianity than disbelief altogether, and an outright blasphemy, especially when it involved elements from Buddhism, Hindu, Islam, Baha'i, et al. Whereas I thought it sounded like a darned good idea. In fact, I'd come to something similar on my own, as I'd liked parts of each of the churches I had attended and their beliefs. And, in my youthful naiveté, though I probably didn't even know the word, the general idea of ecumenism made eminent sense to me, as opposed to sectarian tussling and warfare. (My full-body immersion among the Southern Baptists probably helped here too.)

So I decided to form my own "ism," based not so much on faith in anything as on reason and hope. I loved nature, I saw the all-embracing sense of pantheism, and I sympathized with various teachings behind the denominations. Jesus's embrace of pacifism and poverty appealed to me, for example, though I beheld few examples of it in practice. The Sunday paper preacher was all I needed to react against and found my own creed. I called it "Naturo-Pantheistic Syncretism." Not that I sought followers, or to broadcast my "religion." I simply felt I'd now dealt with that aspect of life, and could comfortably put it on the back burner for the duration, in favor of butterflies and girls.

Many, many years later, I was visiting my younger brother, Howard, just a lad at the dawn of my new credo. "So, Bob," he asked, "are you still a *naturo-pantheistic syncretist*?" I guess I'd acquired one follower, at least enough so to remember the name. I assured him I was.

I never got too far with the details, because I didn't care that much. I just figured the name was enough. The pun on Pan was a bonus, harking as it did to both the Piper at the Gates of Dawn and to "all." I thought I had arrived at the central tenet on my own while naturalizing my holy ground along the High Line Canal in eastern Colorado, as reinforced by Darwin's all-encompassing metaphor of the "tangled bank" at the end of the *Origin of Species*. Once in college, studying conservation, I began to encounter eloquent restatements, as in John Muir: "When we try to pick out anything by itself, we find it hitched to everything else in the Universe." And, a little slant, in Aldo Leopold: "To keep every cog and wheel is the first precaution of intelligent tinkering." Endless iterations of the same principle jumped up from Buddhist translations such as Gary Snyder's, and in his own poems. Further on, in John Steinbeck and Ed Ricketts's *Log from the Sea of Cortez*, I read: "all things are one thing and that one thing is all things," and "ecology has a synonym which is ALL." But maybe the ultimate boiling-down of the idea to its greatest simplicity and absence of ambiguity came along in Kurt Cobain's "All Apologies," from Nirvana's 1993 album *In Utero*: "All in all is all we are." Says it all.

* * *

Next day I visit the *malecón* in Ajijic, farther up the lake. The water hasn't been higher in Lake Chapala in forty years. The morning wind laps it to shore, almost up to the promenade. The feet, legs, and waists of the shoreline trees and palms are all in the drink, their branches dotted with black-footed, yellow-billed great egrets and yellow-footed, black-billed snowy egrets, side by side in a field guide picture. They eye the same small fish the terns and brown pelicans dive for and the white pelicans and fishermen seine. Walkers, both Mexican and *norteamericano*, and their legions of dogs steadily progress along the *malecón* and back again in the harsh sunshine. On the opposite shore, berry fields and white roofs of greenhouses line the banks.

The egrets, their plumes flying like high cirrus clouds in high winds, plumes that started conservation wars and Audubon societies, still look glamorous; though few of these walkers even note them now, eyes ahead and not a single plumed hat to be seen on the promenade. Brilliant pink-and-purple bougainvillea and pale blue plumbagos backdrop a scene otherwise like any other waterside walk anywhere, except in their particulars. At the end of the *malecón*, a great egret stands atop a red swing set, a lone coot paddling almost at the level of the seats. The slides disappear into the drink, as a kiskadee makes a racket in the willow above, and grackles glide by, checking out the shore wrack.

* * *

A few years after my founding of Naturo-Pantheistic Syncretism— funnily enough, its acronym, NPS, was the same as the National Park Service, about as close as I get to a godhead—I took Philosophy 101 in college. I found it only reinforced my apostasy. The preoccupation of many of the thinkers with labored proofs of God made eminent nonsense to me. The arguments of Berkeley, Aquinas, and others seemed anything but parsimonious (a concept I was just getting at both ends of campus; Occam applied equally well to the natural and social sciences). Their attempts to justify evil in a godly world utterly failed, in my mind, without the most extreme mental gymnastics. Only the fact that my philosophy prof, John Chambless, was a birder with a puckish wit, who demonstrated many of the concepts through ornithological metaphors drawn from his morning walks across the same marshes I cut other classes to bird, maintained my interest and tolerance in the course. I certainly came out as no less of a nontheist than I'd been going in.

As for models and heroes, I found the figures I was exposed to in Melville Hatch's History of Science and Richard Cooley's Conservation of Natural Resources classes far more compelling: Aristotle, Buffon, Hooker, Humboldt, and Darwin, Marsh, Pinchot, Muir, Leopold, and Brower. And when David Brower came to campus, I felt I'd received a seraphic visitation.

All of which left me where, from a metaphysical (or solely physical) stance? Certainly nontheistic. Certainly "naturo." But that began to feel almost a redundancy, as I realized more and more that there is, was, and can be no real nature/non-nature divide. The "pantheistic" part still applied, but I was put off by all the folderol and mystical trappings that self-described pantheists and pagans adopted during the hippie-into-New Age era, when oatmeal and ideas lost any clear distinction. And as for the "syncretism" part, it still made sense to me, insofar as certain teachings from every tradition I studied—Christian love, Buddhist Tao, Shinto naturism, Jain pacifism, Mormon communitarianism, and so on and on—still spoke to me. As did nature-based church architecture such as St. Basil's in Red Square, full of wildflower friezes; the Blue Mosque, with its red tulips on blue tiles; La Sagrada Família in Barcelona; and St. Mary's in Selborne, Hampshire, depicting all the birds mentioned by Gilbert White in its stained-glass windows.

But those weren't enough to make me a believer. So I had to ask myself, eventually, about outright atheism. Philosophically I am without a god and untroubled by the fact, so you could say that I am (if only by default) an atheist. Yet when a writer I love recently introduced me to an audience as "my favorite atheist," I recoiled. It's not that I want it both ways. I just don't like definitions that rely on negative information—terms that depend for their meanings on their own contradictions. It's why I prefer almost any other available alternative—belles lettres, essay, personal history—to *nonfiction*.

Besides, as an essentially positive person who hates to throw cold water on other people's parades and enthusiasms, I've never enjoyed the negativity, aggression, and anger that seem to go along with the name and practice of atheism. I didn't like it from Madalyn Murray O'Hair when I was young (though I later appreciated her work). I don't enjoy it in the writings of Richard Dawkins today (though his evolutionary biology is brilliant), or in Bill Maher's condescension and bellicosity toward believers (though I agree with many of his opinions).

So when that introduction as "my favorite atheist" occurred, I surprised myself with my response. "I don't really use that term for myself," I said. "I prefer to call myself an Alltheist—either everything is sacred, or nothing is—and I'm not really fussed about which it is." And so I found I'd made my first real revision to Naturo-Pantheistic Syncretism in fifty years plus, and I liked it. It's a lot shorter, cleaner, and easier to say. It eliminates the extraneity of "naturo," since all things are, by my definition of thingdom, natural. It cuts out the woo-woo baggage of latter-day pantheism, though it is, of course, an exact synonym: Pan being (as well as bread and Puck) All.

And, of course, best of all, it hearkens back to those phrases and states of mind and being that so captivated me through my reading life—the Muir, Ricketts, et al.—ultimately reduced to its nub and sanctified by Kurt Cobain and his colleagues Krist Novoselić and Dave Grohl of Nirvana. "All in all is all we are," indeed.

Not that my thoughts along these lines are remotely original.

Kathryn Grayson's "everything is sublime or nothing is sublime," which I have only recently seen, says almost the same thing; as does Bruce Springsteen's "all or nothing at all," and doubtless many others. But I can say that I haven't actually heard "Alltheism" before, and it fails to come up on the Google.

The obvious danger in any all-encompassing outlook is that it might be seen as all-accepting or all-condoning. After all, if everything is divine, sacred, or sublime, what basis could there be for discriminating among actions? Obviously, every attempt to prescribe ethics and define morals has failed to eliminate, and often justified, all manner of enormities, from Aztec heart-ripping to uninvited drone missiles at Middle Eastern wedding parties, with various holocausts and pogroms in between. Perhaps no moral system ever will erase such outrages.

But it seems to me that the full realization that all indeed *is* all would necessarily hobble oligarchy, hierarchy, supremacy, and exceptionalism—four of the worst horsemen of war and repression that I know. You can't as easily objectify, hit, shoot, or bomb the Other when you accept that you and the Other are one and the same. And as for the non-human part of the All: how would it be possible for us to treat it as we do if we really believed in absolute oneness? The way William Glassley felt it in *A Wilder Time*, his 2018 chronicle of wild Greenland: "Then it occurred to me that all was equal here. An absence of hierarchy reigned, everything was beautiful and not."

Hardly de novo, mine is probably one of the oldest ideas alive. But its real application would be new. And what it would look like is what I have tried to describe in *Nature Matrix*, both the essay by that name and this book as a whole. For what *is* the matrix, if not the rich resin that bonds us all together in the glittering amber of

The Whole Thing? And what is that whole, that anything at all could exist outside of it?

Humans have tried, in so many clever ways, to do just that, with surprising (if illusory and temporary) success. But we should know better by now. Or have we entirely ignored our teachers? Such as Walt Whitman, who in *Leaves of Grass* advised us to "behold the great rondure, the cohesion of all, how perfect!" And how does that differ, really, from "all in all is all we are"? Walt and Kurt may have spoken in different vernaculars, but they were speaking the same truth. And we can't ignore them any longer. The jig is up. All in all *is* all there is, the whole is the whole deal, and the sweet current of evolution is running fast. It's time for everyone to recognize that common flow and step inside—the water's fine.

PUBLICATION HISTORY

The following essays appeared previously as indicated, sometimes under a different name or in somewhat different form, though few have been abridged or altered substantially.

Secrets of the Talking Leaf
   Facing the Lion, Beacon Press, 1995

A Mineral King Esthetic
   Unpublished senior thesis, University of Washington, 1969; thanks to UW Libraries, Manuscripts Division

A Different Day on Beetle Rock
   American West, 1972 (as "Can We Save Our Wild Places? National Parks in Jeopardy")

Joys of the Suburban Jungle
   East Side Week (Bellevue, WA), 1991

Eden in a Vacant Lot: Special Places, Species, and Kids in the Neighborhood of Life
Children and Nature, MIT Press, 2000

Nature Matrix
Oryx, the International Journal of Conservation, 2003

The Blind Teaching the Blind: The Academic as Naturalist, or Not
Placing the Academy: Essays on Landscape, Work, and Identity, Utah State University Press, 2007

It Was All About the Beavers: John Jacob Astor I and the Rape of the West
Eminent Astorians, Oregon State University Press, 2010 (as "John Jacob Astor: A Most Excellent Man?")

Swift and Underwing, Boulderfield and Bog: Nabokov's Individuating Details
Fine Lines: Vladimir Nabokov's Scientific Art, Yale University Press, 2016

Real Wilderness: Extinct in the Wild?
Wildness: Relations of People and Place, University of Chicago Press, 2017 (as "Conundrum and Continuum: One Man's Wilderness, from a Ditch to the Dark Divide")

The Semiotics of Sasquatch
Camas Magazine (University of Montana), 2017

ACKNOWLEDGMENTS

First I wish to thank Jack Shoemaker for asking me to produce such a book; Harry Kirchner for heroically helping me to do so and for his always-adept edit; and all their colleagues at Counterpoint Press for bringing it to be, including Sarah Brody, Jordan Koluch, Jennifer Alton, Megan Fishmann, Alisha Gorder, Kathleen Boland, and Miyako Singer. Along with them I also thank with affection my longtime and trusted agent, Laura Blake Peterson, and her colleagues at Curtis Brown Ltd.

My warm thanks could and do extend to everyone mentioned in these essays and all of those editors and others responsible for their first appearance in books and journals (see Publication History); and for the new pieces, their very existence. That is way too many names to name, or even to remember. But among the more significant and recent influences, too many of them now gone, I do indeed thank Victor B. Scheffer, Aldon Bell, Susan Kafer, Carol Jane Bangs, Knute "Skip" Berger, Stephen R. Kellert, Peter H.

Kahn Jr., Jennifer Sinor, Steve Forrester, Michael Bales, Karen Kirtley, Kurt Johnson, Stephen H. Blackwell, Gavin Van Horn, John Hausdoerffer, Mike Houck, Phil Condon, Jessica Eller, Robert Gimlin, Kenn Kaufman, and Jay McInerney, who has no idea who I am.

Kind thanks to the folks at the University of Washington Libraries Special Collections, especially Sandra Kroupa and James B. Stack, for helping me to locate and copy the earliest manuscripts.

Finally, loving thanks to all my family and to many dear friends who have supported me daily throughout this project and all that went into it, particularly Neil Johannsen, David Branch, Jon Pelham, Fayette Krause, JoAnne Heron, Holly Hughes, and Krist Novoselić, and most especially Florence Sage.

ROBERT MICHAEL PYLE is a biologist and writer who has worked in conservation biology around the world. His twenty-four books include *Wintergreen, Where Bigfoot Walks, Mariposa Road*, four collections of poetry, the novel *Magdalena Mountain*, and a flight of butterfly books. Founder of the Xerces Society for Invertebrate Conservation, he was recently named an honorary life fellow of the Royal Entomological Society. Pyle lives, writes, and studies natural history in rural southwest Washington.